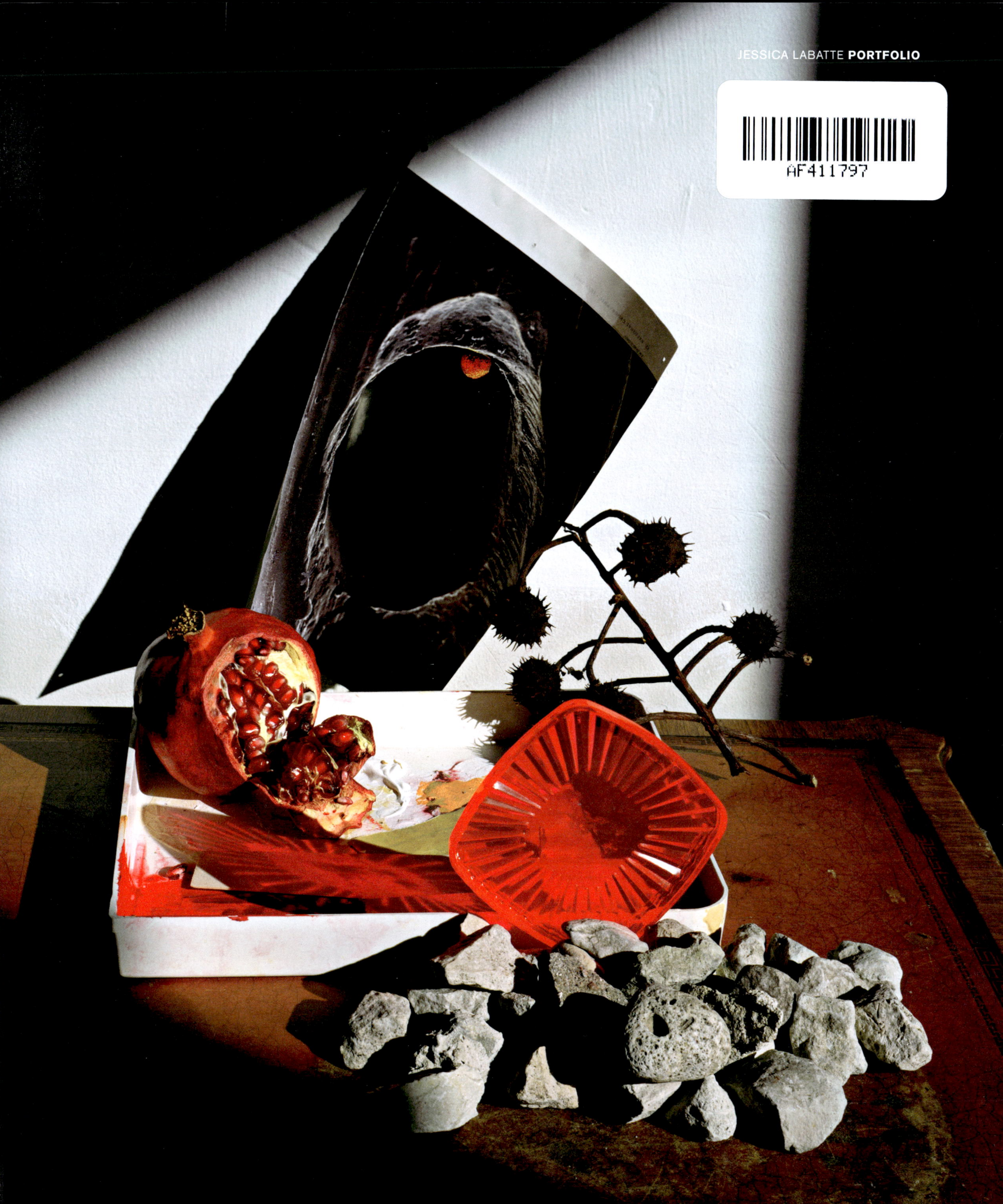

# JESSICA LABATTE Surface Effects

In their meticulous arrangement of chaos, Jessica Labatte's photographs breathe new life into refuse and household items. Freeing these objects from their customary associations and signifiers, new relationships are forged. Labatte's assemblages, almost entities in themselves, are creations fully aware of their two-dimensionality. By the flattening that comes with image reproduction, the contours and angles of the objects are dislocated, producing sculptural deconstructions of surrealist still lifes. The captured image becomes a multitudinous array of visual planes and symbiotic dimensions, inviting the eye to scrutinize and uncover subtle clues left by the artist, coaxing the viewer to distinguish foreground from backdrop, beginning from end. In her latest series, *Surface Effects* and *The Brightness*, Labatte adds another layer to her practice, quite literally a 'reflectivity.' Using detritus material from previous projects, including foil, and carefully considering the mechanics of sight and color perception, she constructs images that are both optically and spatially deceiving. In her words, "the resulting photographs resemble small crystals or geodes each uniquely reflecting the installation. These works continue my investigations of photographic space, as well as my interest in the relationship between photography and sculpture." - Jessica Labatte, born in 1981 in Salt Lake City (USA), received her BFA and MFA from the School of the Art Institute of Chicago. In 2010, she exhibited at Humble Arts Foundation in New York and Golden Gallery in Chicago. Her most recent solo show was installed as part of *UBS 12 x 12* series at the Museum of Contemporary Arts in Chicago, where she lives and works.

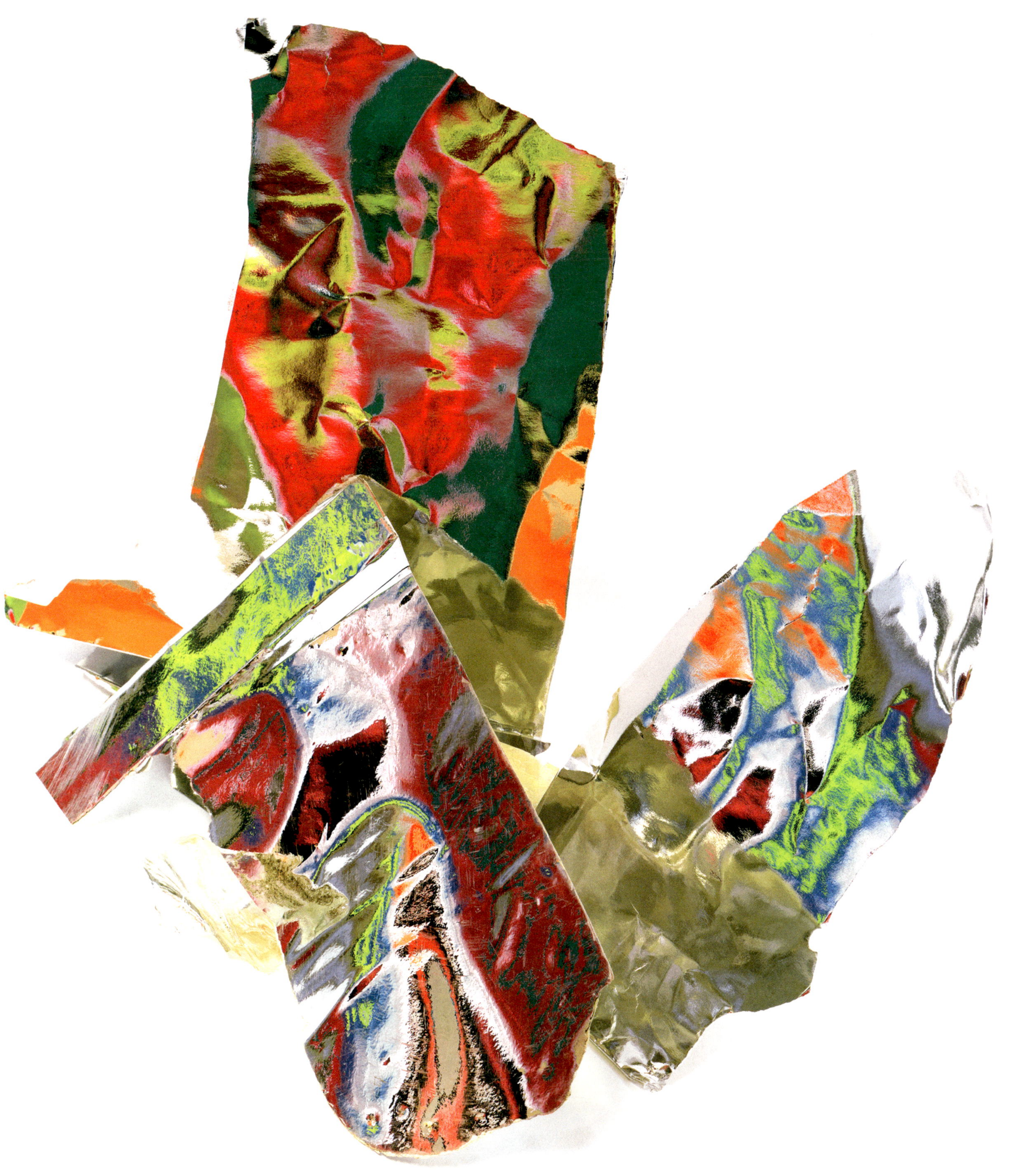

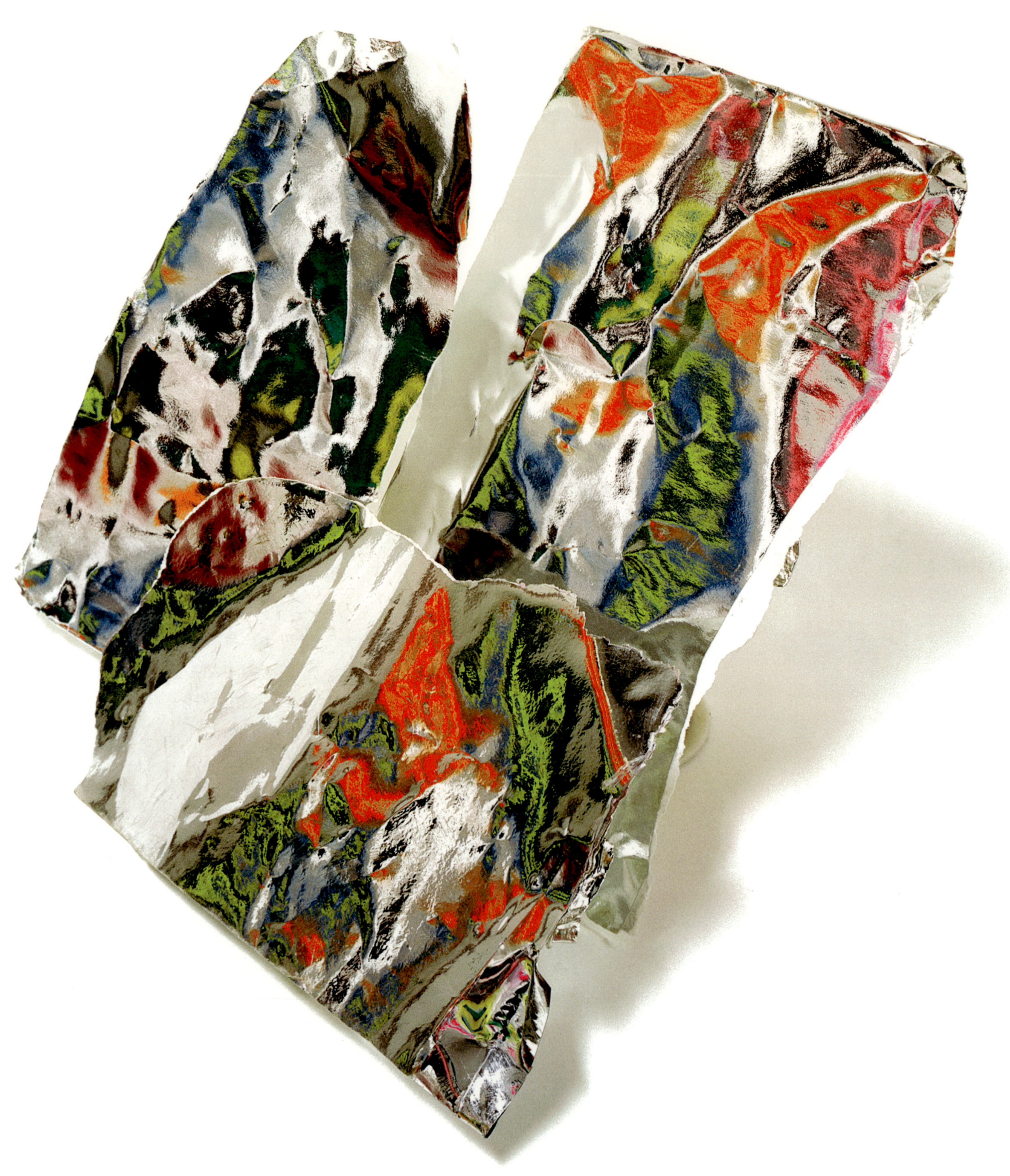

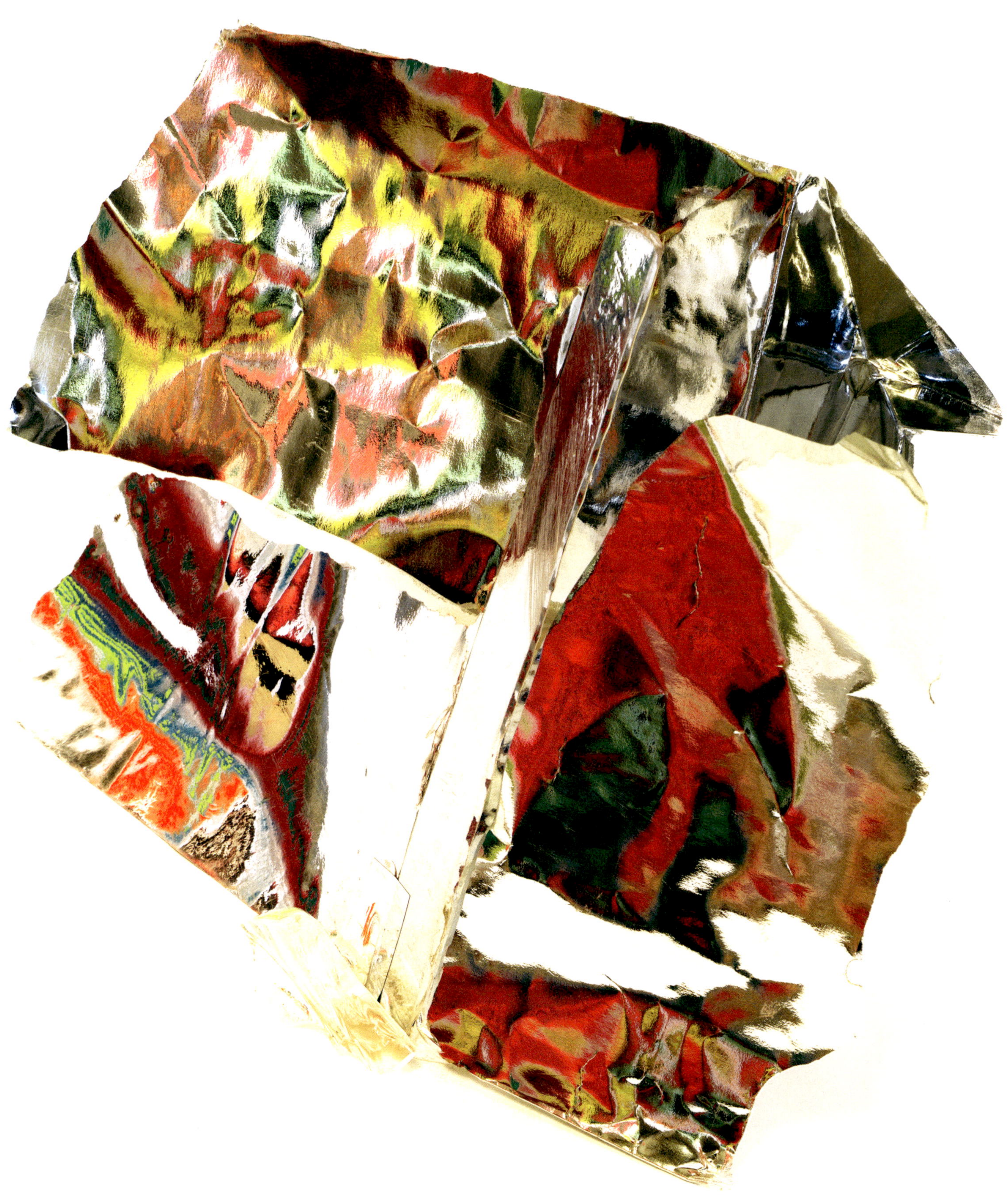

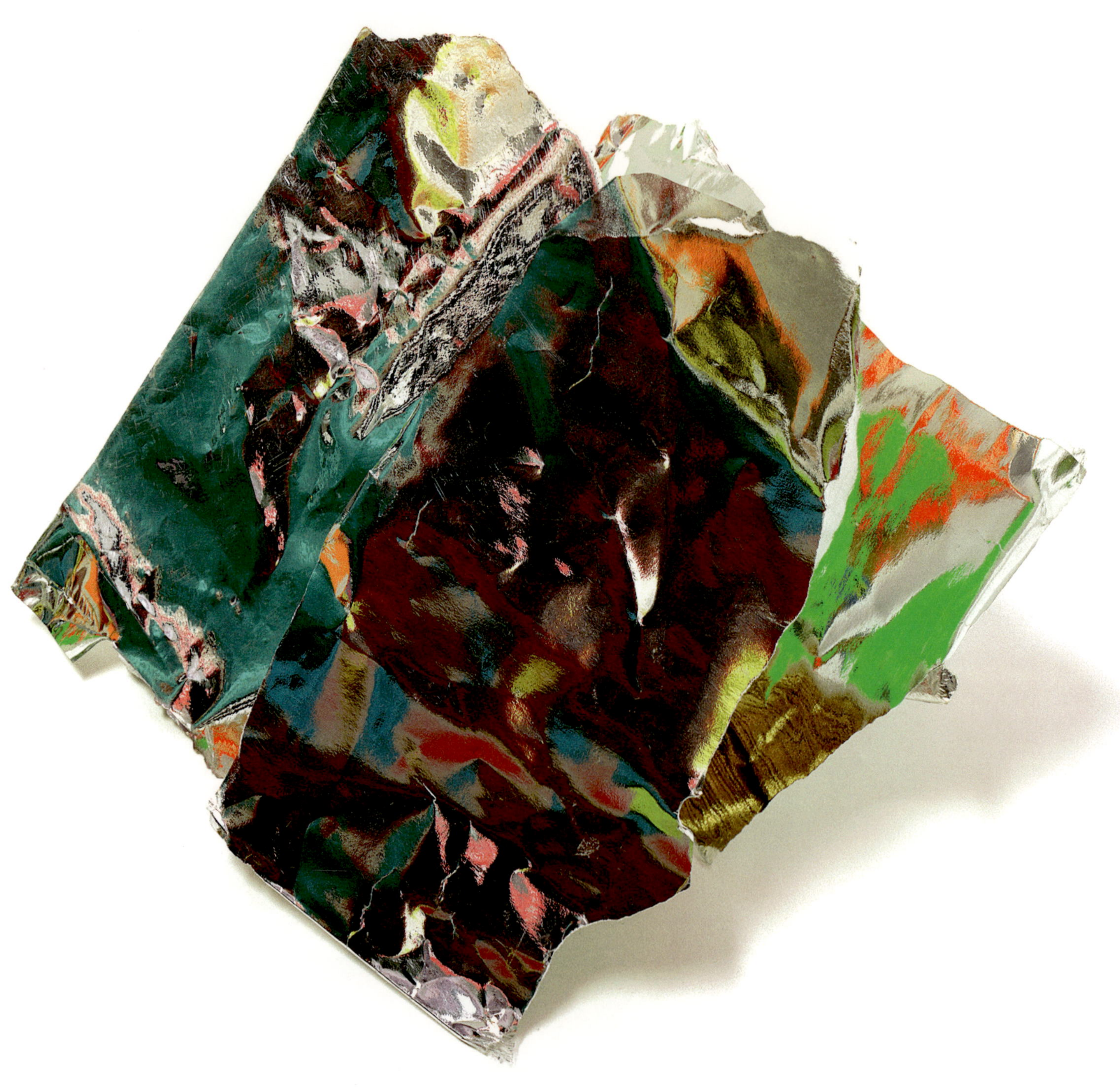

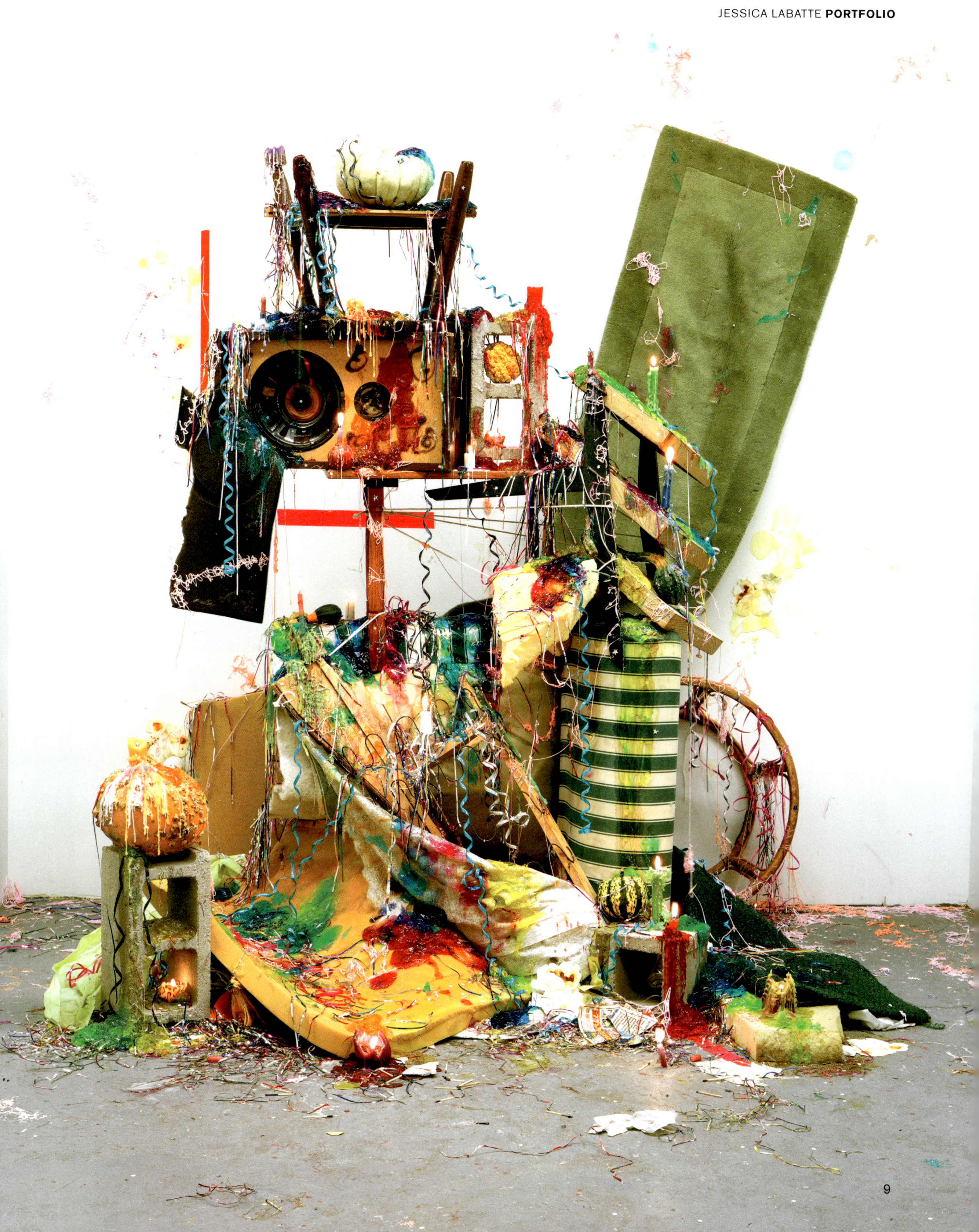

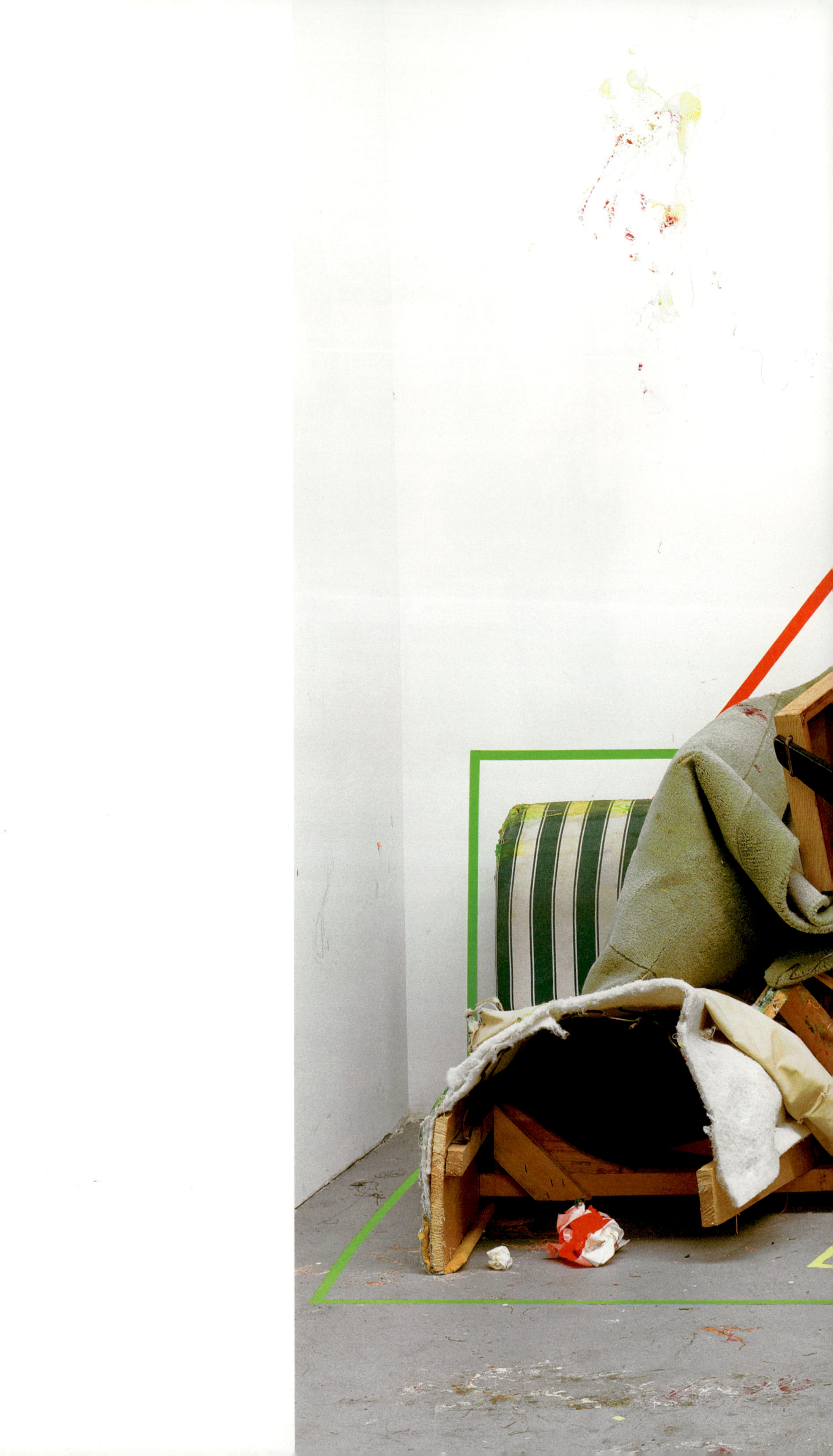

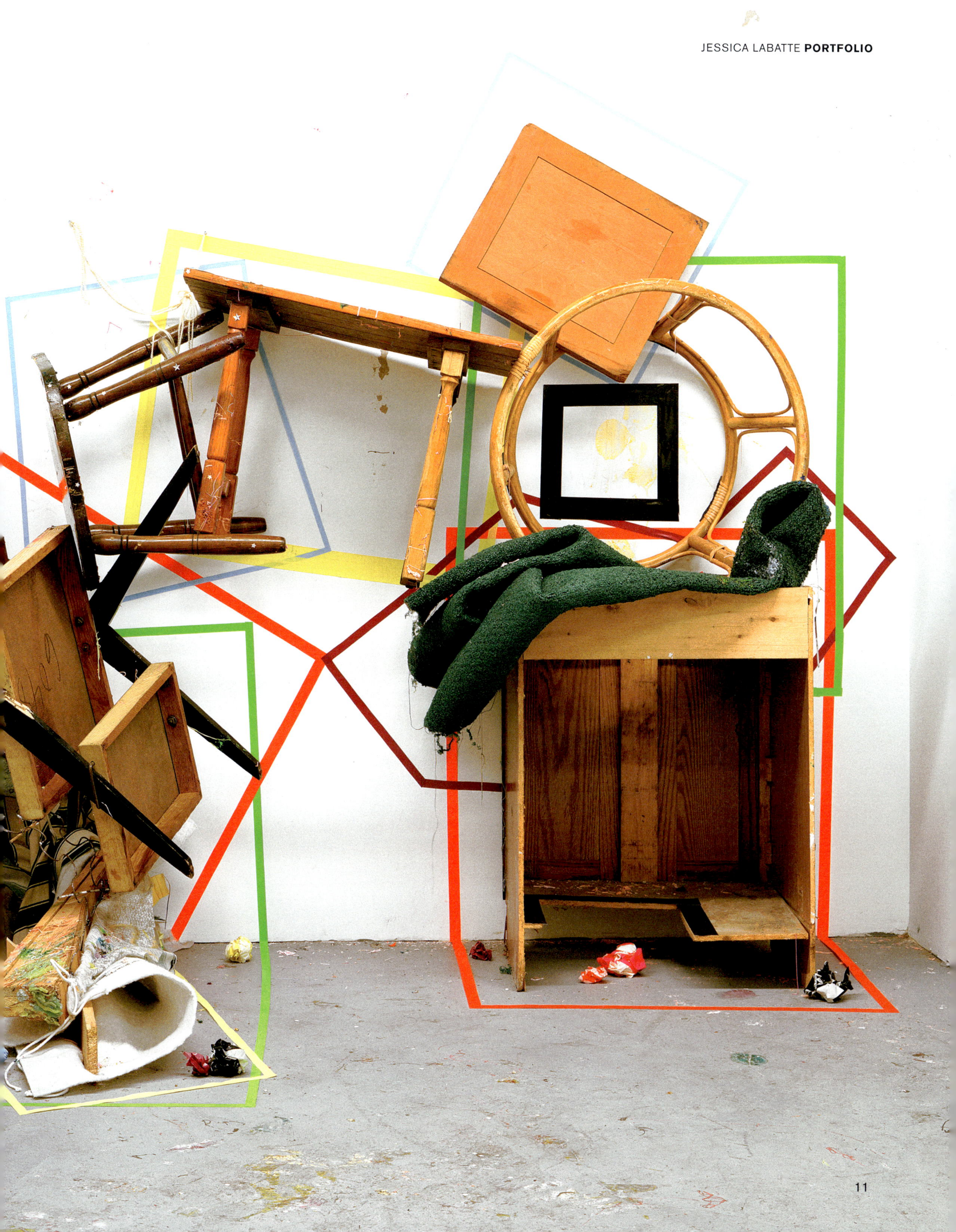

# RÄ DI MARTINO No More Stars

Rome native, di Martino is best known for short films that combine visually rich and cinematically evocative images with enigmatic and often fragmentary storylines. Narratives can begin in mid-action or be repeated with slight unexplainable alteration. Something very meaningful either just happened or is about to commence. Her most recent series of photographs, *No More Stars (Abandoned Movie Set, Star Wars)*, 2010, reiterates this suspicion. Shot in Chott el-Djerid in Southern Tunisia, the largest dry lake in the Sahara and a site of many fata morganas, these photographs document abandoned sets made in the 1970s for the *Star Wars* trilogy. Like a mirage, these structures appear out of place, and yet are rendered almost achingly sharp. The visual impact of di Martino's motifs, ruins of abandoned bunkers of a dystopian war far away in the future, is combined with the universally popular knowledge of these films to great effect. The series recalls another work that was shot in the same location, Bill Viola's seminal video *Chott el-Djerid* (1979), with its glimmering images of figures reflected in the sand. Fata morganas both, Viola's video and di Martino's photographs are two different ways of looking at what exists most vividly in our mind alone. - Rä di Martino has been featured in international film festivals and group exhibitions including MCA, Chicago (2009), Manifesta 7 (2008), Artists Space, New York (2006).

*All images from the series* No More Stars (Abandoned Movie Set, Star Wars). *Right page* 33°59'39 N 7°50'34 E, Chott El-Gharsa, Tunisia, 03 September 2010. *Page 14* 33°59'42 N 7°51'00 E, Chott El-Gharsa, Tunisia, 01 September 2010. *Page 15* 33°50'34 N 7°46'44 E, Chott El-Gharsa, Tunisia, 01 September 2010. *Page 16* 33°50'34 N 7°46'44 E, Chott El-Gharsa, Tunisia, 01 September 2010. *Page 17* 33°59'42 N 7°51'00 E, Chott El-Gharsa, Tunisia, 01 September 2010. *Page 18* 33°50'34 N 7°46'44 E, Chott El-Gharsa, Tunisia, 01 September 2010. *Page 19* 33°50'34 N 7°46'44 E, Chott El-Gharsa, Tunisia, 01 September 2010. *All images © the artist, courtesy Monitor, Rome*

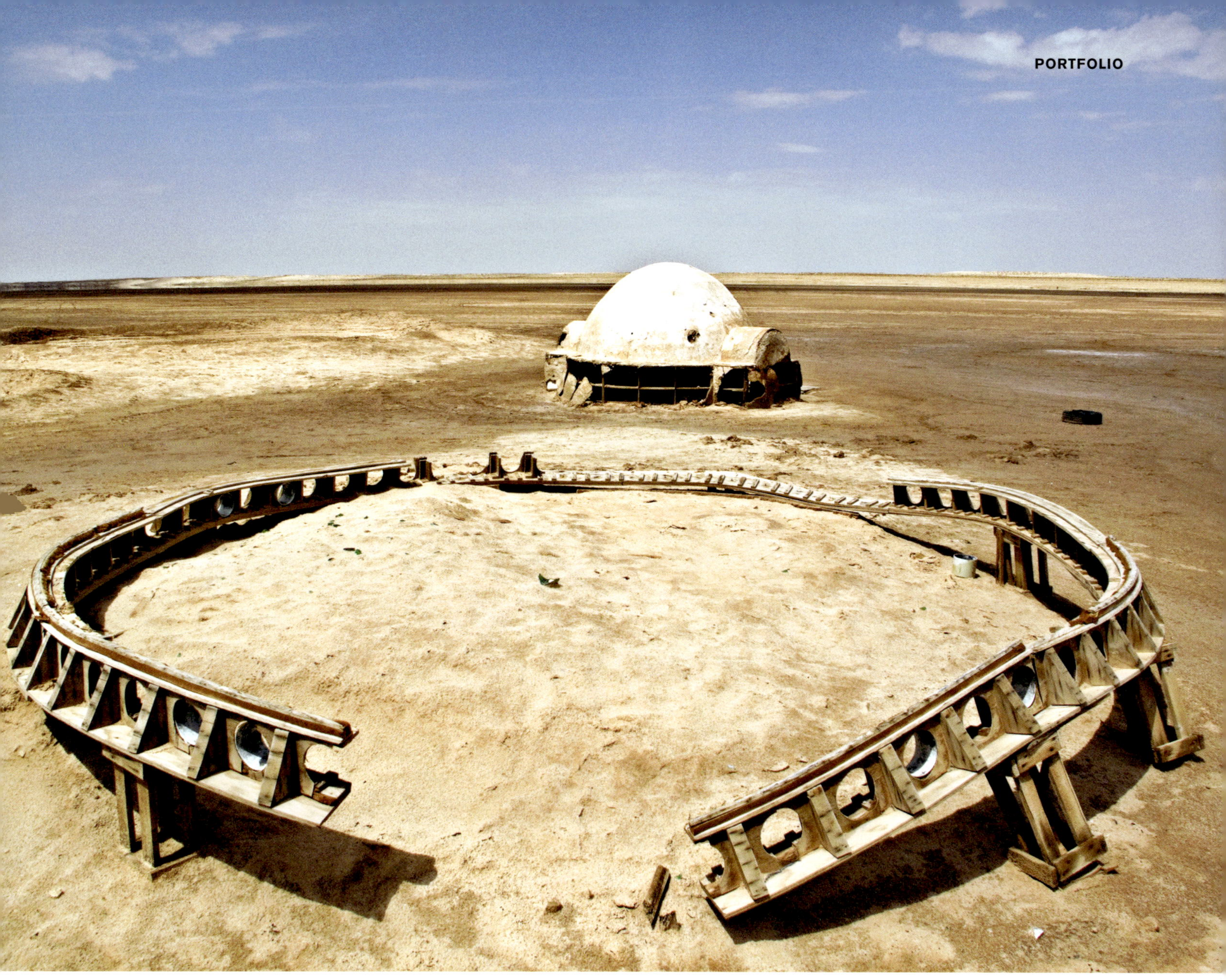

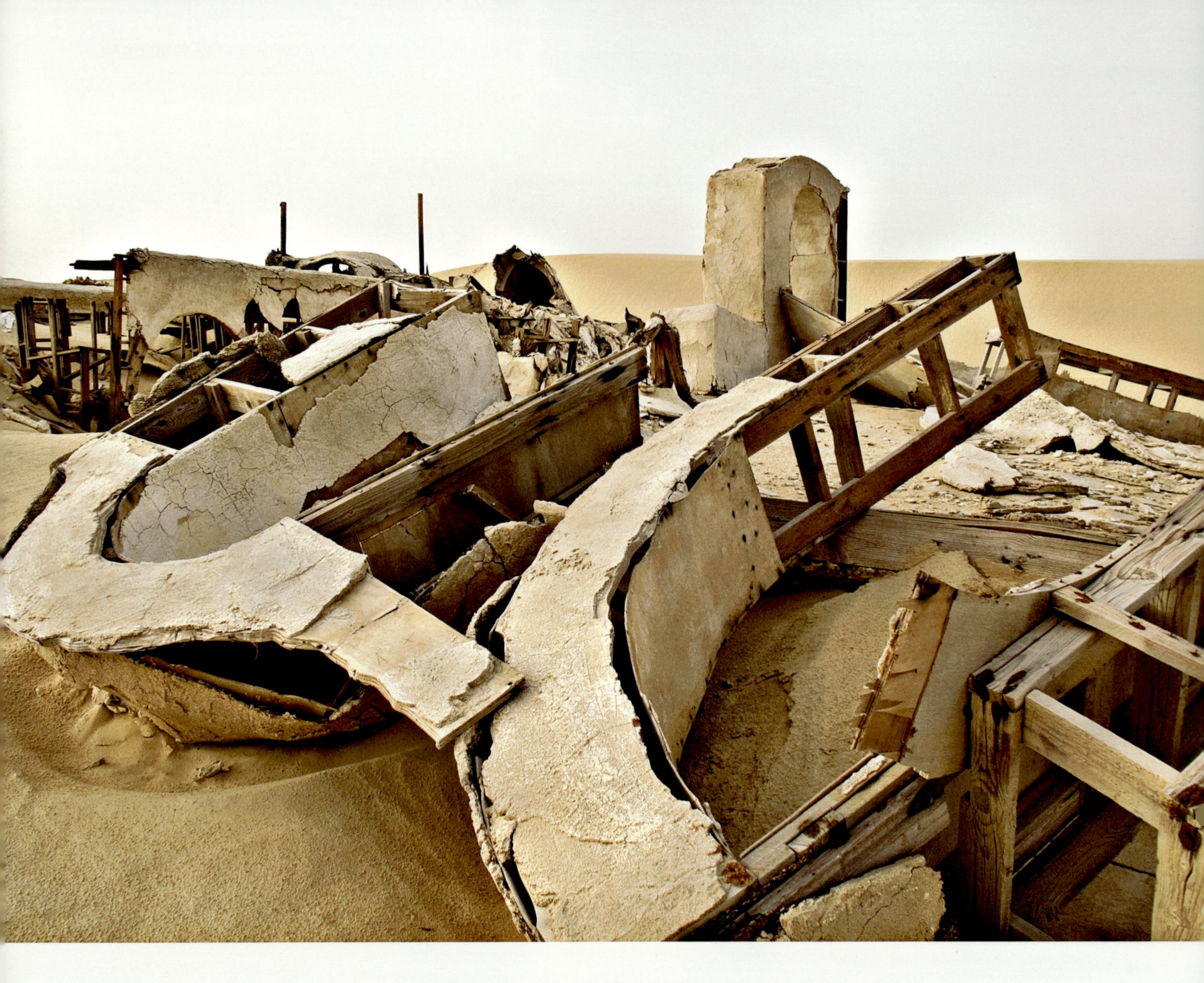

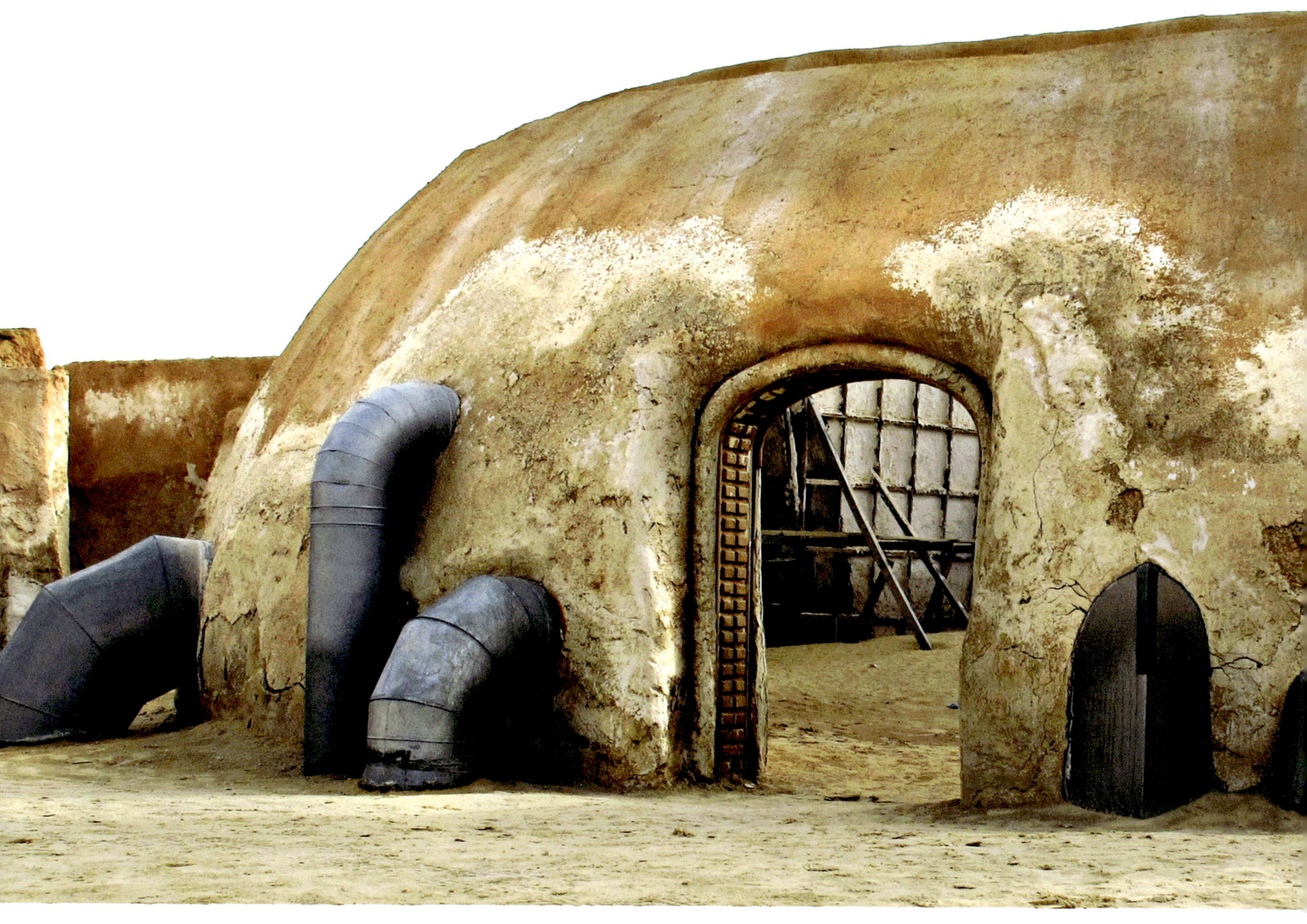

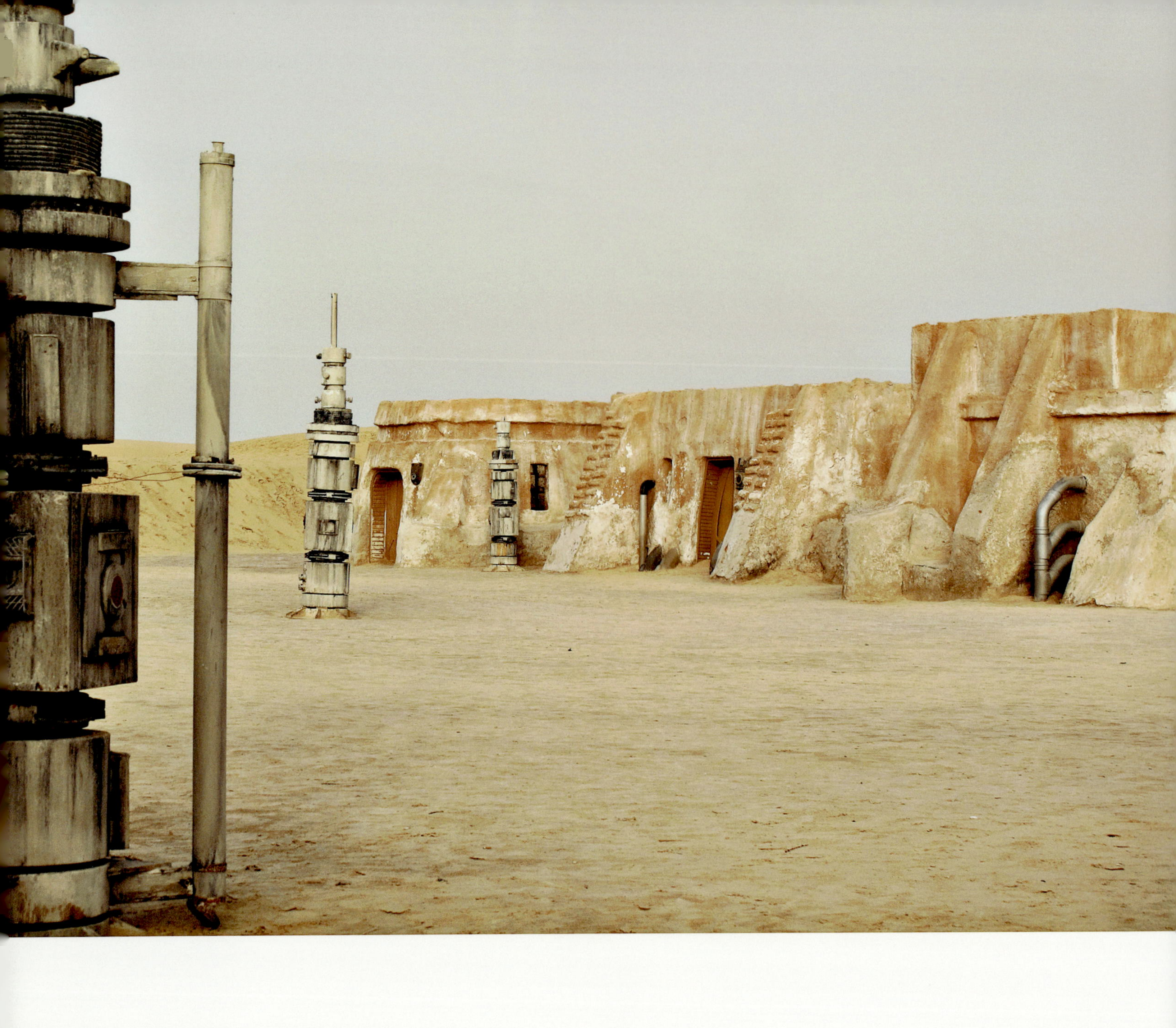

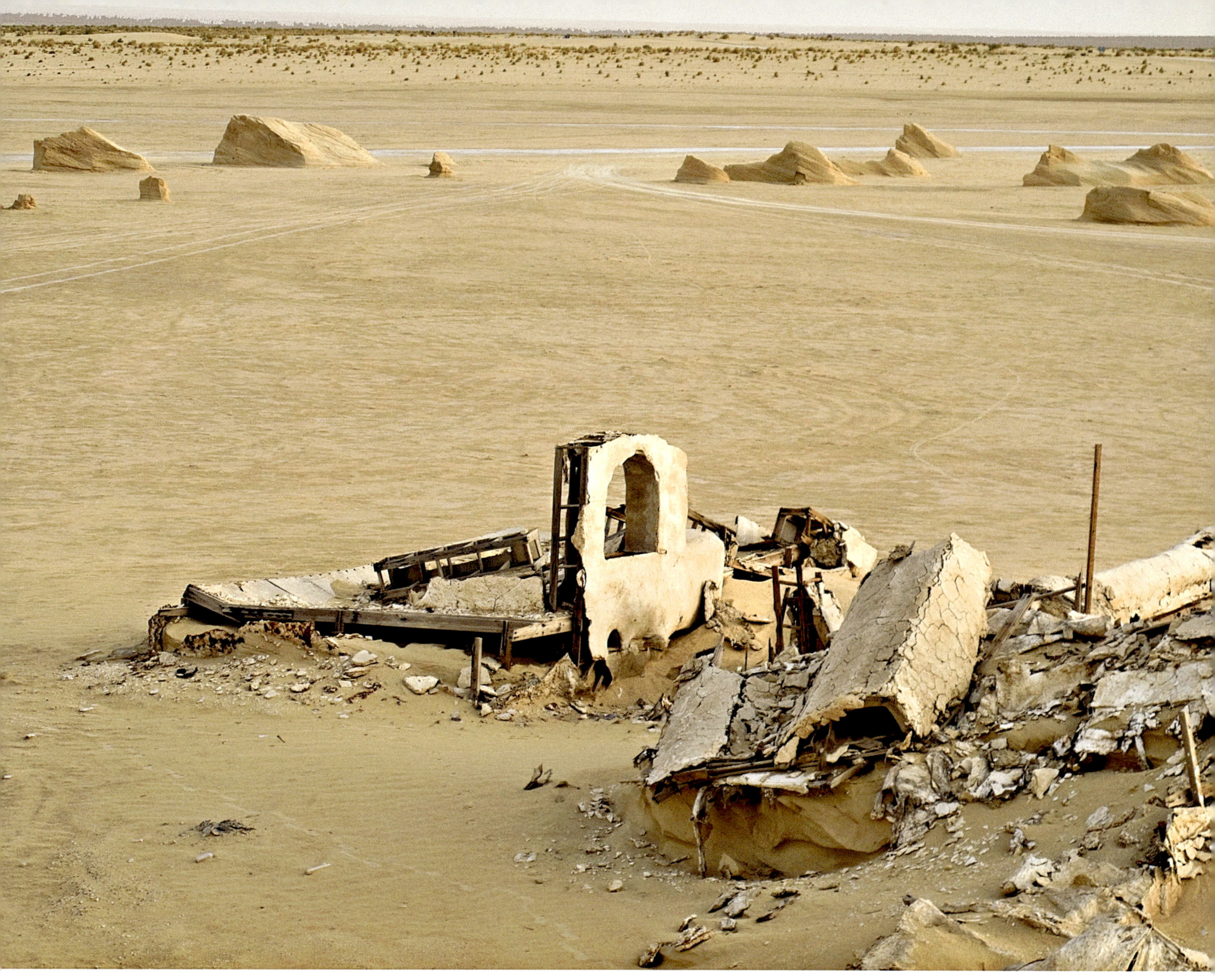

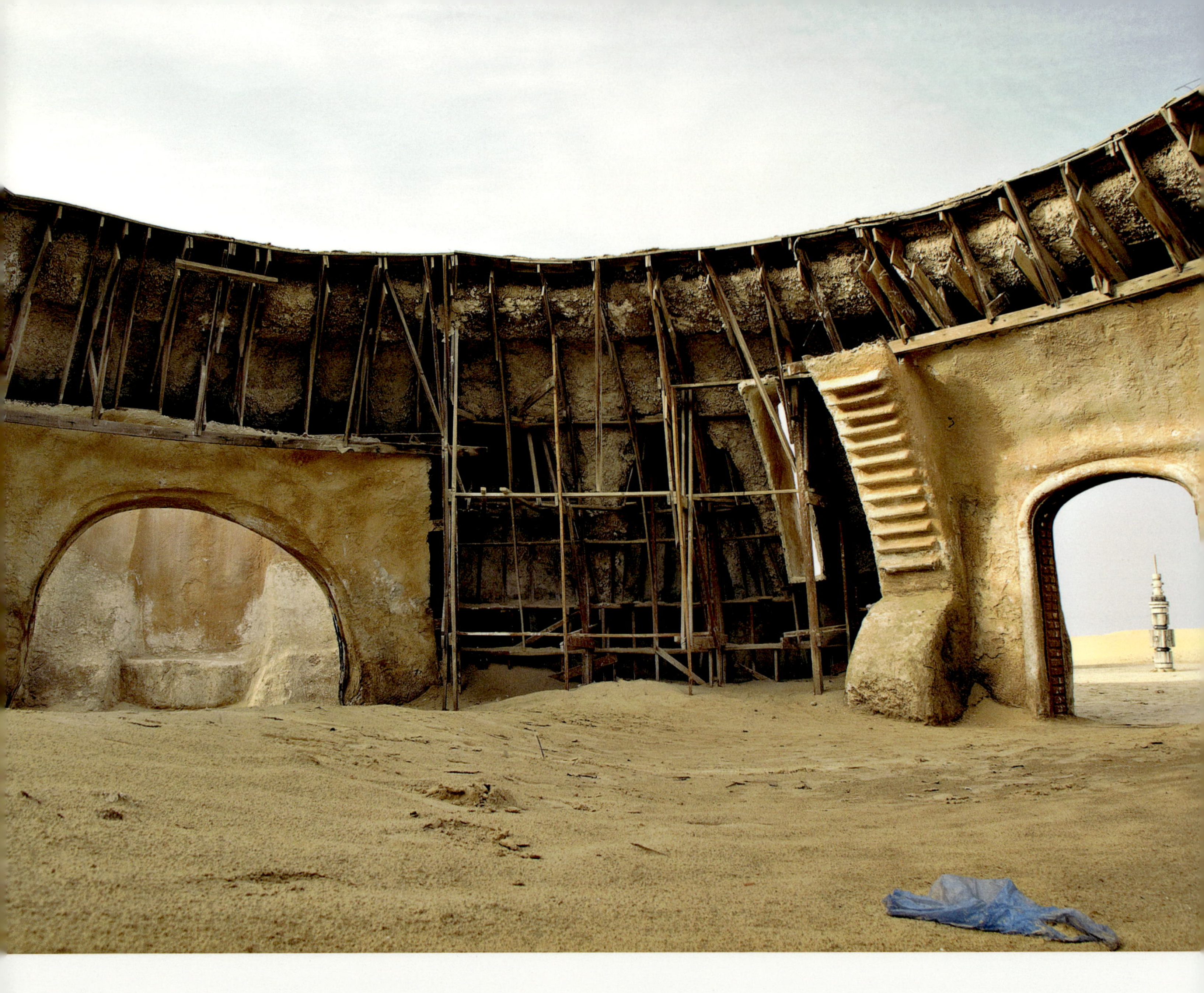

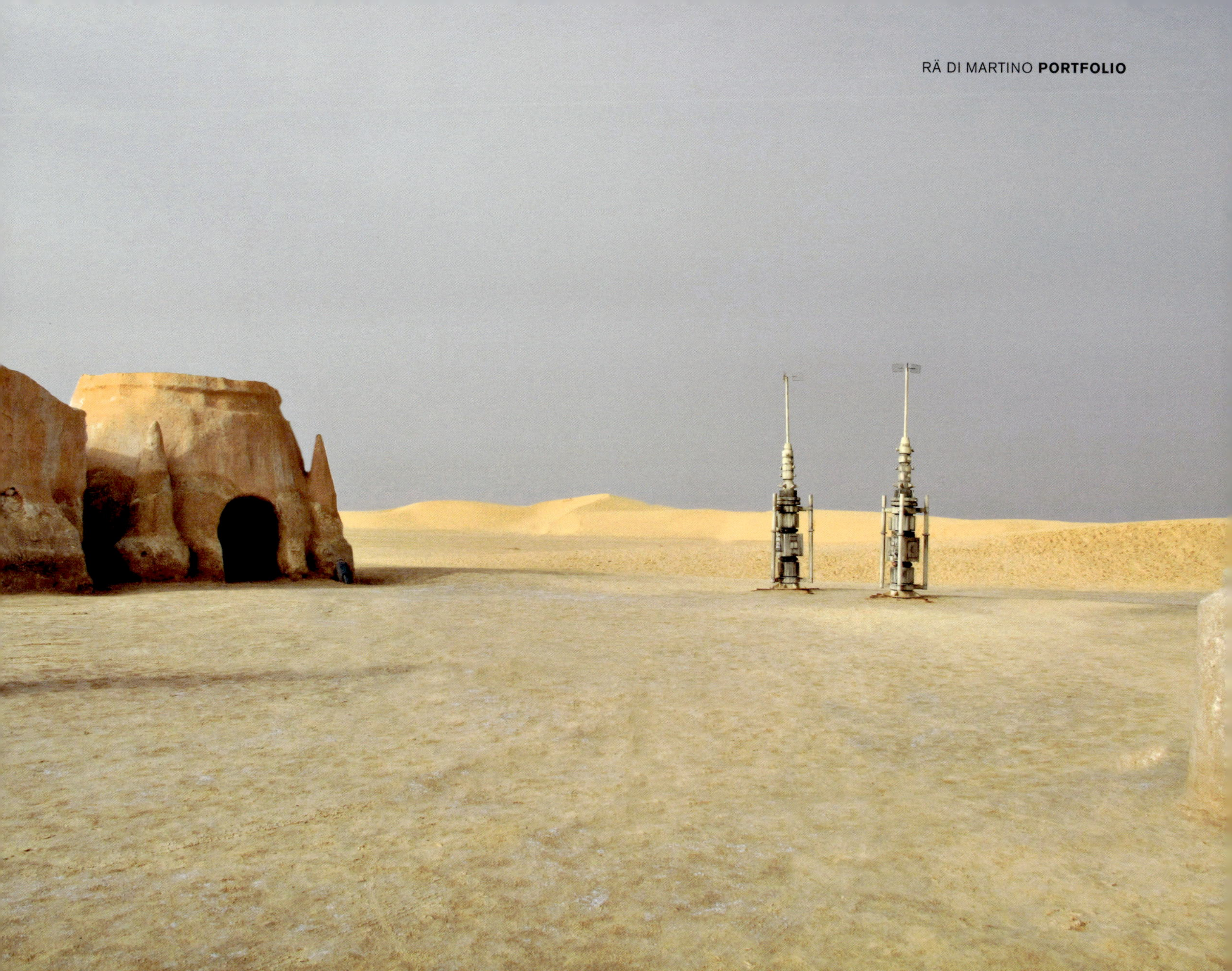

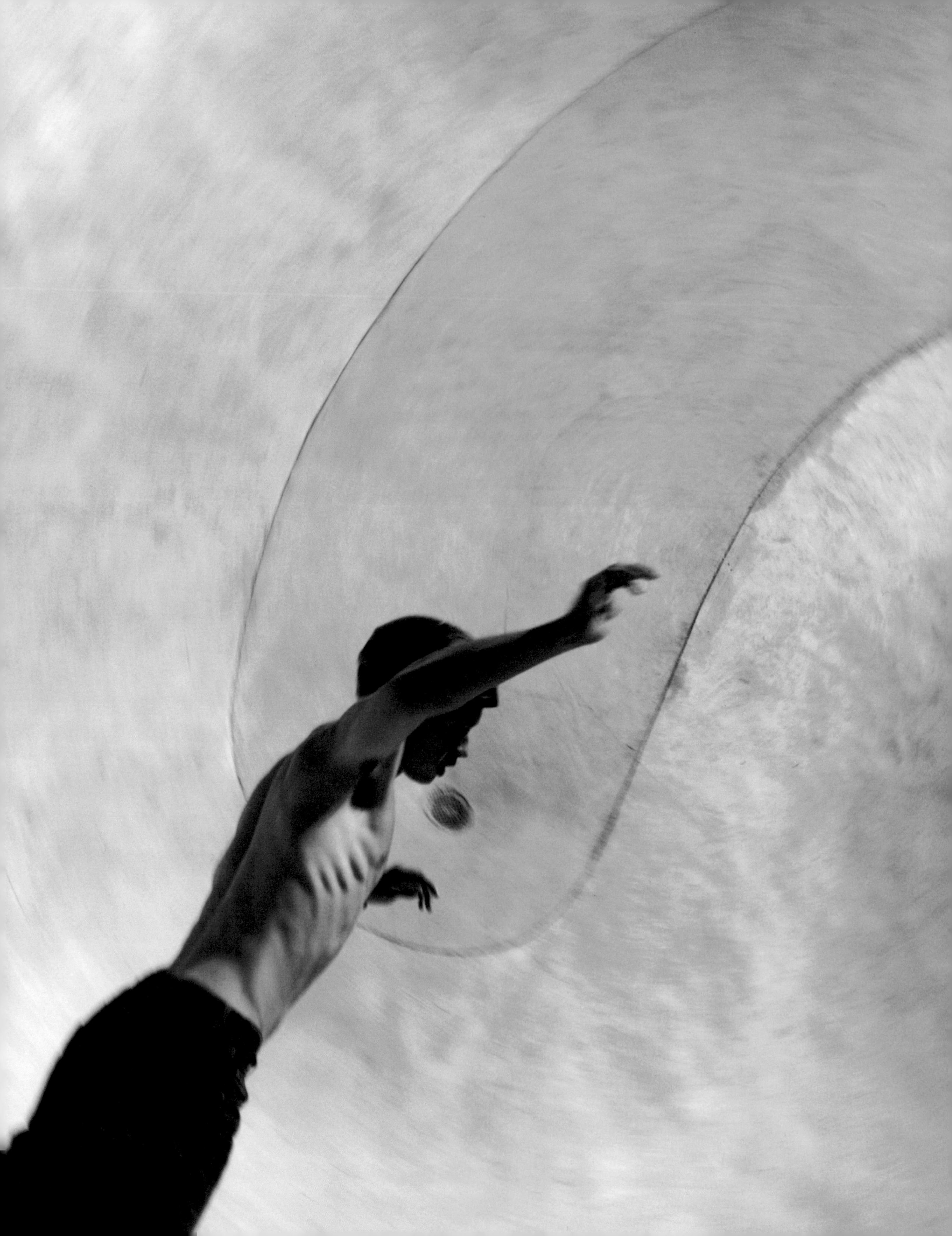

# Camera Consciousness
# ARTHUR TRESS
# by Jordan Hruska

BORN IN NEW YORK IN 1940, TRESS TRAVELED WITH HIS OWN CAMERA TO FARAWAY CONTINENTS FROM THE 1960s TO THE 1980s TO DOCUMENT SUBJECTS IN THEIR NATURAL ENVIRONMENTS. DESPITE HIS OFT-CITED SIMILARITY TO HENRI CARTIER-BRESSON, TRESS DIDN'T PRESENT UPLIFTING GLOBAL ALLEGORIES. HE LABORED, INSTEAD, WITH A MORE MELANCHOLIC AND ATAVISTIC RENDERING OF SUBJECTS - A WHOLE SERIES, FOR EXAMPLE, ON CHILDREN'S SOLITARY PLAY HABITS IN THE POST-INDUSTRIAL PERIPHERY OF URBAN AMERICA. BUT AFTER SEVERAL FIN-DE-SIÈCLE STYLISTIC EVOLUTIONS, TRESS PRESENTS A BODY OF WORK THAT MANIFESTS A SENSE OF DURATION THAT UNITES BOTH PHOTOGRAPHER TO SUBJECT AND ALSO SUBJECT TO SPACE AND TIME.

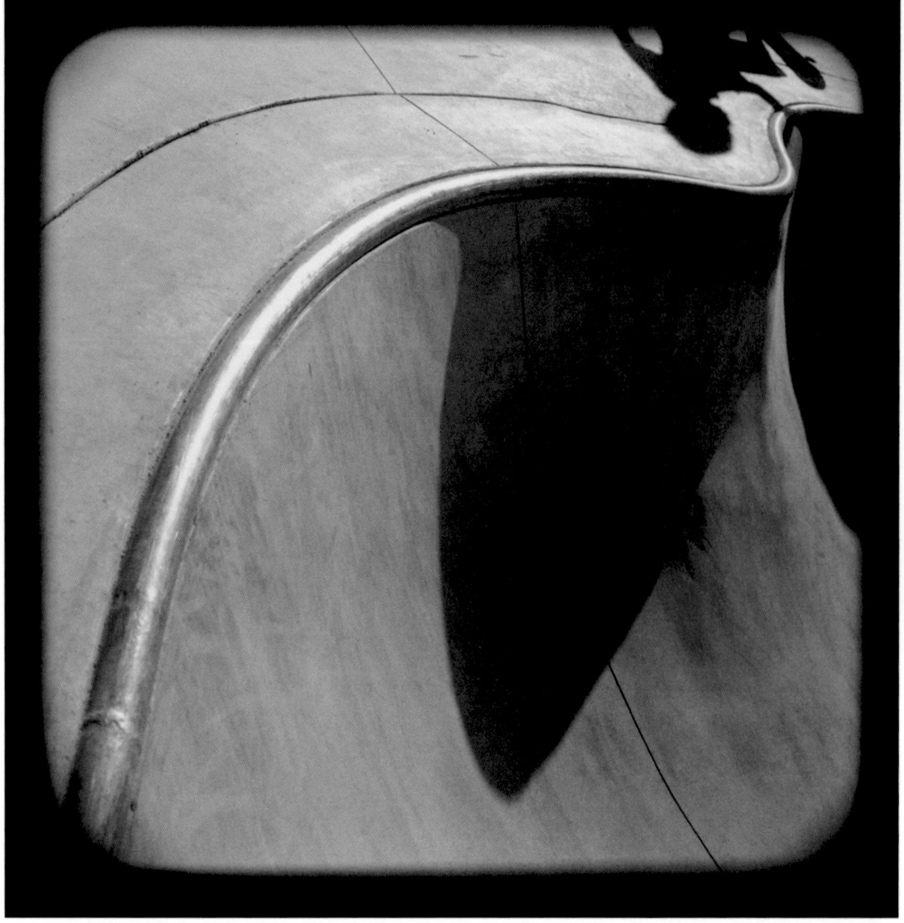

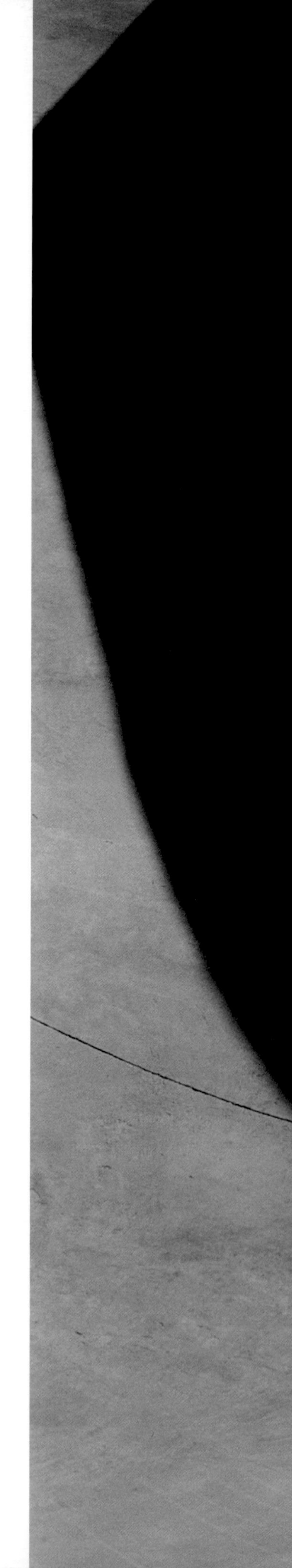

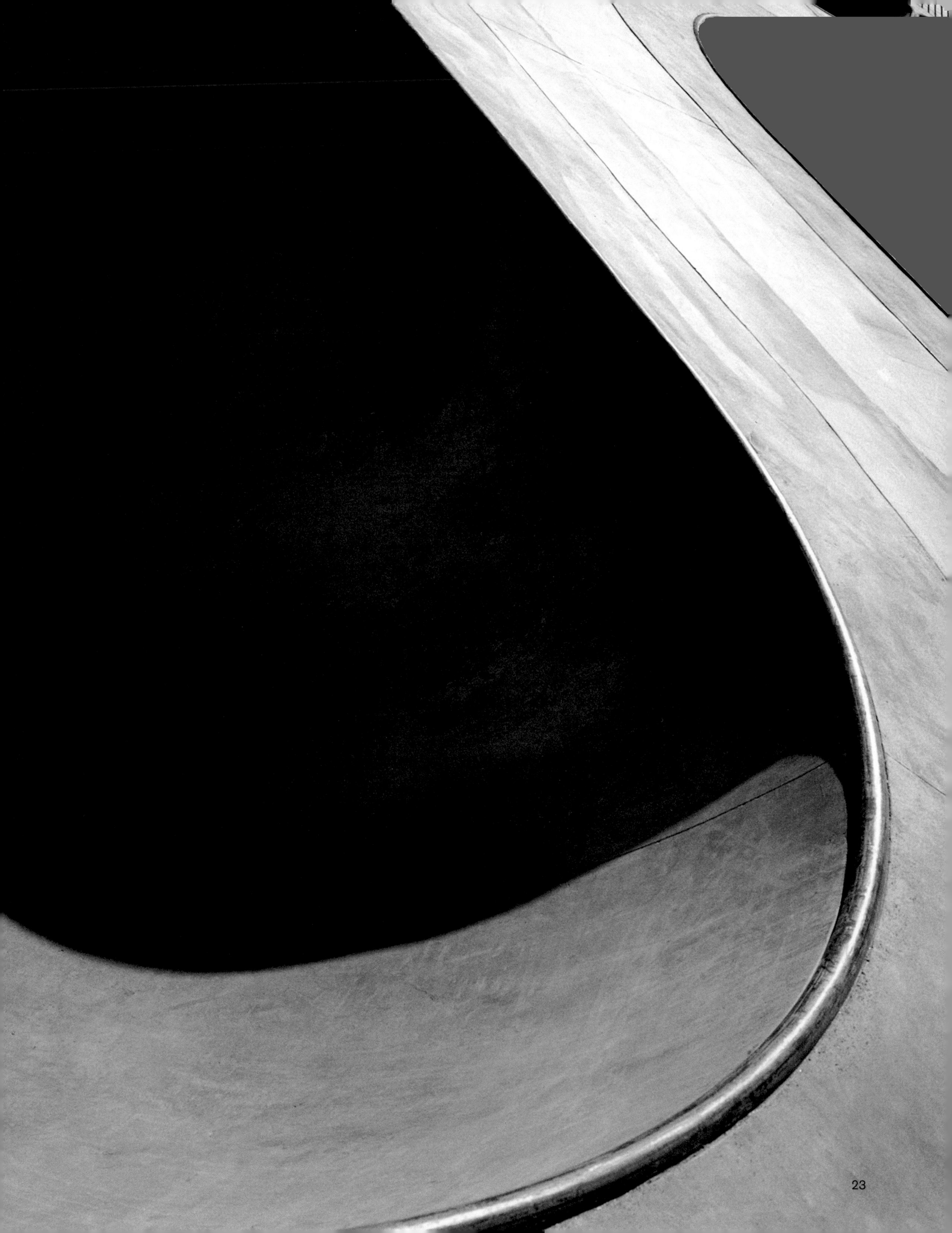

For several years, Tress documented the skaters in his adopted home of California. His photographs in *Skate Park* (Birch Books, 2010) capitalize on the notion that skateboarding is not a finite gesture. Instinct and reaction govern each second of a ride - not a prescribed choreography. Furthermore, in his *Skate Park* series, the skate park architecture itself is a record of the ride, in the same way that the photographer corrals a moment from the grasp of time with a photograph.

In black and white compositions, Tress first presents these concrete bowls and wooden half-pipes as objects without figures - architecture without people. Rubber and wax accrue in swirls and skids, offering mesmerizing records of time that manifest in a warped continuum. But then, skaters come into the frame - first as shadows, then as blurry forms hovering mostly out of frame, set against the molded landscapes activated both by the gesture of the skids and the velocity of the skaters. To a capricious eye, the photographs seem like unfinished compositions, or images better left to the red 'X' of the editing room. Collected, they comprise a powerful portfolio of the reciprocal struggle of skater and photographer - the desire to articulate time with form.

A possible connection between the two practices lies in Henri Bergson's 1896's work *Matter and Memory,* wherein the philosopher presents an indexical definition of space and time beginning with the collapse of two 'universes' of perception: one of his own body in relation to images around him, and another where those same images react to every other image. Already 100 years before Tress, for Bergson, 'images' indi-

cate each moment, "like a compass being moved about." To translate these images, an intermediary, such as the aforementioned compass or body or even the brain, which directs ideas and an argument throughout the book. And similarly, one could argue that the camera functions as such a device to record images or movements for the photographer. An image received by Bergson's body may produce one of two reactions: an instinctual response or movement that begets other images, or one that doesn't produce an instinctual reaction, and instead "spiritualizes itself into consciousness."

Similarly in the photographs, two actions take place: Tress internalizes the images and impressions of his subjects through his camera, and at the same time the skaters resemble an image in perpetual reaction to other images. They limn with great speed and instinct across a space designed specifically to move them in a constant, fluid state of flux… an act that Tress spirits into memory. A photograph becomes the common ground while viewers assume a participatory role by becoming aware of the caprices of image capture.

Outside of the bowl, however, the skater subjects take on a new form - not one of reaction, but one of perfection. Here Tress' gaze slows down to muse on their shirtless, Grecian forms - timeless in a different, wholly aesthetic, plastic context. When not in motion, Tress sees them as a different kind of ideal image, leaving only the viewer to react.

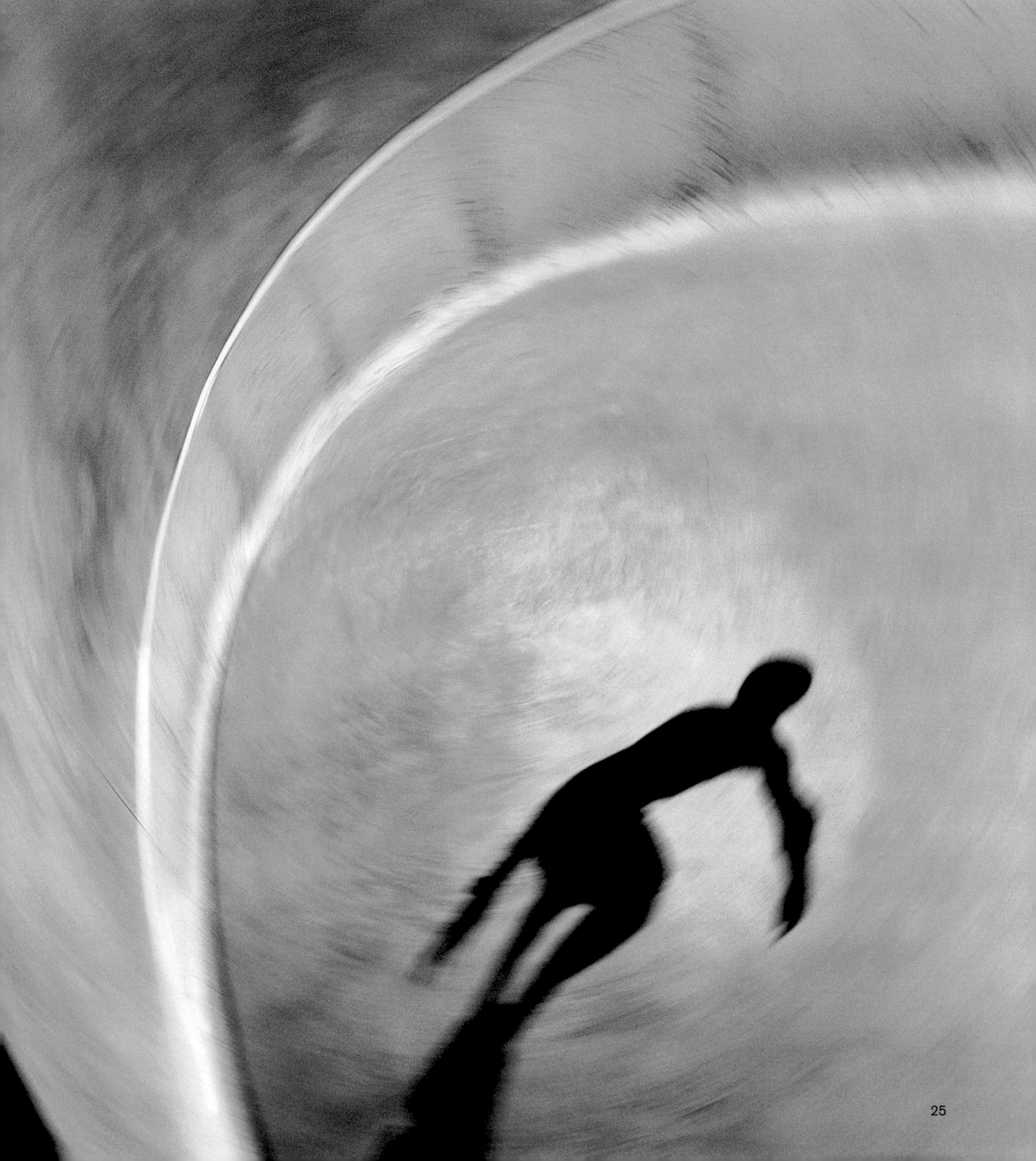

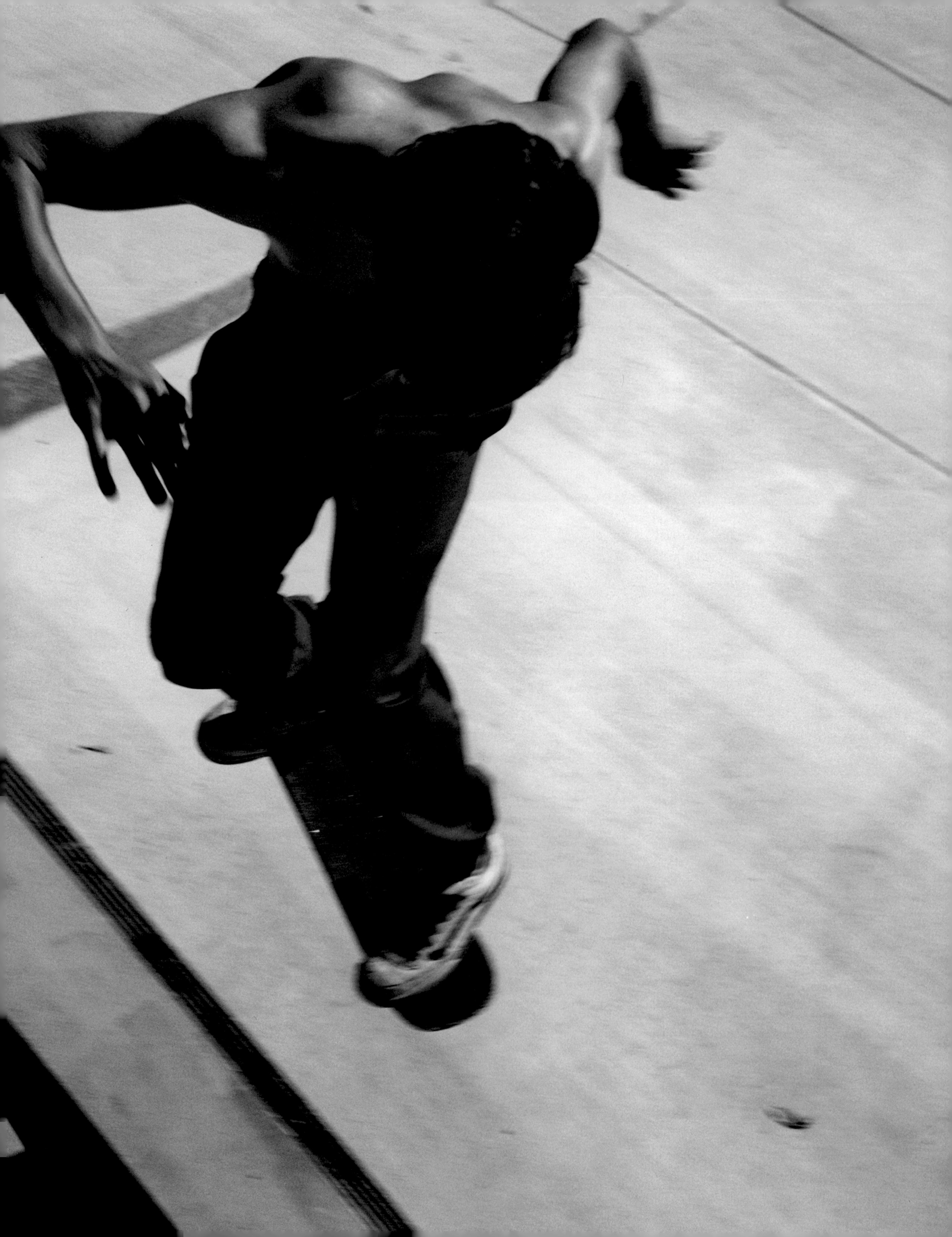

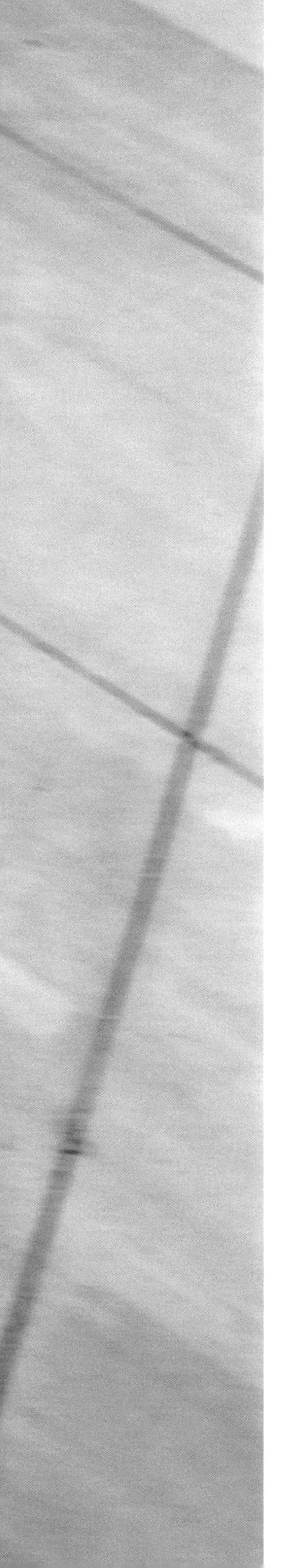

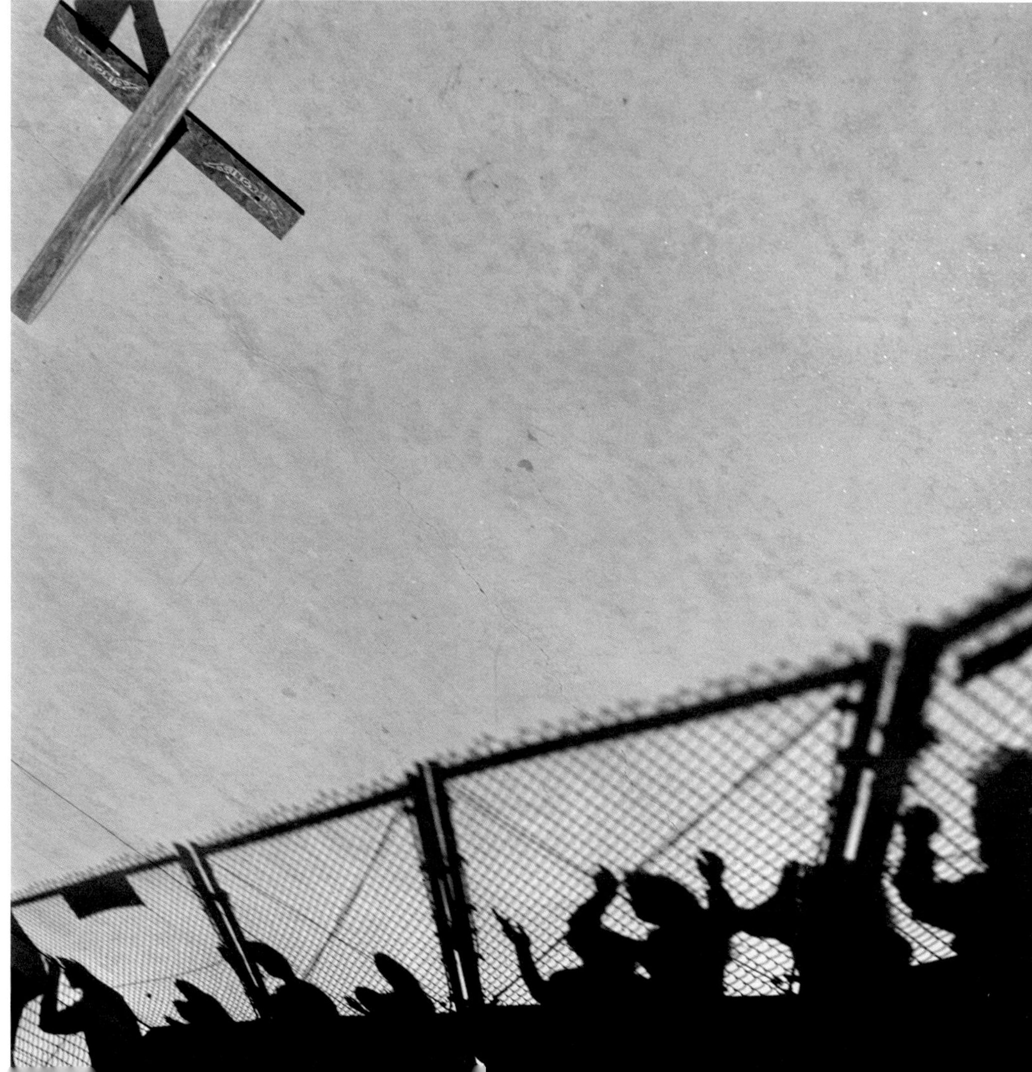

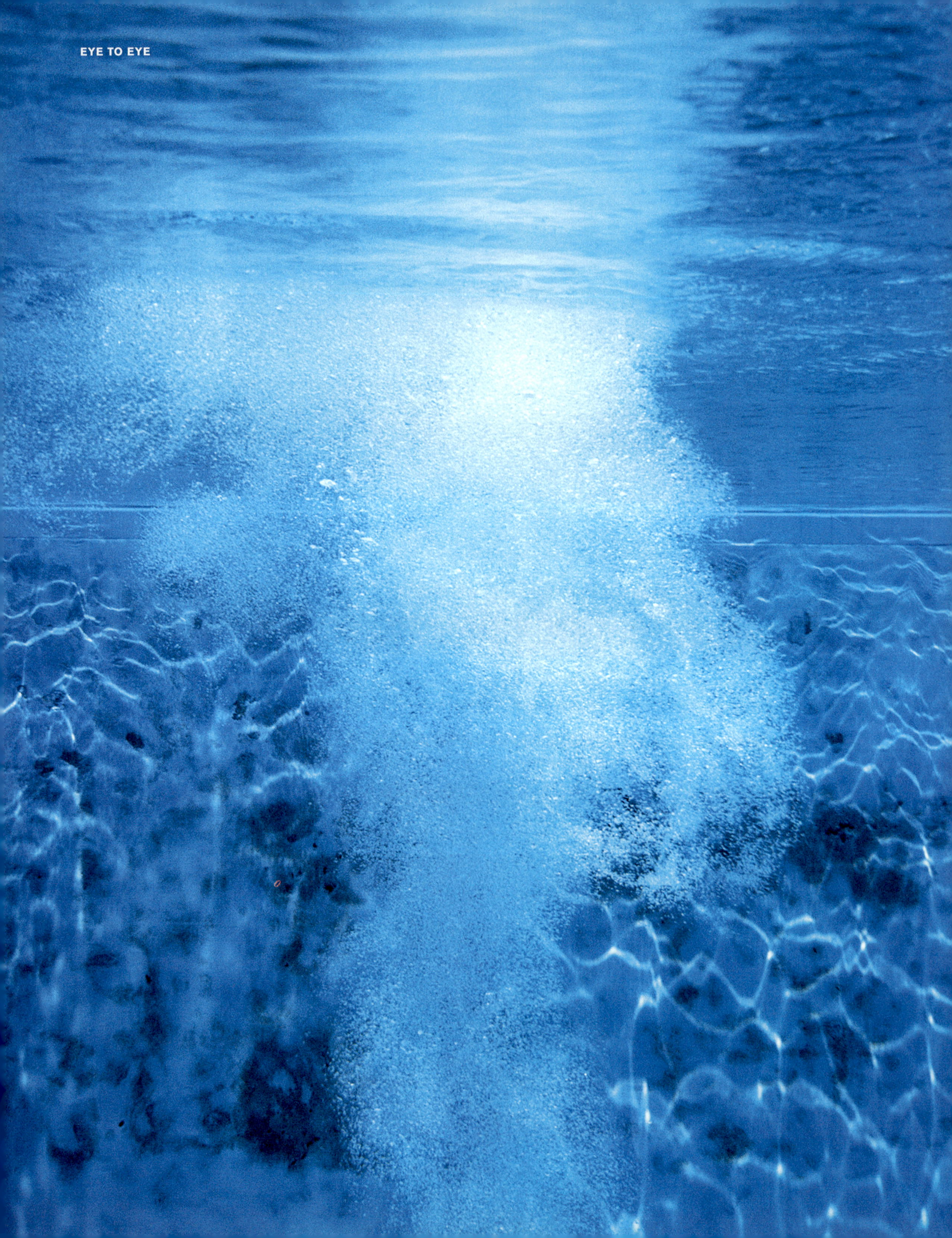

# *Formatting the Future*
# Giorgio Barrera in conversation with
# JOEL MEYEROWITZ

**Joel Meyerowitz decided to be a photographer in 1962 when he was working as Art Director for an agency on Fifth Avenue. The motivating factor for this professional shift was seeing Robert Frank during a commercial shoot, which almost immediately compelled him to follow the Swiss master's example. Meyerowitz started as a street-photographer in the Big Apple, and eventually began to stand out from his colleagues for one crucial element in his work: color. Since the very beginning he chose to depict the urban world he was living in without excluding any of its nuances. His pictures influenced the acceptance of color photography in the art world in the late 1960s and mid 1970s. Color was key to his production in the following years, when Meyerowitz started using an 8x10 view camera, which allowed him to realize some of his best-known photographs. His most recent series is committed to representing the natural elements: water, fire, wind and earth. In the following conversation with Giorgio Barrera the two photographers, who both have refined the use of large format film, talk about the past and the present and their favorite topic, the future.**

**GIORGIO BARRERA** *In an interview you gave in 1981 for a TV program called* Visions and Images *you stated that "technology has always changed photography." At that time you were referring to your switch from B/W to color photography. Being one of the pioneers of color photography and having been experiencing lots of changes in the last decades, now B/W photography is getting more and more rare and technology has changed photography into digital. What do you think photography represents now?*

**JOEL MEYEROWITZ** Today's photography represents an opportunity for artists, and even the general public, to easily cross over from other disciplines as access to photography's methods are now so available and seem so simple, as opposed to the days when the darkroom and its mysteries kept many people away. Technology once again has enlarged the territory of photography's influence and brings us now a new kind of playfulness that the demands and costs of film held at bay. We are in the new age of 'everyone is a photographer now.' From being near the scene of a disaster or crime, to being in the presence of popes and kings and movie stars, to simply maintaining a blog of all one's thoughts and visual experiences, today's limitless opportunities, and the access to the web's broadcasting power makes this time a rich mix of possibility for anyone who is open to looking at their immediate world. At the same time, let's be honest, there is an immense amount of meaningless crap being generated; it's sort of like boring conversations that one can't get away from fast enough, but in spite of that there remains the new possibility that fresh voices - unconstrained by schools and academic formulas, and even history - will say original things in ways that we haven't considered as yet. My sense is that this is a moment of great significance in photography and an invitation to millions of people around the world to find a way of saying something of importance for themselves, and with millions more speaking we have a greater chance for genius to appear.

*Last April, SFMoMA opened a symposium titled* Is Photography Over? *where major art critics and curators were invited to answer this question. Lavoisier stated that "nothing can be created or destroyed, but rather it can be rearranged." Do you think that this sentence may fit to that question?*

Well, Lavoisier may be wrong. We do have a new creation,

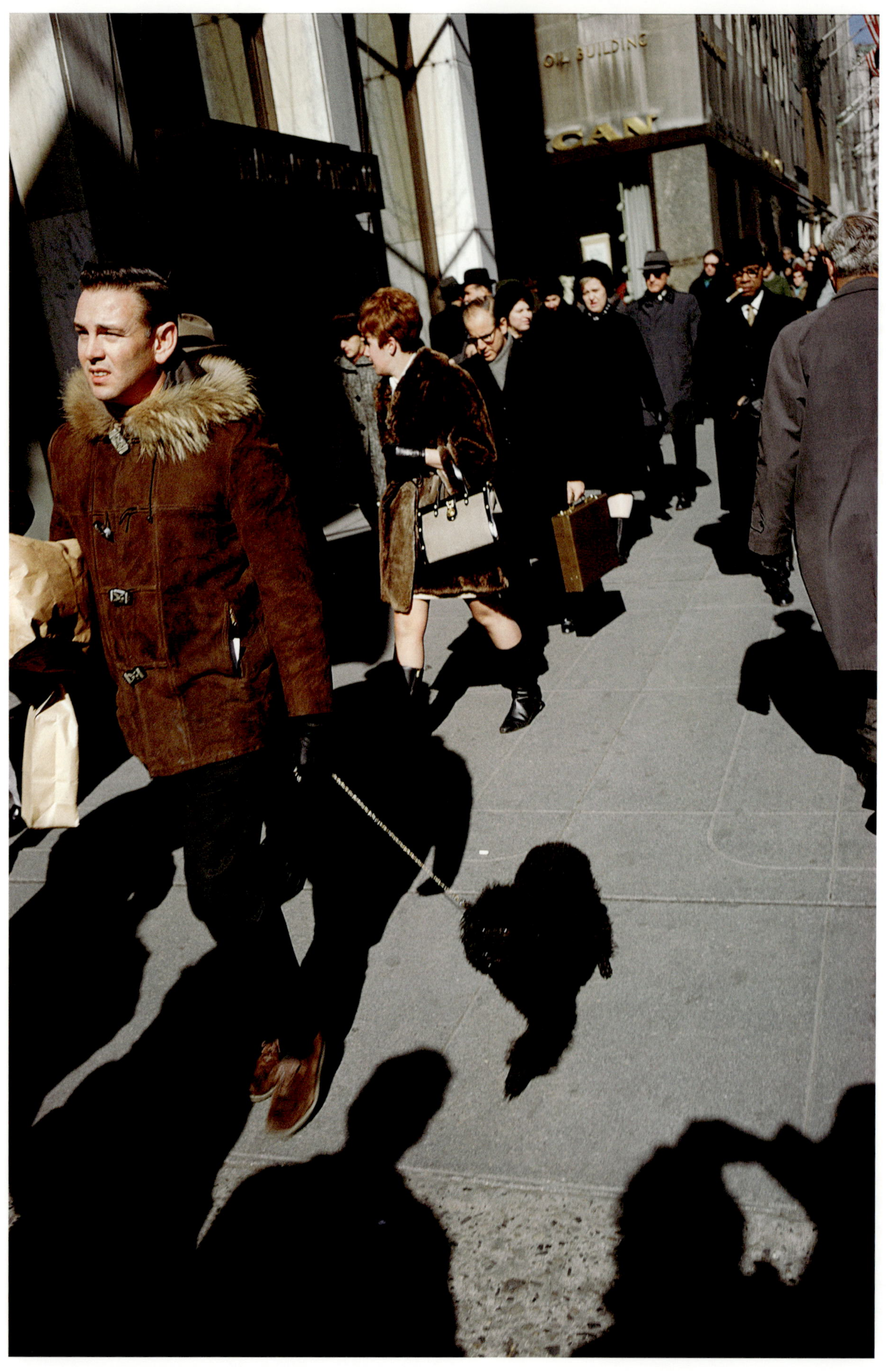
OIL BUILDING
CAN

which happened when we moved from light activated salt crystals to ones and zeros, thereby expressing through pixels what we can see and say and remember. This new technology has liberated us to re-imagine the way we view our world. So, from that point of view we can say that photography is over, or dead, whichever sets up a more dramatic position for argument. Photography as we knew it is over. Now it is a much more plastic and fluid form than ever before, and with this flexibility we invite more creative activity to be unleashed. Much of this takes place in the space that Photoshop has provided for us, a space where fictions can easily be attached to 'truths,' or let's say to direct observations. The metaphysical view of reality we took for granted has been somewhat stretched by photography now. We have subjective reality, objective reality, and finally reality itself uninflected by any connection the observer 'I' brings to bear on things.

When observing the use of the new tools of photography, we can see how blurry the boundaries between subjective and objective reality can become, and how presentation of these visions as reality are closer to Lavoisier's concept of things being merely 'rearranged.' In that sense he is correct since it is the rearrangement of details or elements from one image to another that brings us to the 'mashup' mentality - to use a word that covers a lot of the aesthetic opportunities and strategies of today - which is often fearless about reassembling bits and pieces of images to create a new presentation. We see this in music, video and the performance works which combine all these elements.

*Your series,* The Elements: Air/Water, Part 1 *is a work in progress with a conceptual approach that is pretty different from other previous works of yours. Images are kind of abstracts and it seems to me they depict another world. It's odd, somehow, that the representation of natural elements may need and be shown through abstraction. Are they an abstraction of a straight experience? And, why this need of representing those natural elements?*

*The Elements* series came about by chance plus the cumulative observations I've been making for a long time now. This work poses a fresh photographic problem for me to consider as well as how to approach this new idea and whether it has any validity at all, but only by raising the question in the first place can one take the risk and feel the excitement of the challenge. A brief background; I was making an installation video to accompany an exhibition in Cologne and what I went to film suddenly changed direction and opened me to the question of what would lead me to this *Elements* work. I was in an underwater viewing room beneath a professional diving pool in Florida watching Olympic divers practice. I kept observing how when each diver entered the water they brought in with them an immense cloud of air bubbles which surrounded them, and then when they had passed through it on their way to the bottom, the cloud of bubbles cohered in a cosmic cluster and slowly rose to the surface and dissipated. After a number of these events, I had a flash of recognition that the two basic elements, Air and Water, were in a momentary union within the water but then, as they must, they separated back into their individual forms. It was then, in a flash that I saw how Air Water Fire Earth were each their own phenomena and it came to my mind that that would be an interesting challenge to see how each phenomena might be photographed. But now, in a way that presented the phenomena as an experience rather than a picture of it using the photographic conventions we are all used to. For example, I have photographed air and water for 30 years now, and there is always the horizon line to distinguish between top and bottom, and even though that is a fairly flat representation we still incur some sense of

Renaissance perspective, where things near are larger than those far away. I had a sudden urge to do away with the convention of deep space and instead resort to the image being only the thing itself, and printed at a scale that would present the image at a size that was similar to what the viewer might experience if they stood in a field looking down at earth or at the water's edge looking at the sea. A one-to-one scale image. I was on fire with this idea and I saw immediately how risky the attempt could be, how possibly boring and familiar photographs or dirt, air, water, etc would look. But the idea that 'Phenomena' might be brought into a space and visitors could suspend themself in front of it and be taken in by it was all I could think of. My feeling was to make large format still images as well as videos and I have been pursuing that now on and off for 3 years in different parts of the U.S. and the world.

The issue of 'abstraction' is one that follows photography everywhere. These photographs don't seem to me to be abstractions since they are representations of an elemental experience, but at the same time they are a fragment of that experience and therefore an 'abstract' of it, a quote from it, a reduced, but also possibly heightened version of it. So this boils down to language; abstraction vs. representation, but once we stand and dismiss the horizon line and look into moving water, simply stare into it, it has the immediate power to become an abstraction, and the same for earth, fire, etc - just watch flames leaping, and how you dissolve into them in that primal dream state of humans at the edge of a fire and you'll feel the power of abstraction. It's what I believe the latent forces of phenomena can bring to us.

*This year will be 10 years after September 11. You worked in Ground Zero for many months, taking pictures of what happened and was happening inside the site. Do you consider that work a documentary one? Many of those images remind of 17th and 18th century paintings. What were you looking for in the midst of the rubble's site?*

I worked inside Ground Zero for nine months and although I brought my past memory of what can happen on streets anywhere in the world into the work down there, it became a different, larger, and more complex kind of project for me. One that contained some of the chance qualities of street photography, but also one that required a historical point of view. I went in because I felt a deep need to help out in a time of disaster, and photography was all I was capable of doing. I told myself that since I was the only one who was going to keep a record of all the efforts down in the zone, and if that was my goal, then I would have to do it in a way that treated the experience with dignity, and I'd use a visual approach that allowed for very large scale images that could work on a visceral level rather than merely for the eye. I was inspired by images from as far back as the American Civil War, where large format cameras recorded every small detail so that the enormity of the carnage could be understood by whoever stood in front of the photograph. I wanted the same clarity for my work.

What became of interest to me was that I began to think like a historian and found myself drawn to content that I would normally not be interested in; for example, the practice they had of washing every vehicle that left the site so that no pollutants or asbestos fibers left the site and entered the life of the city. This was a mundane task beneath artistic notice, but it happened all day at 4 points in the site, so I became aware of it and always added to my collection of images about it. This was true of every practice down there and it was only by becoming conscious of it that I was able to function as the historical record keeper. This was all new to me and I believe that the opening of my mind in that way actually made me more ready to receive the inspiration to go forward with something like *The Elements*.

*You have worked almost on all fields of photography from street photography to landscape, from portrait to cityscape. It often seems to me that, behind the image, a story is hidden. It appears very clearly that a photograph - be it a large or 35mm format - is an interruption of the flow of time. If you feel this to be true, can you tell us something more about it?*

It is true as you say that a photograph is an interruption, but in our flow of time, not in time itself. It is we who are shaken out of our dream state for a brief moment of consciousness where we suddenly see with the clarity of a newborn who is gifted with an old eye. Well, wait a second, it may be that is not so correct because I was once more naive than I am now, most certainly. And back then everything was new to me, and the world was delicious, and I wanted to eat it all, take it inside of me so I could savor it and know something about it. We are all innocent once and then we build our experience and if we are lucky we maintain some core place where the sweetness of innocence still resides. I believe it is that space between knowing and innocence that the art spirit stays alive. Lose the innocence and you've lost the essential connection with the spiritual, intuitive self. Look around you at all the works you admire, including your own, and you'll see where that pure vision is intact, and then look at the rest of the work and if you can't tell the difference then you are doomed to wander until you recognize what is of essential quality. Even so, we will all wander off the track. Photography's nature is such that we are always experimenting, wishing, reaching out for, and consuming our experiences. In some ways this is the gift of photography, this bounty of the world pouring itself into our eyes every day as, armed with this glass cup in our hands, we take the drops of nectar from the gods. And there is another gift that I believe plays an essential role in photography's delicate and sometimes elusive search for meaning. And that is ambiguity, which is what the world presents every day. There are few, if any, guaranteed meanings the world offers. Everything is tangential, oblique, marginal, momentary. For me the all of photography has been about relationships. How do things relate to each other, and from their simultaneous appearance in the frame, what meanings are offered? When I have been asked about what it is that I photograph, the first and clearest response is: relationships between things or moments. Simple as that.

The idea of putting an object into a frame no longer holds appeal to me. It's too much like collecting artifacts. I find that too simple an act of observation, too much like still life - and I certainly accept the remarkable works that are made in that genre - it's just that I can no longer find passion in pursuit of that idea. It's the ambiguity that thrills me and this is where I see photography's unique strength; we have an instrument in our hands which has the amazing capability of recording with exquisite detail everything we turn the camera towards, and yet... and yet, more often than not what we have in the frame does not tell a coherent story - if it did, we would not have needed captions for as long as we have relied on them. So this break between the concrete description of things and the open ended meanings that attach to them make photography a medium for minds that are open to this kind of conjecture, this playful, philosophical, humanistic tool.

*Page 28* The Elements, Air/Water 16. *Page 30* NYC, 5th Avenue, 1968. *Page 34 top* Florida, 1965. *Page 34 bottom* NYC, 5th Avenue, 1973. *Page 35 top* NYC, 6th Avenue, 1975. *Page 35 bottom* NYC, Riverside Drive, 1974. *Page 36 top* NYC, 8th Avenue, 1978. *Page 36 bottom* NYC, Puerto Rican Parade, 1963. *Page 37* NYC, Puerto Rican Parade, 1963. *All images © the artist, courtesy Edwynn Houk Gallery, New York*

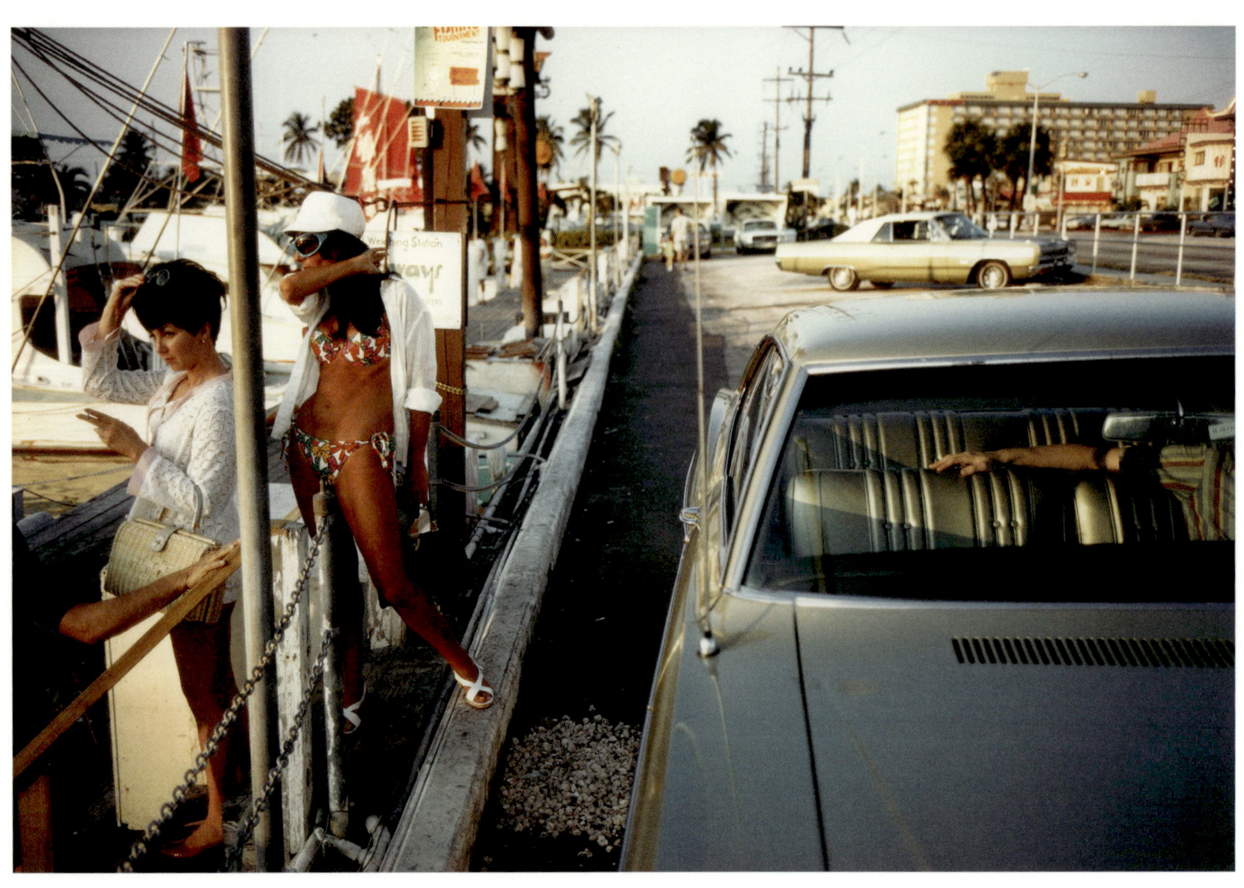

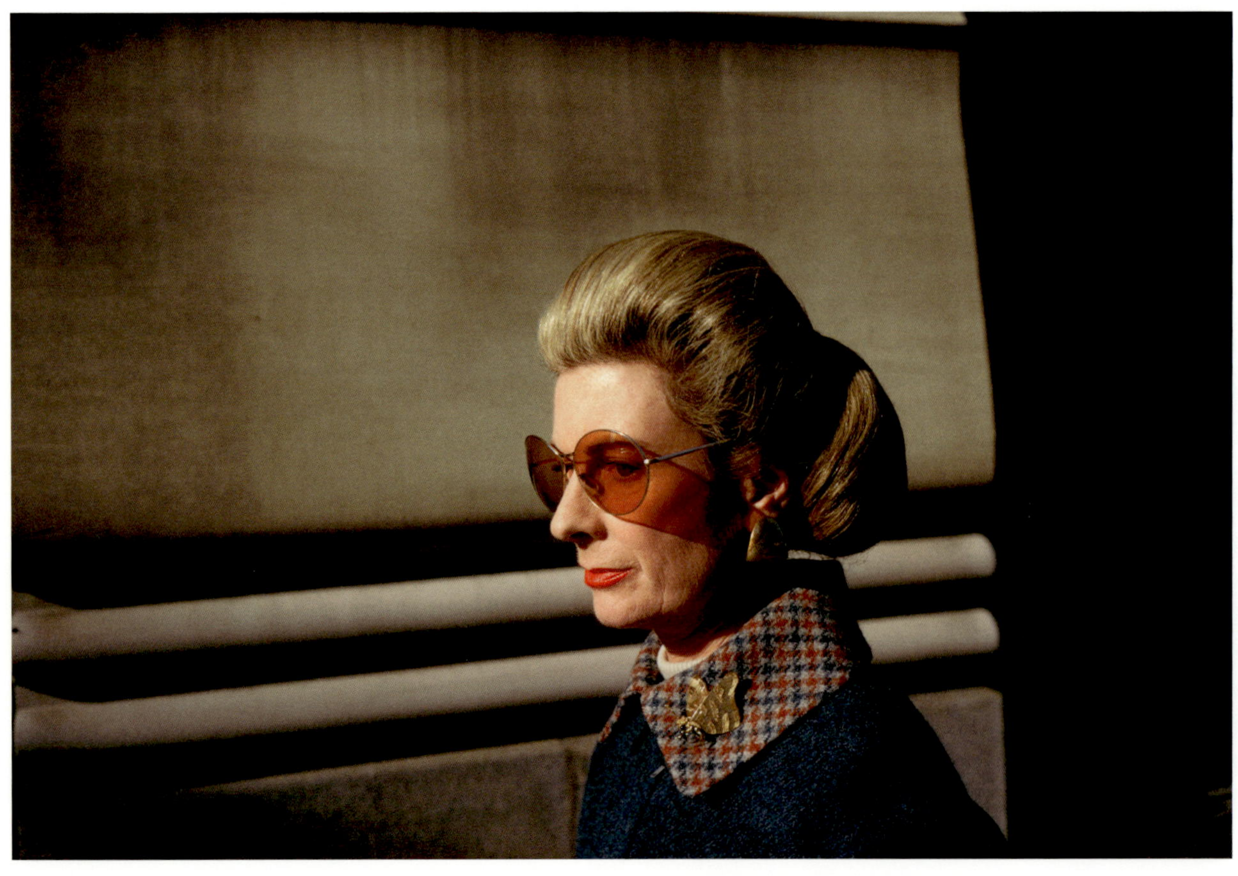

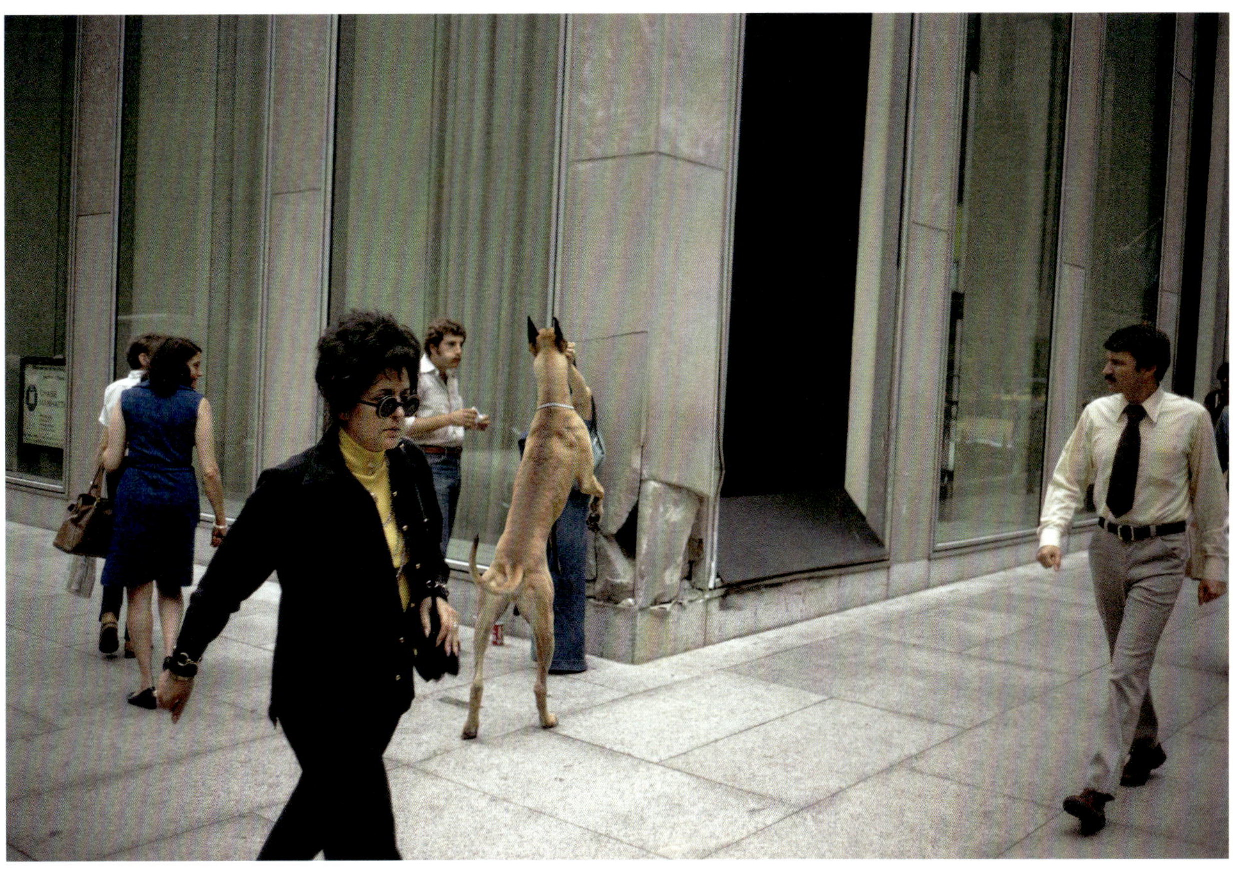

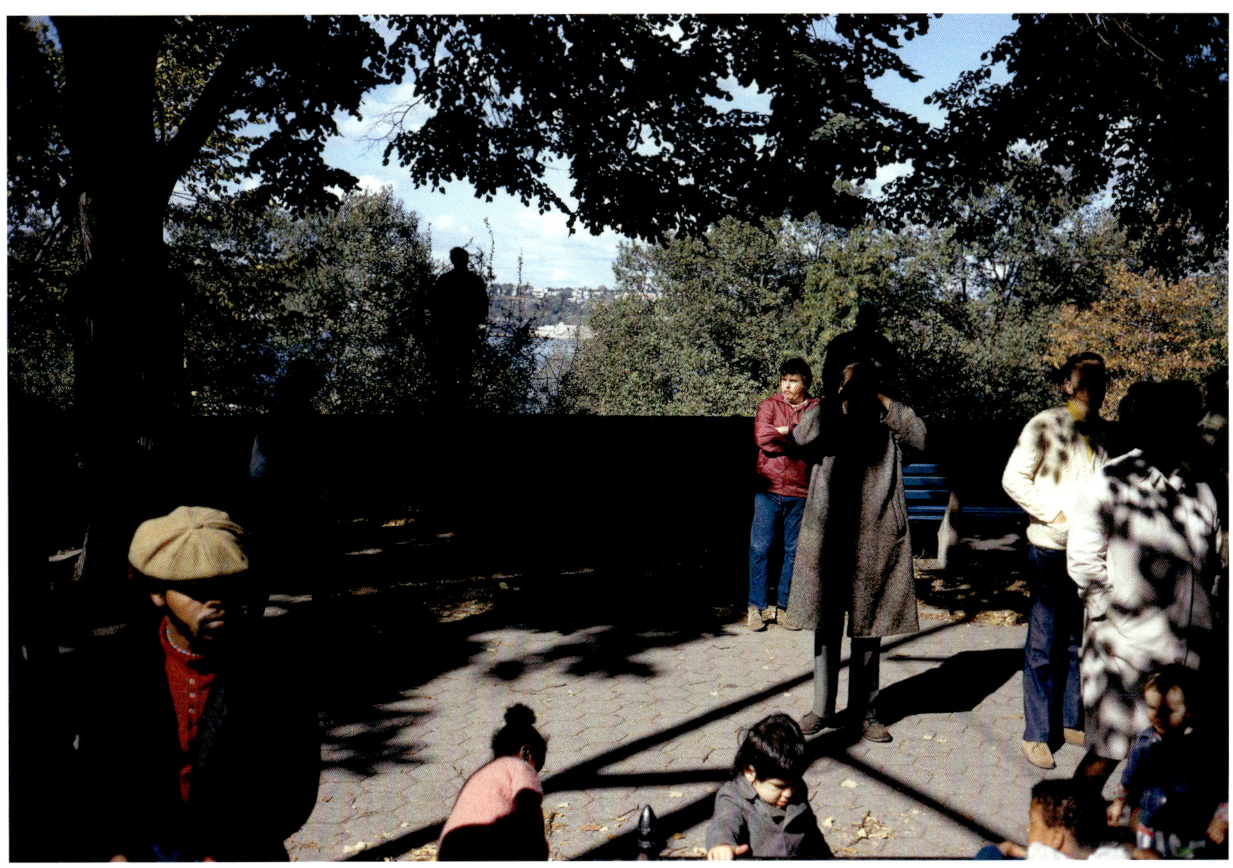

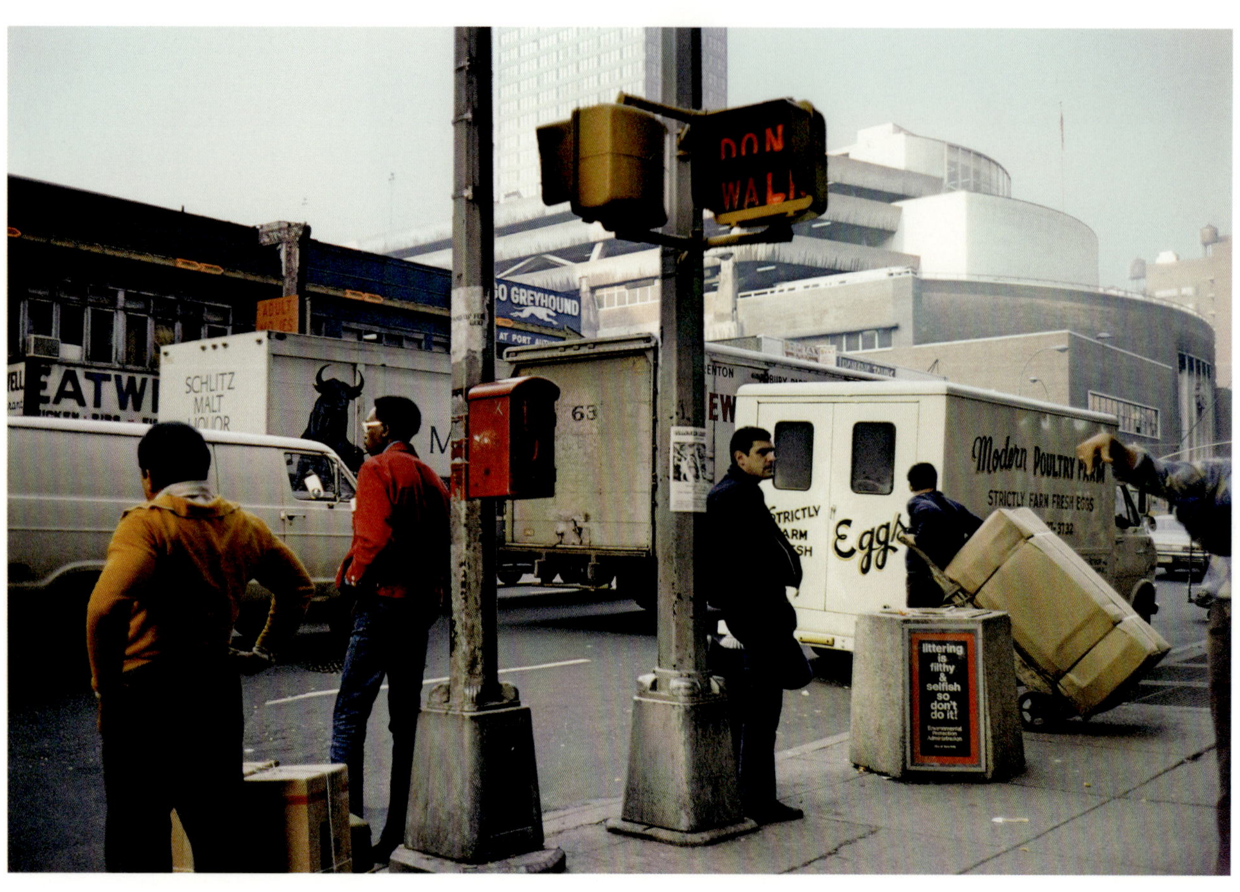

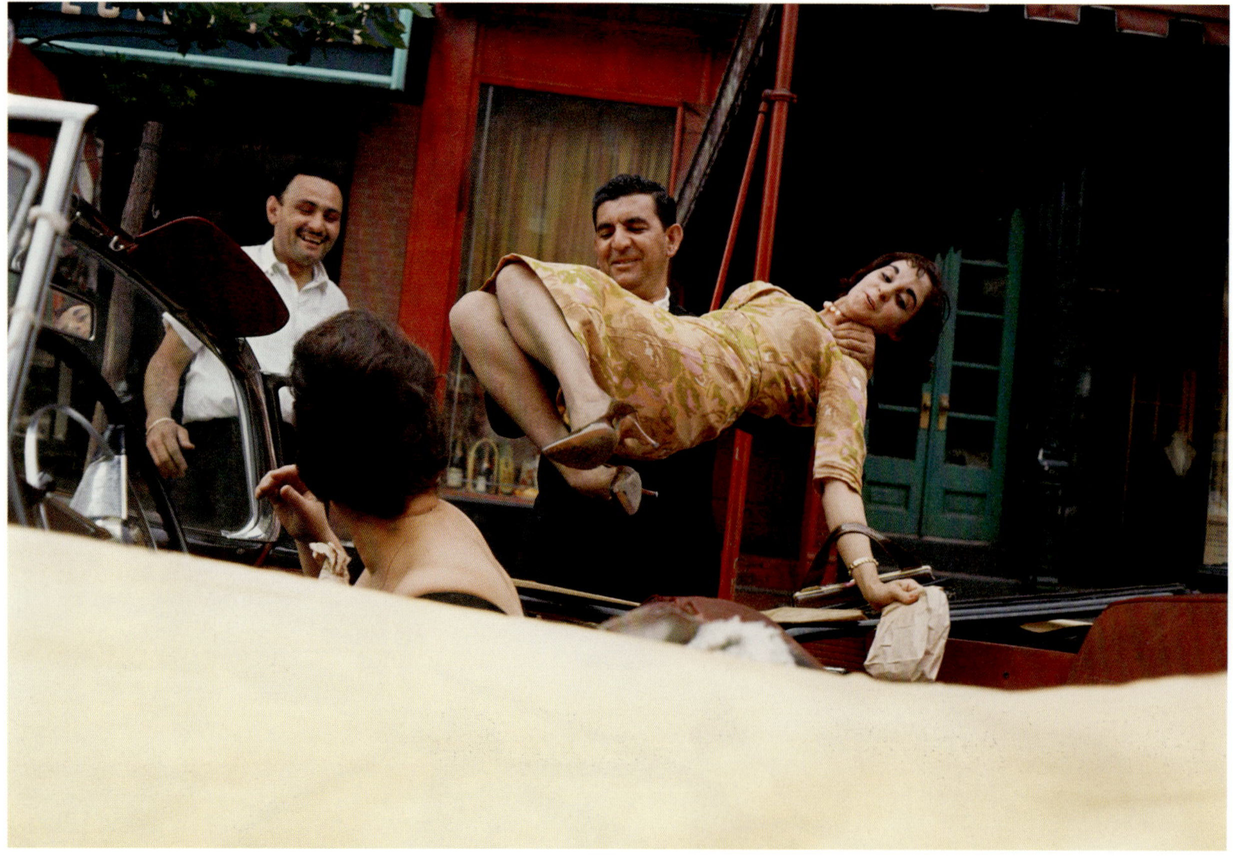

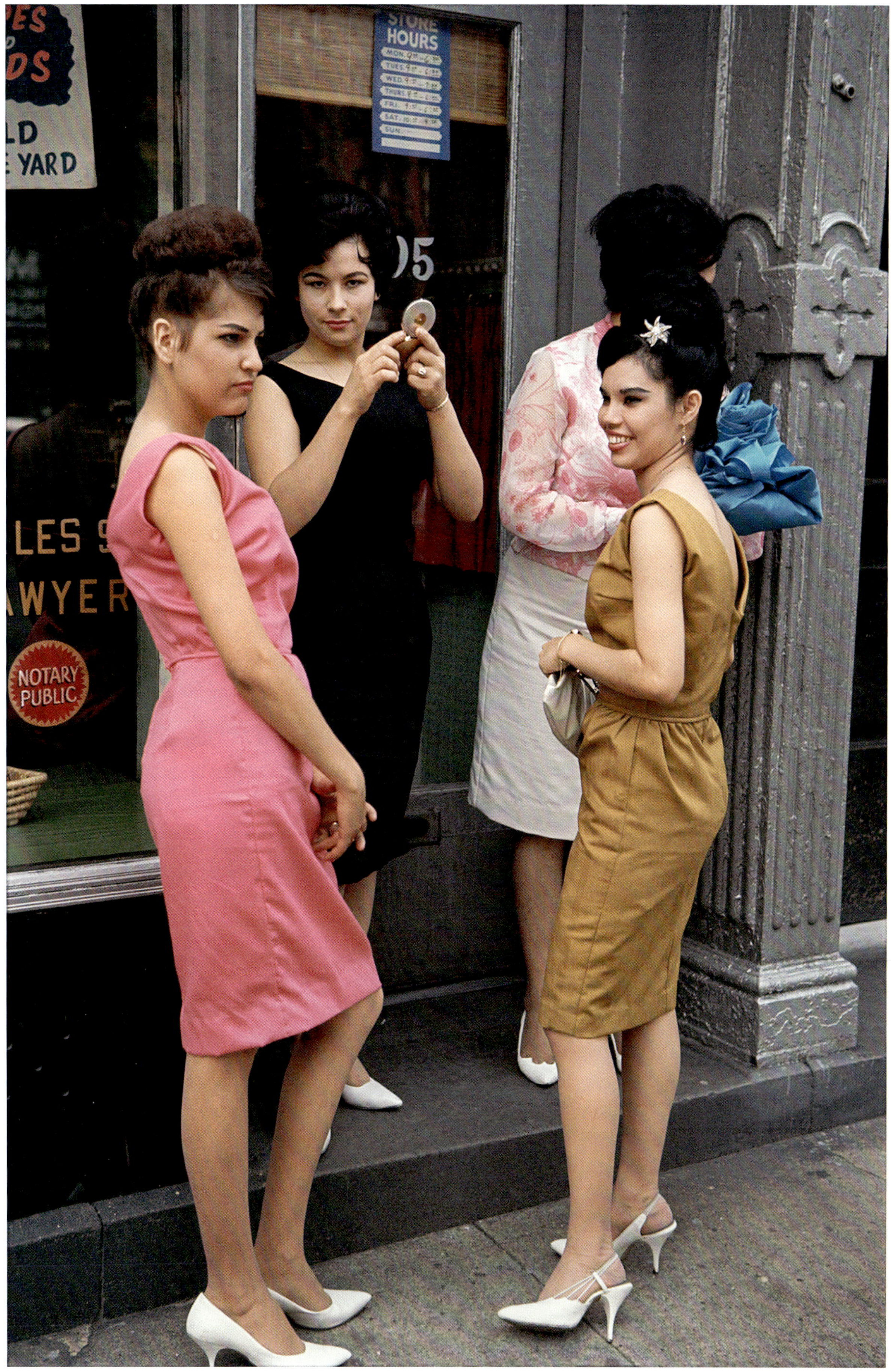
STORE
HOURS
MON.
TUES.
WED.
THURS.
FRI.
SAT.
SUN:
NOTARY
PUBLIC

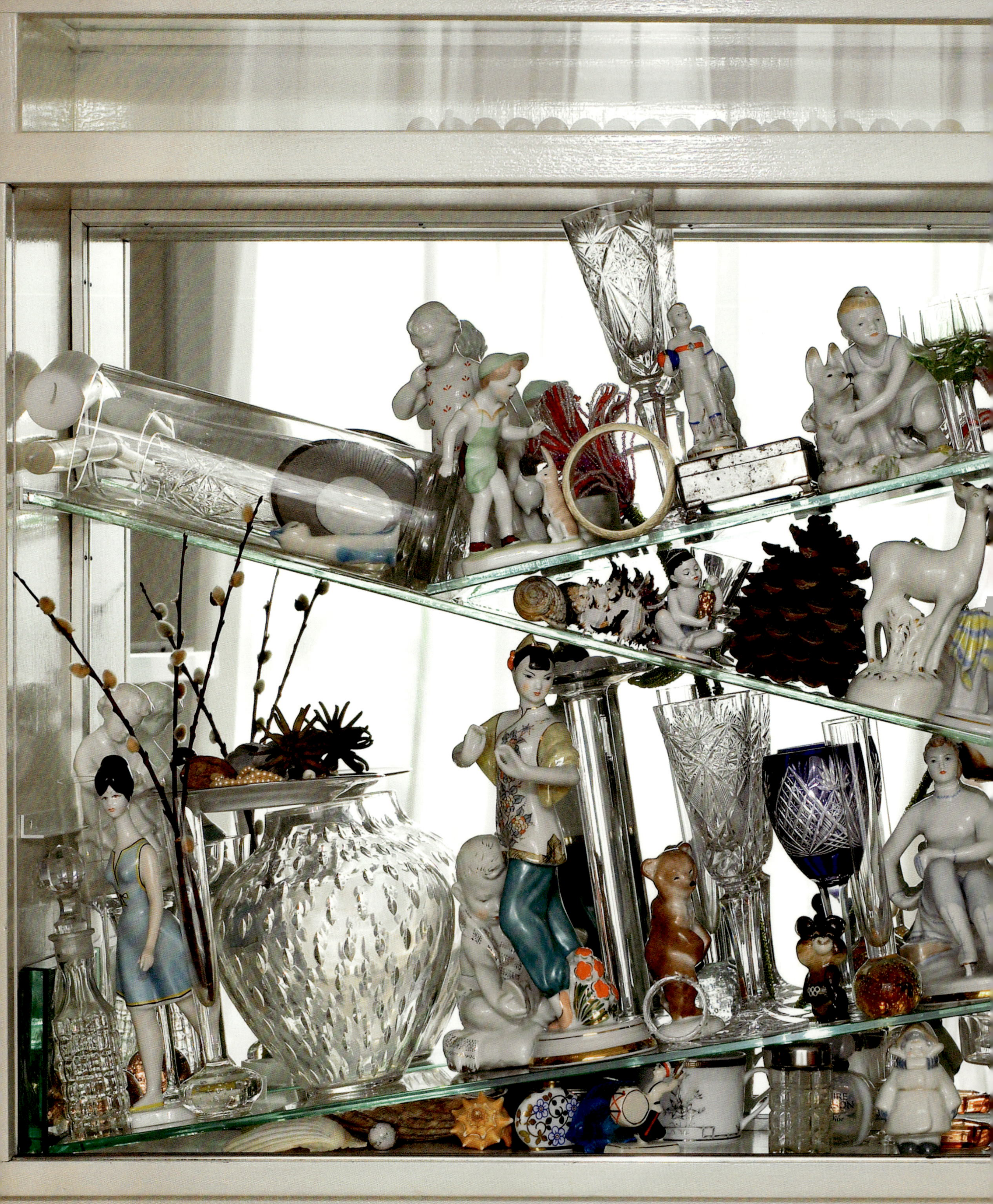

My Collection *from the* Show-Cases *series,* 2008, pigment print, cm 100 x 140. *Image © and courtesy the artist*

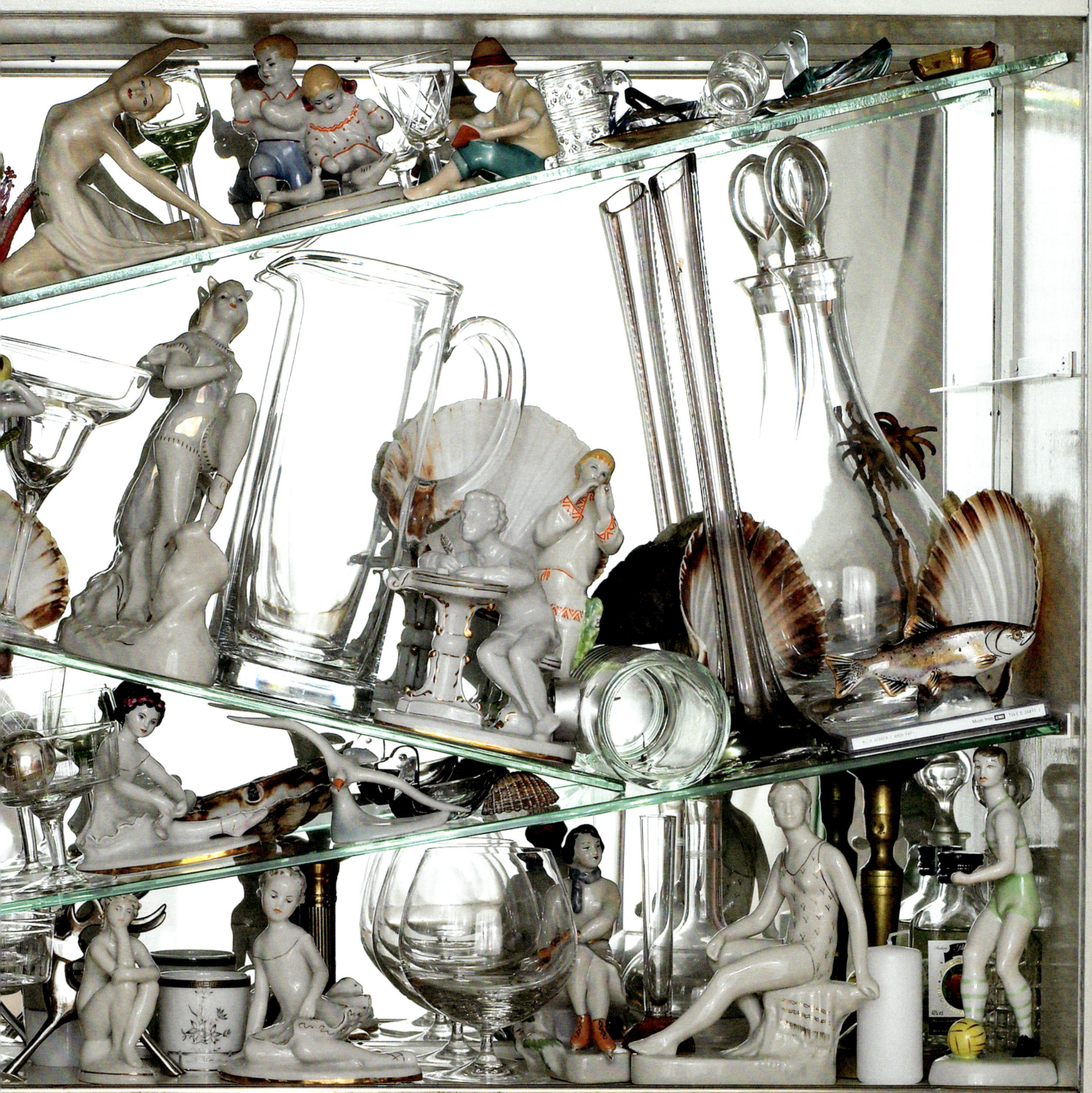

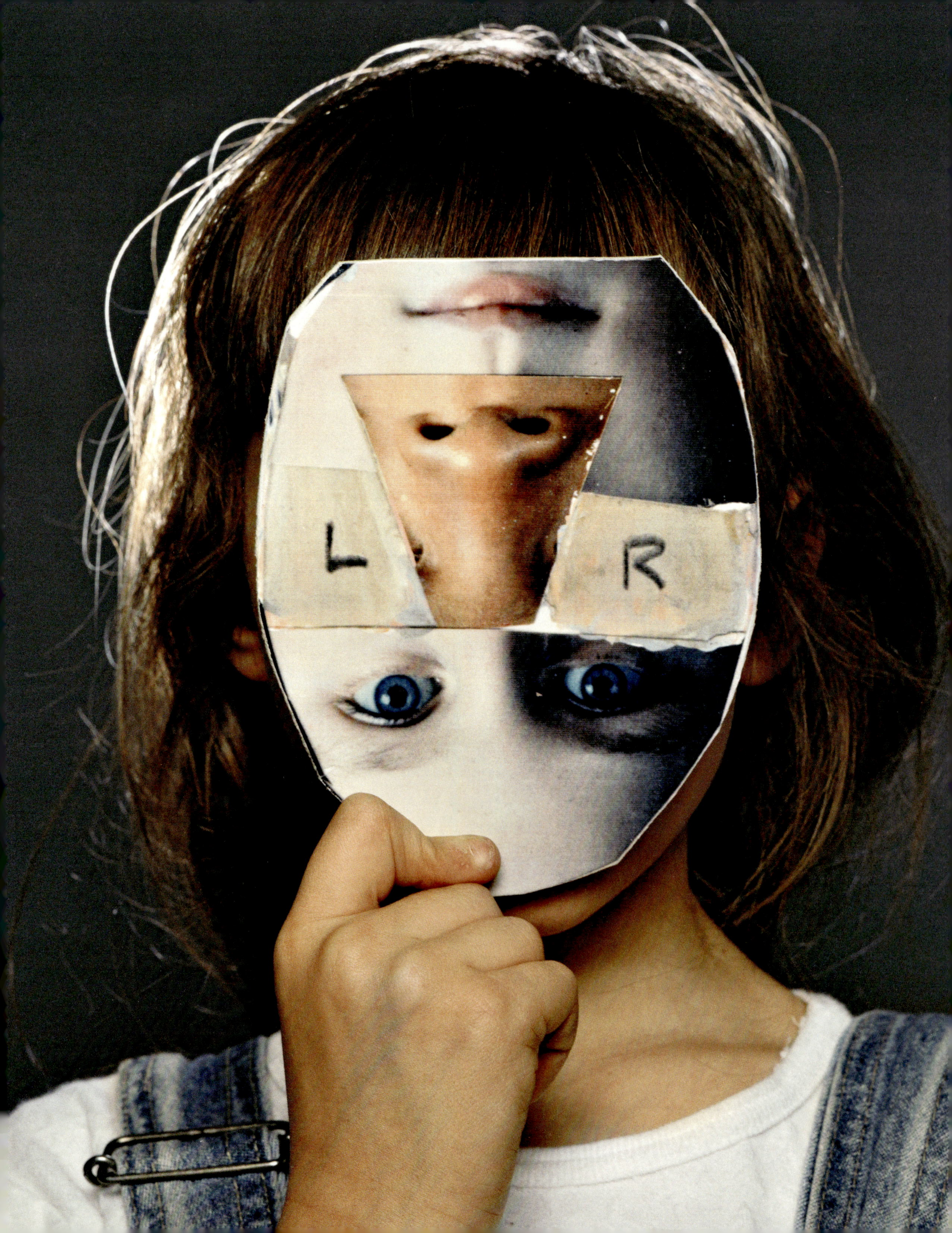
L
R

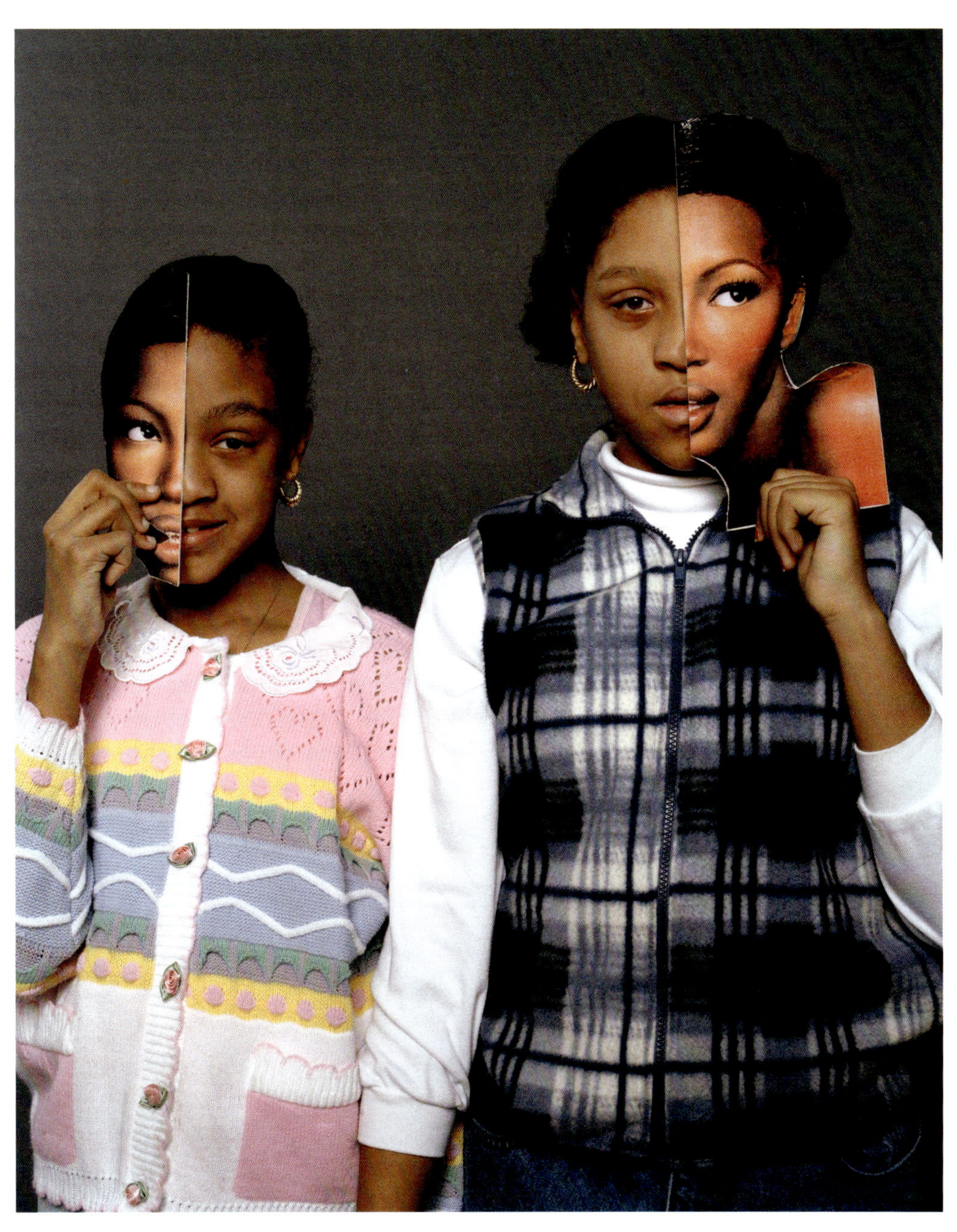

# Auguring the Future
# AURA ROSENBERG's
# Vision of History
# by Stephanie Snyder

Aura Rosenberg's family fled Nazi Germany in 1939. One year later, Walter Benjamin committed suicide in France, his exit visa denied at the border. But not long before entering the past about which he cared so deeply, Benjamin completed, and hid, *On the Concept of History* - a poetic, and prophetic, rumination on Fascism, oppression, and historical materialism. Here, Benjamin gave the world his most enduring image: the Angel of History, flung backwards into the future by the winds of Paradise, condemned to witness civilization as a ruinous bricolage. Over the last ten years, Rosenberg has authored a group of remarkable photographic projects in conversation with Benjamin's proleptic, mystical, and, at times, melancholic vision. Like Benjamin, Rosenberg gazes unflinchingly into German history, embracing magical thinking as a form of insight.

In 1991, while living in Berlin with her husband and young daughter, Rosenberg created a series of one hundred and seventy five images in response to each entry in Benjamin's 1932 memoir *Berlin Childhood Around 1900*. The photographs capture the remains of the past - those not irremediably lost through systematic annihilation - in the context of the everyday present. In the photograph Kaiserpanorama, for instance, a child peers into the public stereoscope of Benjamin's youth. A form of mass spectacle, the Kaiserpanorama sat twenty-four people simultaneously, constructing visions of geographic and ethnic otherness for the German public. There, Benjamin wrote, "… the desire these worlds awakened would call them not into the unknown, but home." In her own imaginary Berlin childhood, Rosenberg summons a vision of place that never came to pass - one steeped in innocence and fantasy, with a sense of menace lurking at the edges. The photographs offer the viewer a trans-subjective experience of a disappeared past blanketed by time and the recurrence of trauma.

Rosenberg has also re-imagined the Angel of History in human form. In *Black Noise* (2006), Rosenberg created an intricate graphic novel (in memoriam of artist Steven Parrino) that immerses the viewer in the Angel's point of view. The last image in the book is a haunting absence: a bite, taken from another book by Parrino himself. The metonymic body of the artist is transferred directly into the work. Such explorations of sensual and sexual transference permeate Rosenberg's work. Her black and white study of male erotic gestures, *Head Shots* (1996), studies the faces of men, up close, while engaged in real and fictive sex. And in her expansive, ongoing collaborative project, *Who am I, What am I, Where am I?* Rosenberg invited artists to create portrait photographs of children, which Rosenberg shot. Here as well, the work is predicated upon the transference of meaning between subjects. The children are covered in face paint and, at times, portrayed in elaborately constructed settings. In a particularly intense image created by

artist Mike Kelley, a young girl is transformed into a weary, delicate, and, perhaps, battered angel.

Particularly in her work with children, Rosenberg summons both tender and unspeakable histories. By convoluting photography's distancing mechanisms through collaboration and physical touch, she captures the transmission of insight, knowledge, and emotion from one place, or person, to another. This, in turn, transforms her photographic projects into vehicles of the kind of trans-subjective awareness described by feminist art historian, Bracha Ettinger: "The [trans-subjective] artwork enacts what are otherwise impossible relations and realizes the passage, onto the screen of vision, of psychic traces from what otherwise remains disconnected from human consciousness or precluded from it and is either absence (the irremediably lost) or a potentiality (the not-yet born) - that which comes into being always in the too early or too late."

Recently, Rosenberg has returned to another text of Benjamin's (this time, his correspondence with writer Gershom Scholem) photographing the residue of coffee grounds at the bottom of antique china cups. The reading of coffee grounds is an old form of divination about which Benjamin wrote, "… a philosophy that does not include the possibility of soothsaying from coffee grounds and cannot explicate it cannot be a true philosophy." The fields of ominous sludge in Rosenberg's photographs possess a mysterious, organic beauty that not only decries artifice, but challenges the viewer's philosophical and spiritual predilections, in effect, enlisting the viewer, alongside the artist, as a reader of signs.

*Page 40* John Baldessari/Carmen, 1996-98. *Page 41* Gerald Jackson/Toni and Ti, 1996-98, *both images from the series* Who Am I? What Am I? Where Am I? *Page 43* Hide and Seek. *Page 44* Zwei Ratselbilder Landwehr Canal. *Page 45 top* Kaiserpanorama; *bottom* The Reading Desk/Eye Exam, *all four images from the series* Berlin Childhood, 1996-2001. *Page 46 top* Coffee Grounds 01; *bottom*, Coffee Grounds 04. *Page 47* Coffee Grounds 06. *All images © the artist, courtesy Sassa Trülzsch, Berlin*

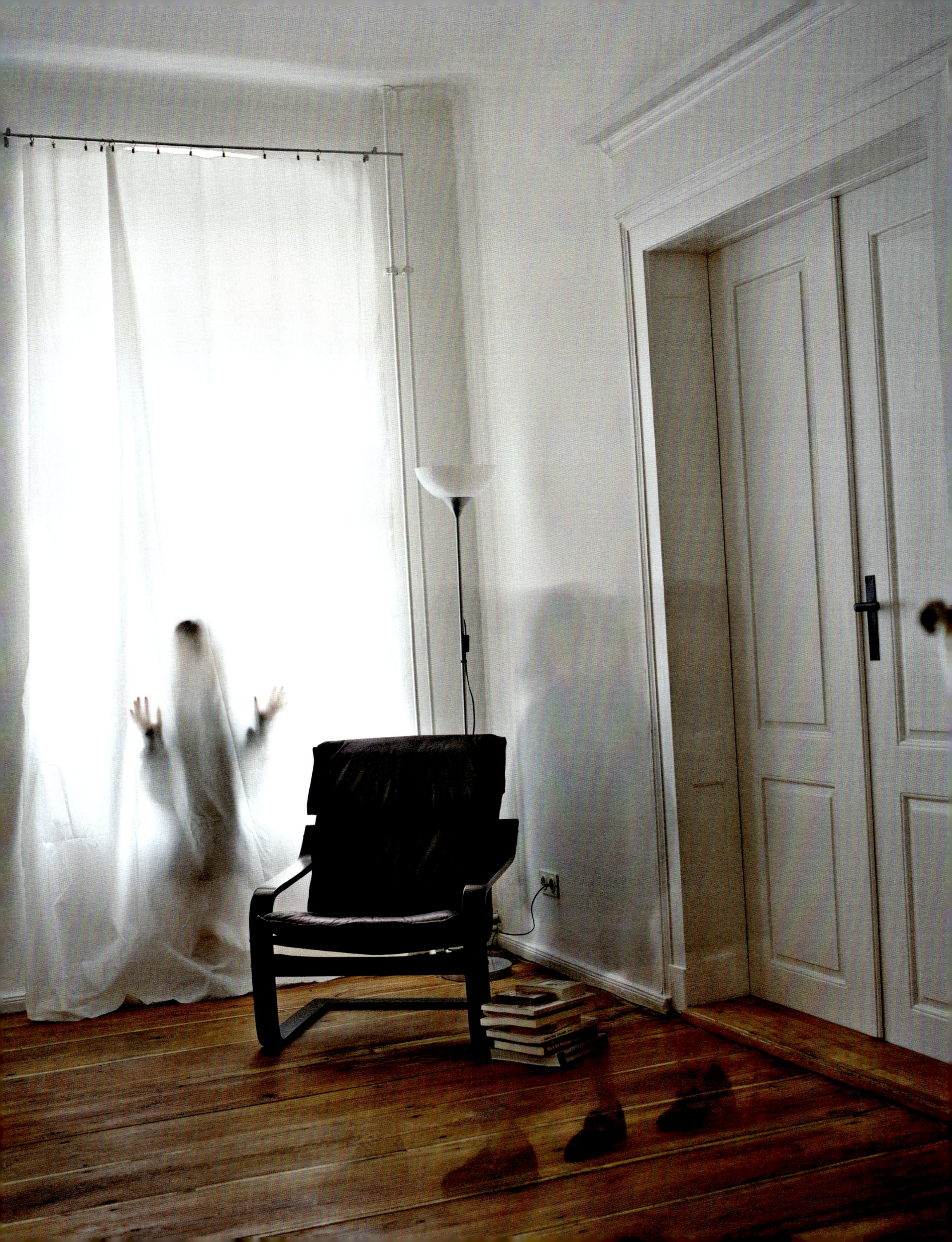

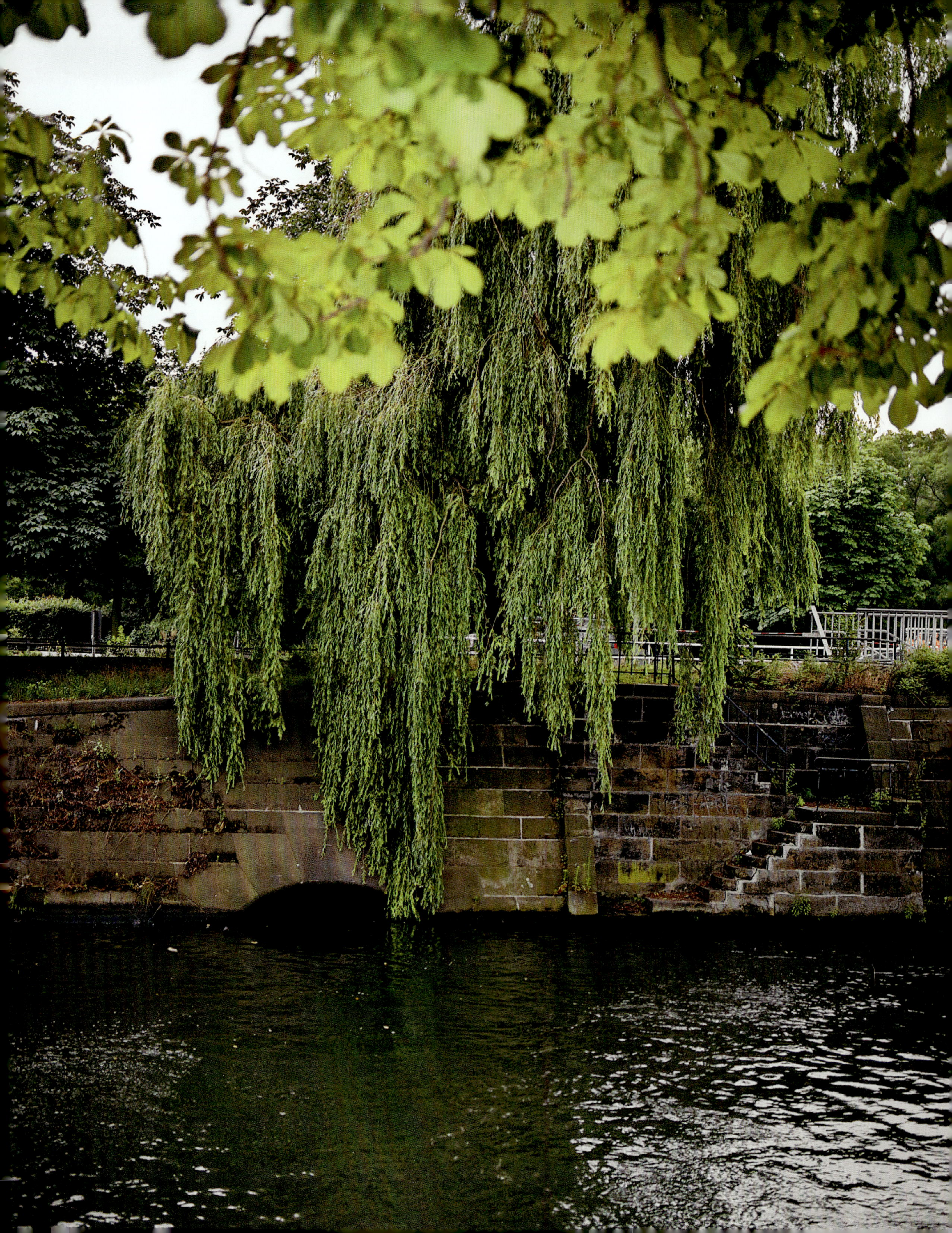

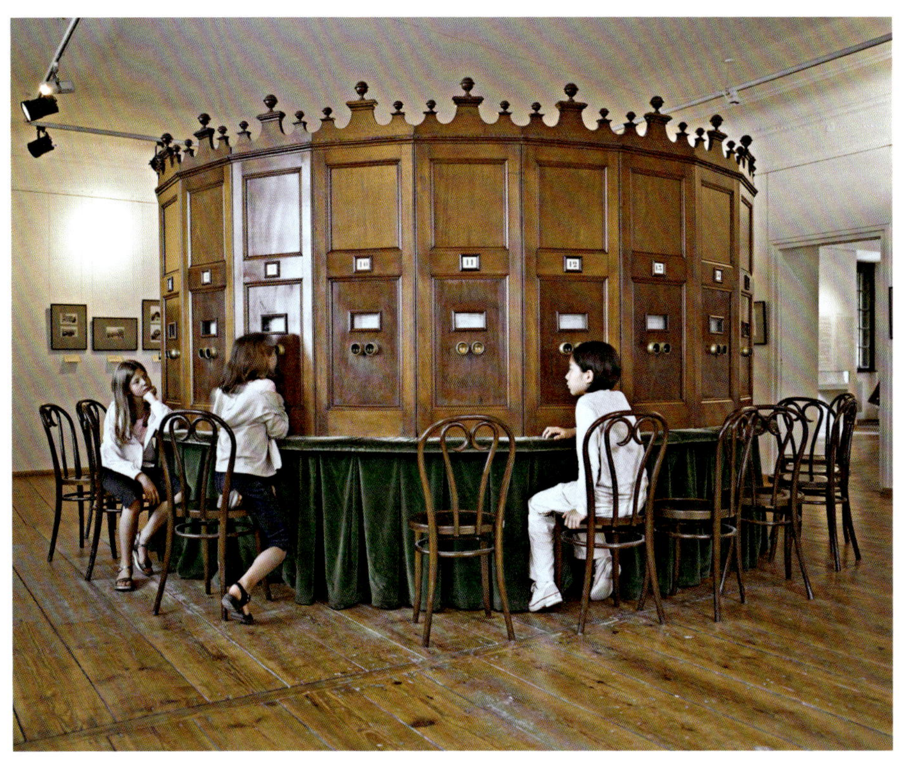

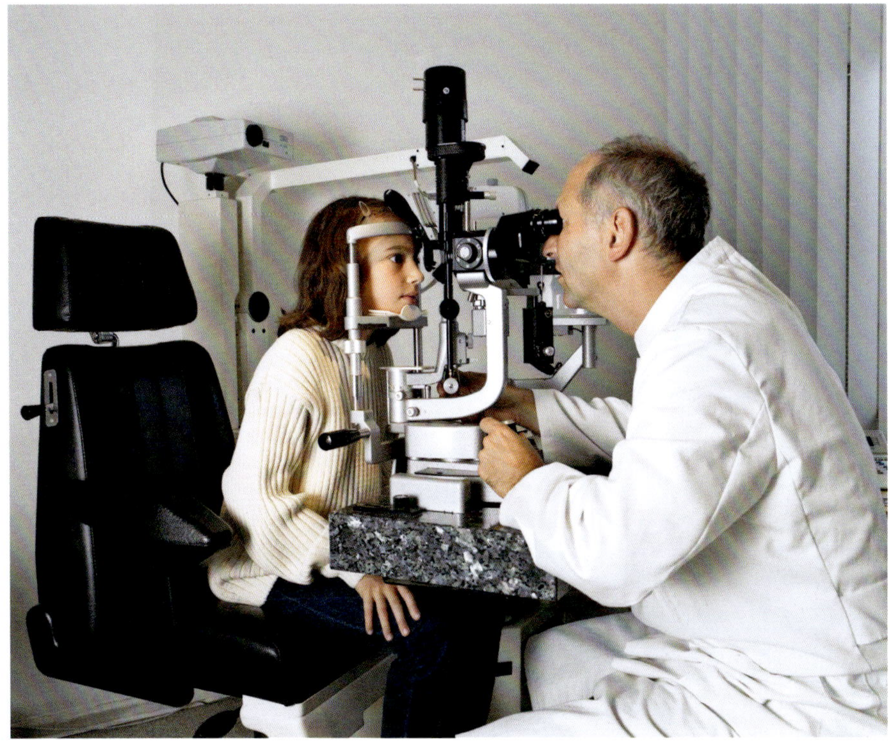

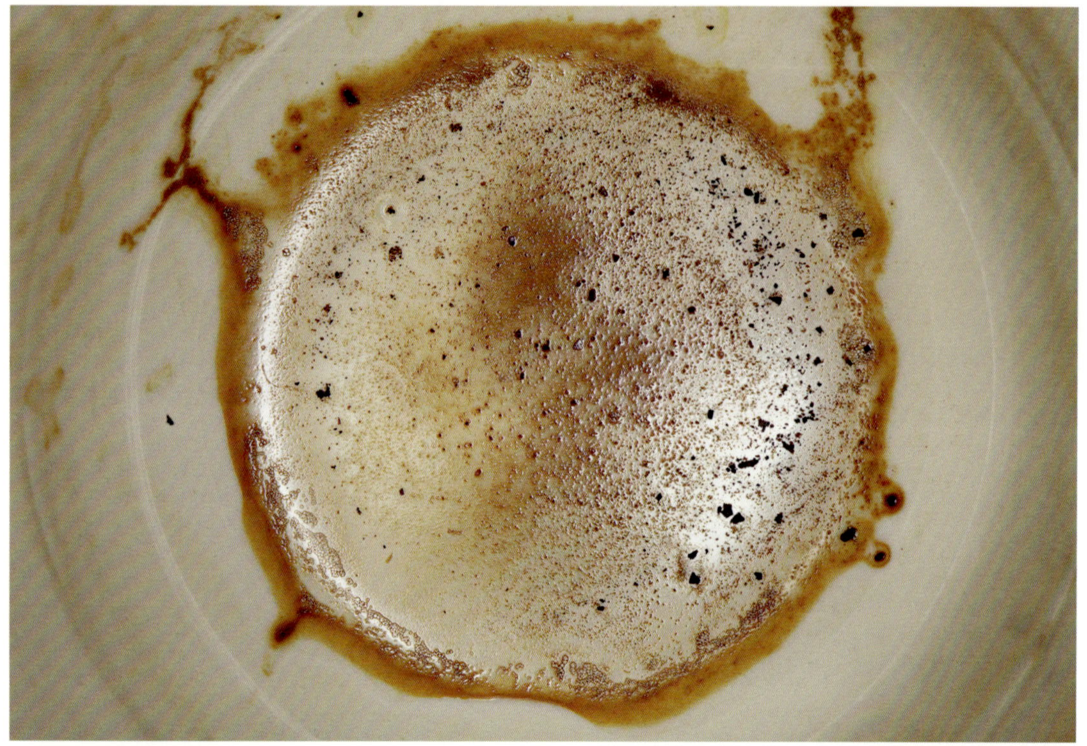

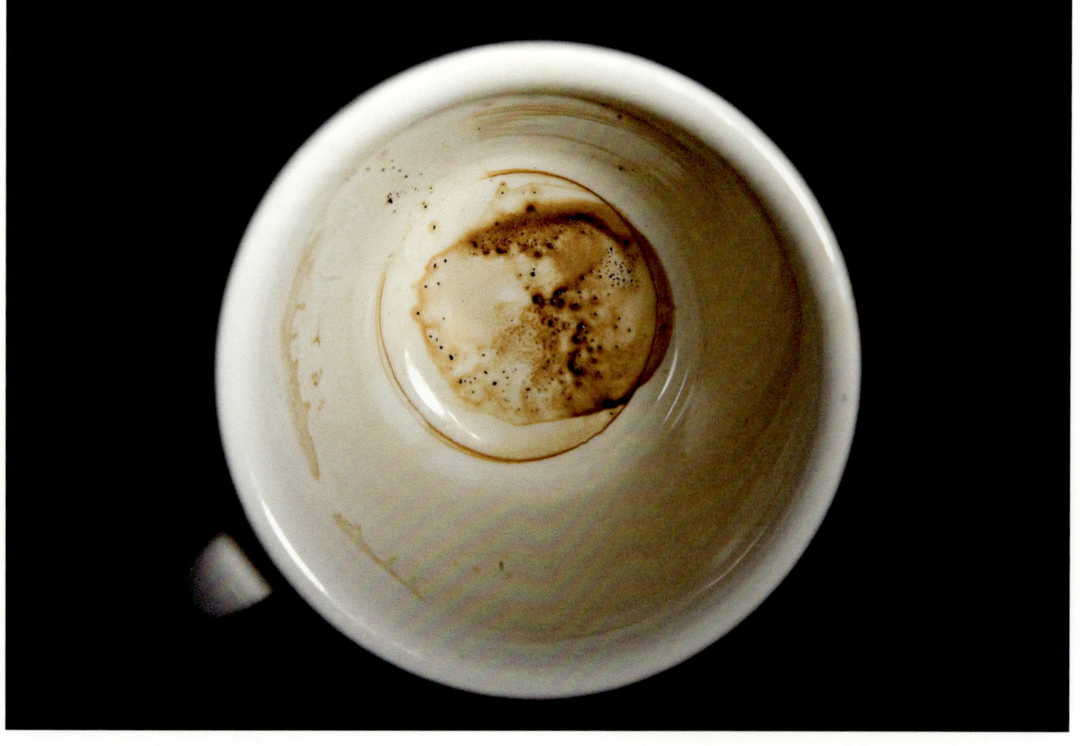

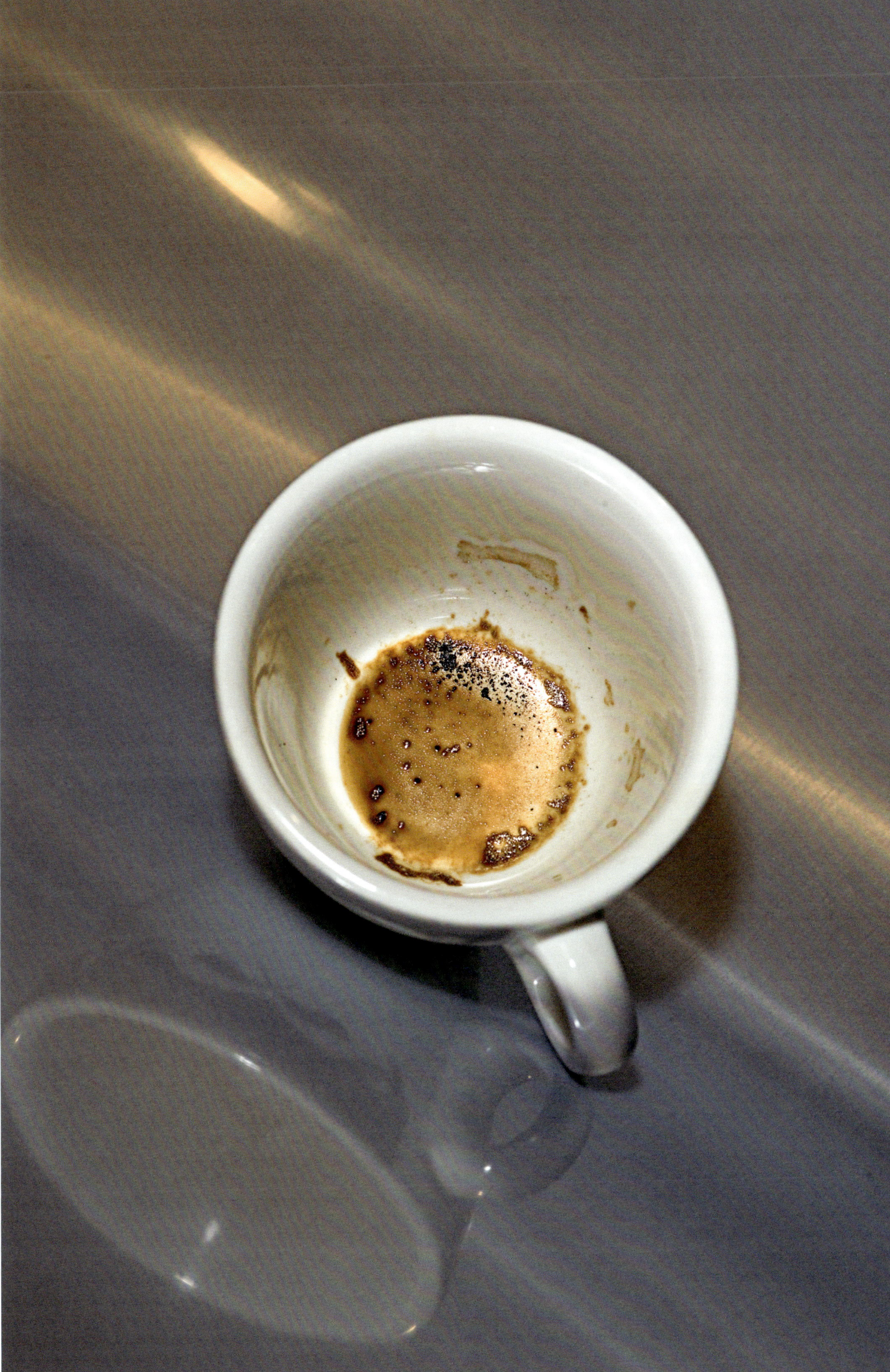

# REAL IMAGES
# MADEIN
## introduced by their gallerist
## David Tung

In a nondescript exhibition space, a young man stares up at a tower bisected in the middle and connected in between by a large steel spring. This is one of the visual clues in the exhibition at the Long March Space *Don't Hang Your Faith on the Wall*, the latest 'solo' endeavor by MadeIn, a young cultural production company founded in 2009 by Shanghai based artist, Xu Zhen. A reading of the exhibition label for the work tells us that it is titled Democracy Is Our Goal, But the Country Must Remain Stable, that the work is made of granite and steel spring, the dimensions are 500 x 500 x 1000 cm, and the work is from 2010. A deeper reading of this information tells us that the title is a quotation taken from former Chinese premier Deng Xiaoping to George H. W. Bush. From here on, we let our interpretive knowledge of China's political system take over. The distance from the top of the tower held aloft 10 meters from the ground sets this up as an unattainable goal, at the same time, the solid granite base gives the sense of unalterable sturdiness that can support the swaying tip and spring. It is at the moment we make this connection in the reading of the work that MadeIn closes the circuit and the trap is sprung, for what we are looking at is an image of the installation. The same can be said of the other fourteen large-scale installations, sculptures and two-dimensional works that comprise the exhibition, although created and in existence, are never to be seen or exhibited.

Xu Zhen has set similar traps before, perhaps none more aggressively than in his 2008 solo exhibition *Impossible is Noth-*ing at the Long March Space, where he recreated the scene from Kevin Carter's famously problematic photo-journalist image of an emaciated baby in Sudan being hungrily stalked by a vulture. Taking place as daily live performance, the work forced audiences to 'refresh' their own standards by confronting the possibilities in the space between collective knowledge and the artwork. Are we more aghast about the work itself, or because of the reference to Kevin Carter's photograph and the vast amount of vitriolic discourse that had been spilled about his actions, or the fact of the travesty being referenced is still ongoing in Sudan? Or are we simply looking at a child playing in the sand? This exhibition was less about the content of the artwork. The purpose is to provoke not by surprise of what one sees, but rather by being made to use our own knowledge to produce a judgment - the result of which Xu Zhen would have no control.

This was to be the last work by artist Xu Zhen, before founding MadeIn, a registered limited company that acts as a proxy for creating his work. The working method for MadeIn is to buy or re-organize the creativity and intellect of others, refining it to produce and fill an order of artwork for either exhibition or collection. This method of a company as an organizational model is not a new way to approach the possibilities of artistic creation. However, MadeIn's practice seeks to go beyond the conventional question of whether a company can be credited as an author for an artwork by seeking out relationships in the art production chain including the gallery, museum, curators,

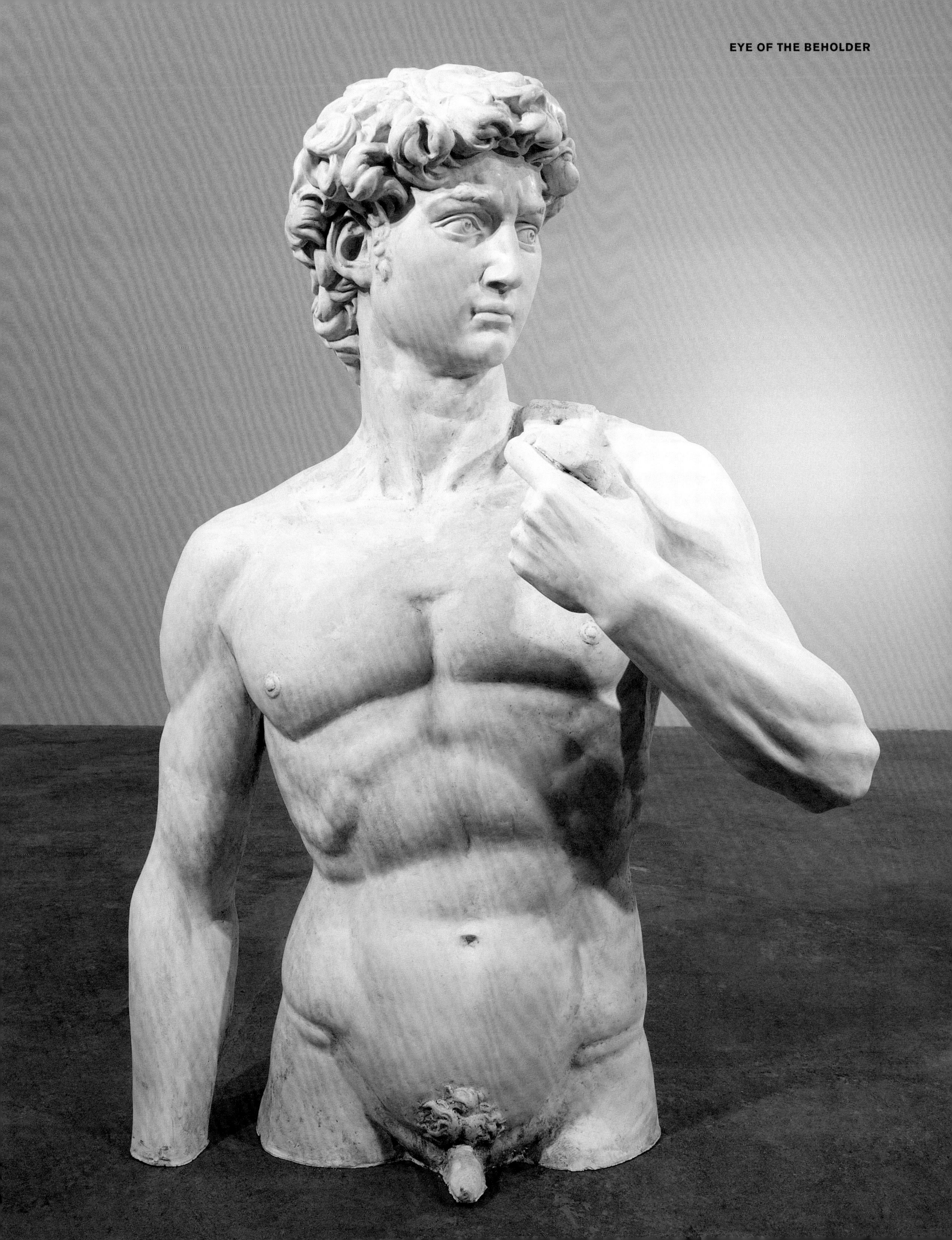

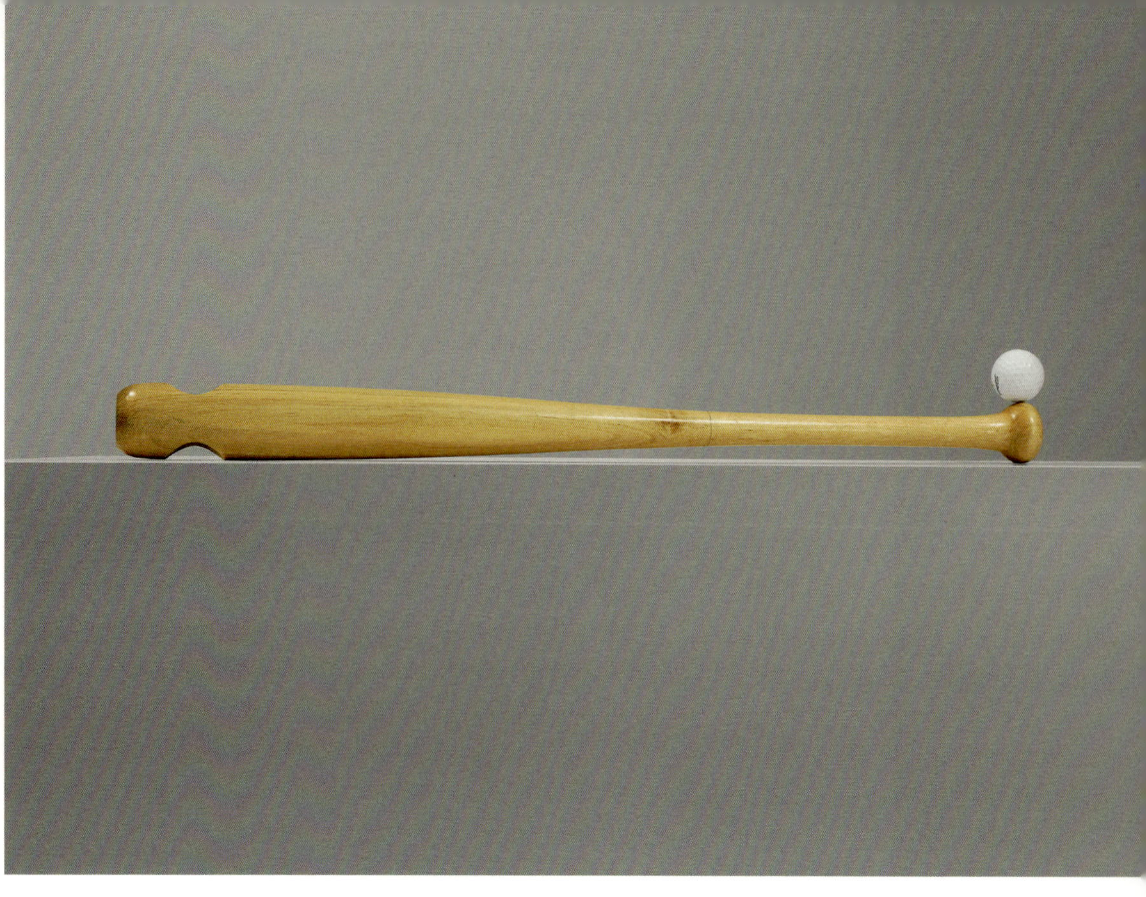

collectors and posing questions that ask how these relationships can be restructured in a new and revolutionary way. Ultimately, it is these relationships that MadeIn makes use of as the material for their art. As Xu Zhen has described: "The relations are constantly changing. At times you are dealing with a relatively concrete issue of audience, at times you're dealing with a systemic issue, and sometimes that systemic issue is grounded in concrete reality, other times it's about the art system. For MadeIn right now, it's possible to turn all those issues into art; the distinction lies in whether there is any effectiveness to that. Our biggest concern right now is the question of how far we can take those issues. How can we express an idea, and why do we want to express it?"

*Don't Hang Your Faith on the Wall* is almost a scientific demonstration of this idea. We are given visual conventions that serve as roadmaps for our understanding and reading. The label informs us about material and dimensions, and the cumbersome title serves as defacto wall text, in which references to Heidegger and Foucault allow our readings to run ahead of what is visually present. Our knowledge allows us to decide upon interpretations by testing them against the situation referenced from our glossary of contemporary art language. This is exactly what MadeIn is doing, testing how much knowledge and information is required to get the viewer to play along and complete the circle of reference to transform the image into a material 'artwork.'

The exhibition is not about representation, the real target is the system of conventions and readings. It no longer matters if the photographs have been 'retouched' or digitally altered, or if the objects are real and exist (they do), the image acts as a catalyst to explore how some representations can actually come not only to look like reality, but become that reality.

Perhaps the most dizzying of these mental re-diversions is the work, Unification Is a Reductive Process Rather Than a Process of Gain, in Which Loyal Believers Never Feel Complete or Secure No. 4. Again, the exhibition label provides the context, the work's dimensions are 150 x 212 cm and it is an acrylic on canvas. Having already been lured into the trap once, we are more cautious this time. The image looks digitally altered, a mixture between graffiti and photoshop collage, but it is a painting. Further inspection reveals the creases of the canvas are visible in the image, and we are convinced that this is actually a painting, and not a photograph of the same size. In both instances we are wrong, it is the image of the painting shown on photographic paper in the same size.

*Previous page* The people is a beast of muddy brain. It does not know its own force; it only knows absolute obedience n.3, 2010. *Above* The path to appearance is always accessible and traveled but one can go around it, 2010. *Right* Crowds do not love logical argumentation, they are not to be influenced by reasoning, and can only comprehend rough-and-ready associations of ideas, 2010

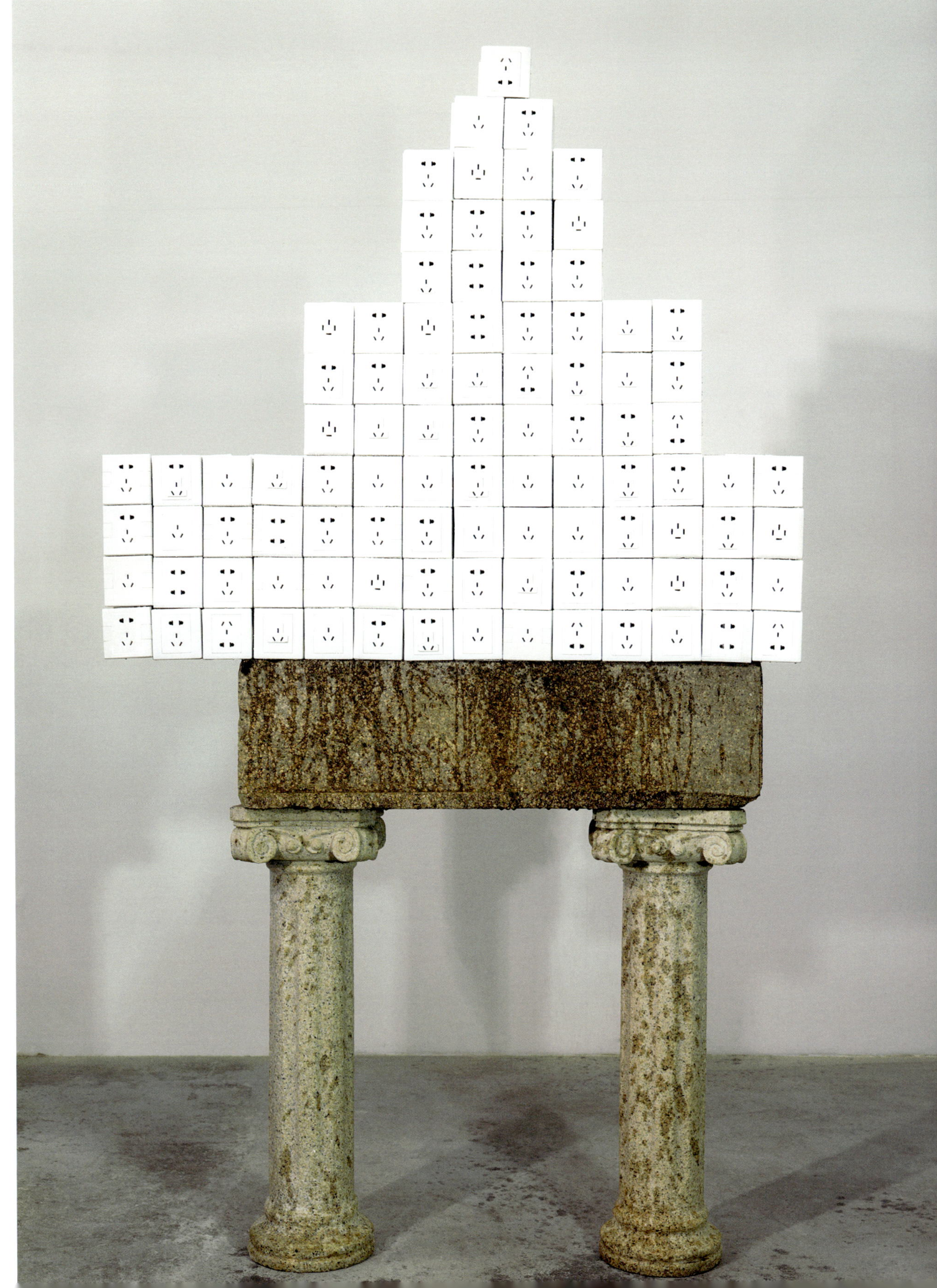

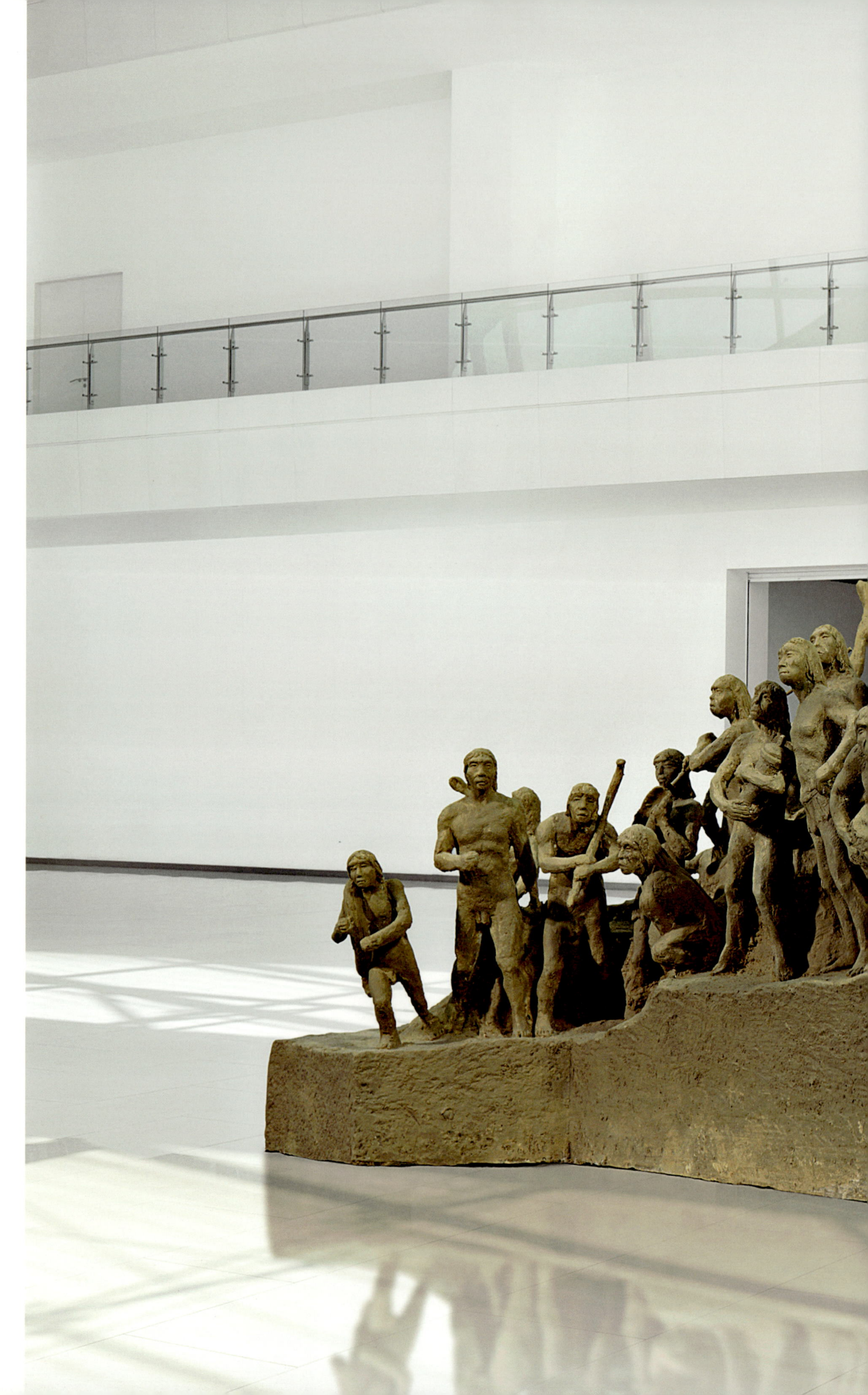

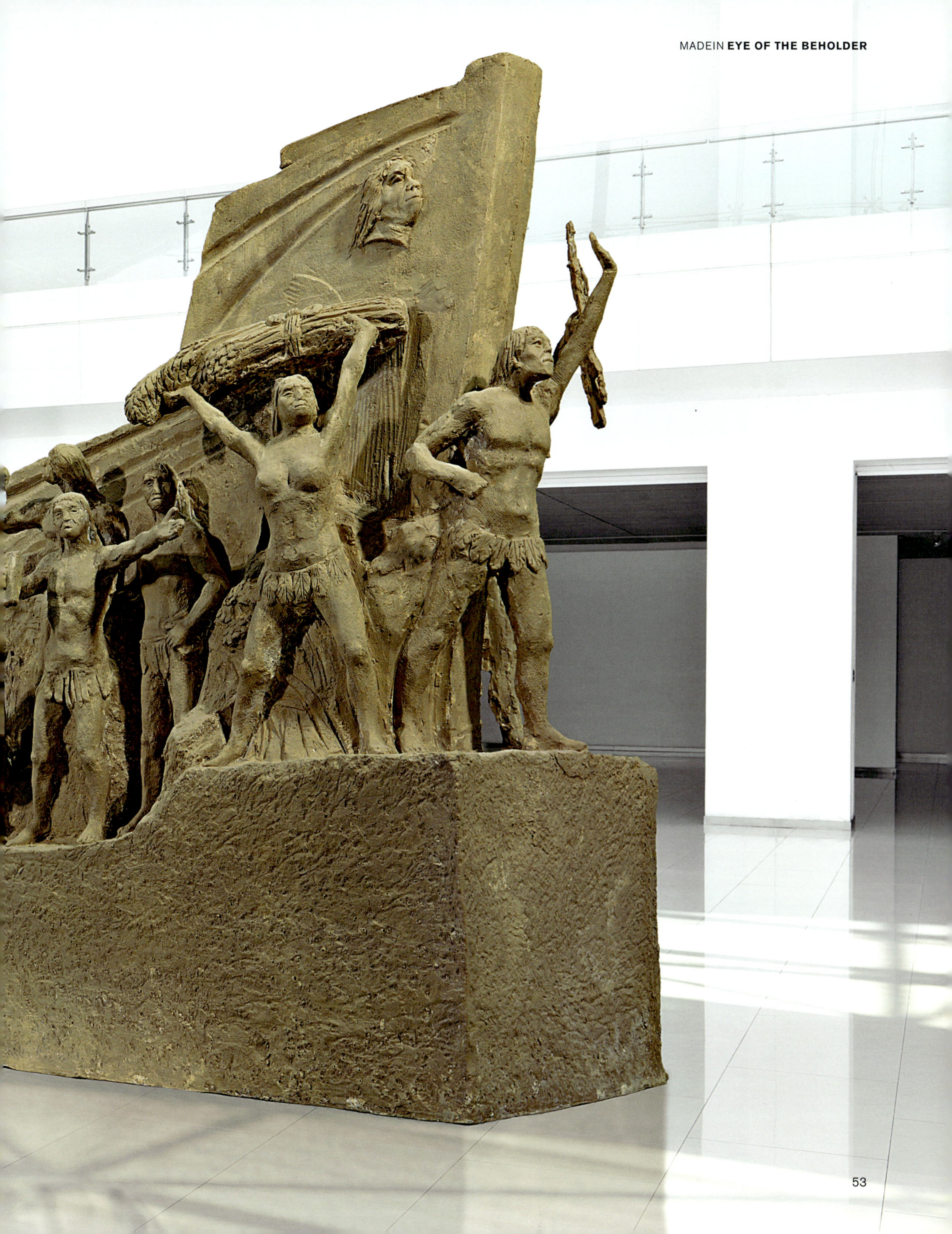

*Previous spread* The struggle of man against power is the struggle of memory against forgetting, 2010. *Below* The people is a beast of muddy brain. It does not know its own force; it only knows absolute obedience n.1, 2010. *All images © the artists, courtesy Long March Space, Beijing*

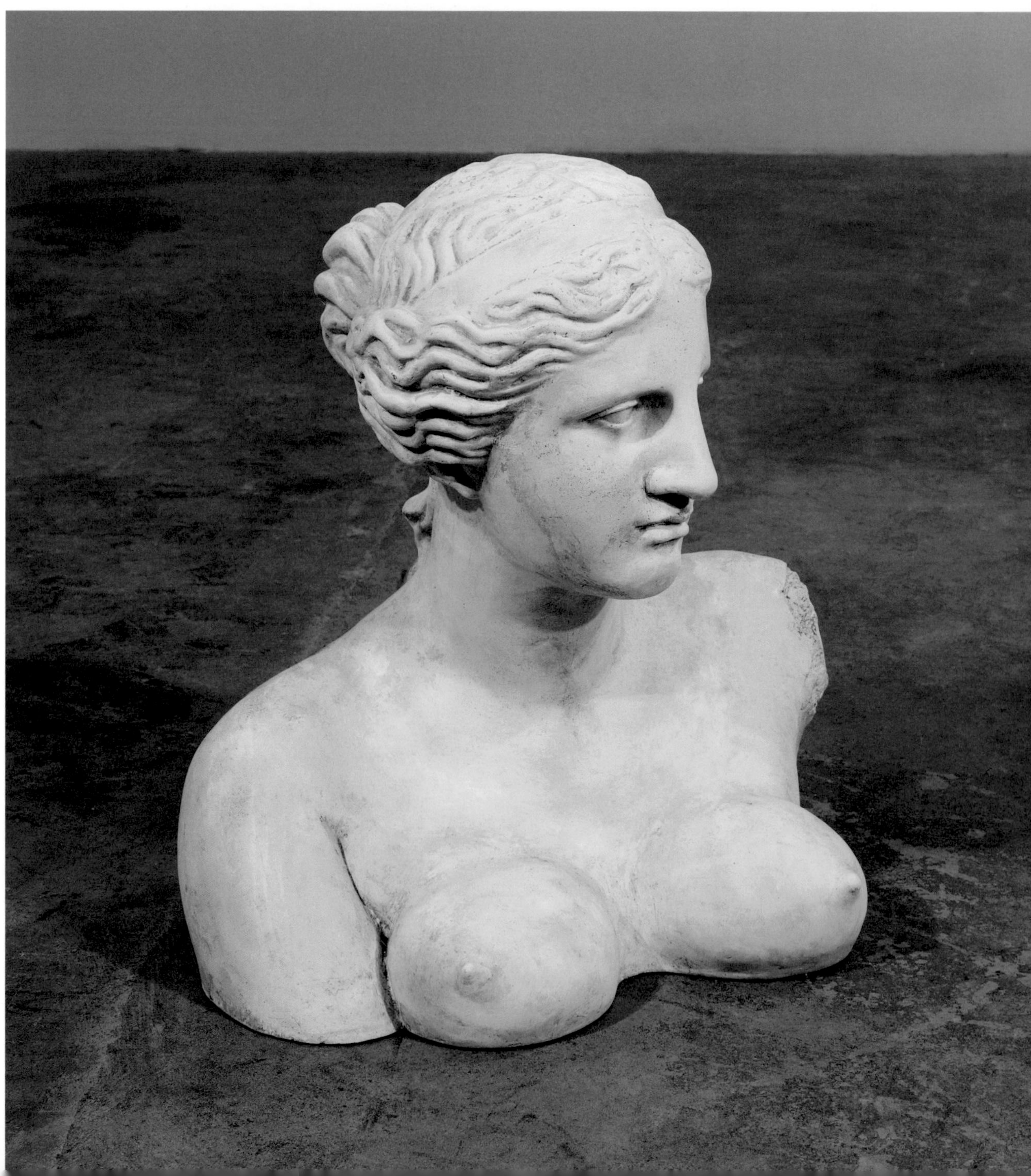

# FRANCESCO ZANOT
# VISITS THE COLLECTION OF
# ARTUR WALTHER

In the late 1990s, Artur Walther bought a typology of grain elevators from the American Midwest by Bernd and Hilla Becher. This was the first piece of the mosaic of a collection of photographs and videos which now numbers more than 700 works and continues to expand, applying a criterion which subtly balances scientific rigour with autobiography. Around this nucleus, Walther gathered an early investigation into typological photography that had been carried out by its principal exponents in Germany, Karl Blossfeldt and August Sander, coupled with some specimens of documentary photography in the United States by Walker Evans and transformations of this approach provided by Bruce Davidson, Lee Friedlander and Mitch Epstein.

Then came his interest in Chinese art and the creation of the second focus of the collection, with works including those of Ai Weiwei, Cang Xin, Chen Shaoxiong, Huang Yan, Ma Liuming, Lin Tianmiao, Wang Qingsong, Yiwu Wang and Xiang Liqing.

Finally, triggered by his peculiar fascination with the images of Seydou Keïta, a further segment of Walther's project dedicated to African photography began to develop and Okwui Enwezor played a fundamental part in taking it further. It currently contains a selection of over 300 pieces which make up the most remarkable existing body of contemporary photography from this continent in the world.

And yet, as was said earlier, all of this is not merely the outcome of consulting experts, studying books and visiting museums, exhibitions and archives. It is also, when it has been possible, the result of a direct and continuous relationship with the artists. Artur Walther does not limit himself to buying a group of prints but shares a trajectory with the artists he chooses, so that often in his collection there are no isolated works but brief sequences by the same photographer collected over time. And there is more: Artur Walther has made the collection part of the story of his family, converting the home he grew up in Burlafingen, a small village in the south of Germany, into a part of a complex of four buildings where exhibitions, which spring from his collection and at the same time determine its future development, have been periodically held since June 2010. It is here that, among other things, the new African and Chinese photography will be introduced to the western public in the next few years. And, above all, in this place a selection of photographs and videos will continuously encounter German vernacular architecture and the story of a man and of a family, generating an experience of extraordinary complexity.

**1. NEOCLASSICISM - SEYDOU KEÏTA** Unlike the other arts, photography has no classics. In literature, for instance, every country has its own classic works of literature. In music, the entirety of European compositions from pre-Christian times until the end of the nineteenth century are classics. In architecture, sculpture and painting we have the classics of Greek and Roman antiquity while, as far as cinema is concerned, you only have to flick through the program schedules of channels such as Sky Cinema Classics or Turner Classic Movies, dominated by American productions of the 1930s and 1960s, in order to get the general idea. The fact is that the basic quality of a classic is that it loses any temporal connotation while, on the contrary, photography is triggered by a peculiar (and paradoxical) relationship with time. A classic does not have contemporaries; a photograph is the apotheosis of the present. Therefore, it can only take its cue from Neoclassicism, which does not establish a universal canon but conforms to it. So, while Antonio Canova represents Venus with the features of Paolina Borghese, Napoleon's sister, reclining on a mattress and two pillows, here a woman from Mali is shrouded in the same idea of elegance and perfection. *Untitled, 1956-1957, gelatin silver print, cm 50.2 x 60.5*

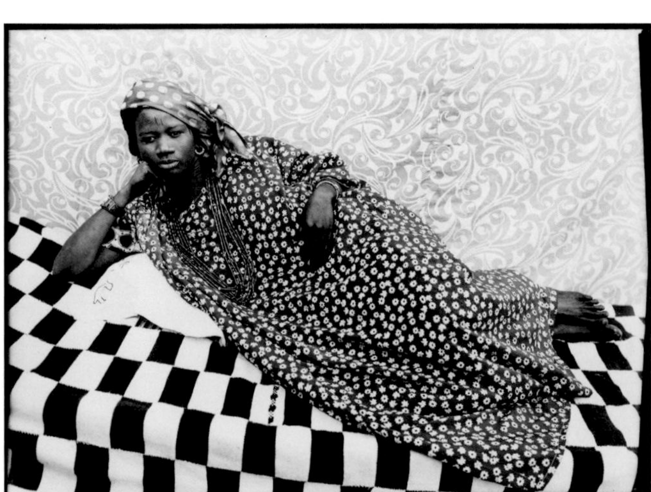

**2. PRECISION - J.D. 'OKHAI OJEIKERE** Photography is a tool of precision. Just like scalpels or chronometers. It enables us to work on reality with a far greater degree of accuracy than can be achieved with normal human faculties. In this sense, it may be defined as a device for measuring the imprecise nature of the world which, on the contrary, behaves according to random laws. Photography, in short, is not just useful for exercising a form of control over what it may represent but is, above all, a means of proving that it is uncontrollable. It is a door onto chaos. This is the source of that slight unease (restlessness) that grips us when we notice that there is a rope of the woman's hair that has been combed to the side in such a way that it leaves far too much space in the center. *Untitled (Agaracha), 1974, gelatin silver print, cm 59.1 x 47.6*

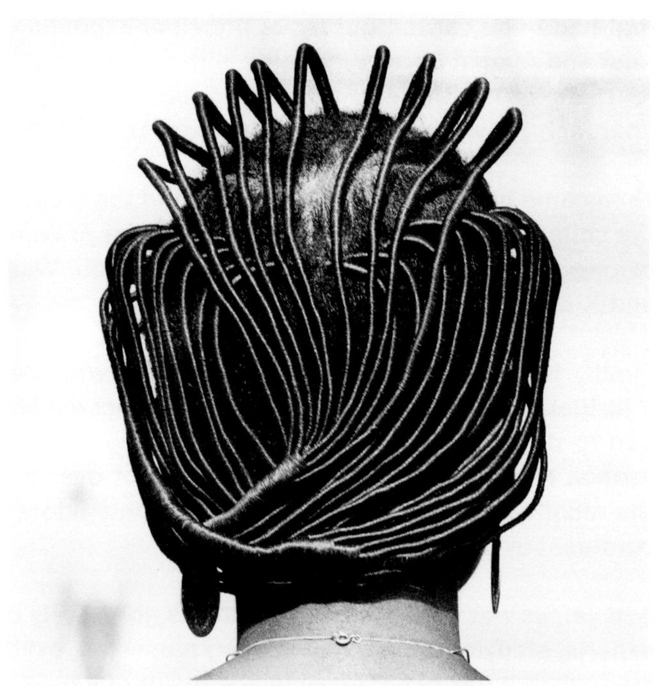

**3. THE INFINITE - MALICK SIDIBÉ** A photograph is an image. An image is a visible phenomenon. Both of these propositions are certainly true and yet it is the photographer himself who challenges them. You only have to read the symbol that is printed on most modern lenses: ∞. Photography pulls the infinite into focus. It is a matter of mathematics, but this does not mean we are not a bit thrilled when we observe its surface, whether we are looking beyond the horizon or at the monochromatic field of a backdrop for portraits. *Lancina Sanogo, the Friend of Mody, Seen from the Rear, 2002, gelatin silver print, cm 60 x 50*

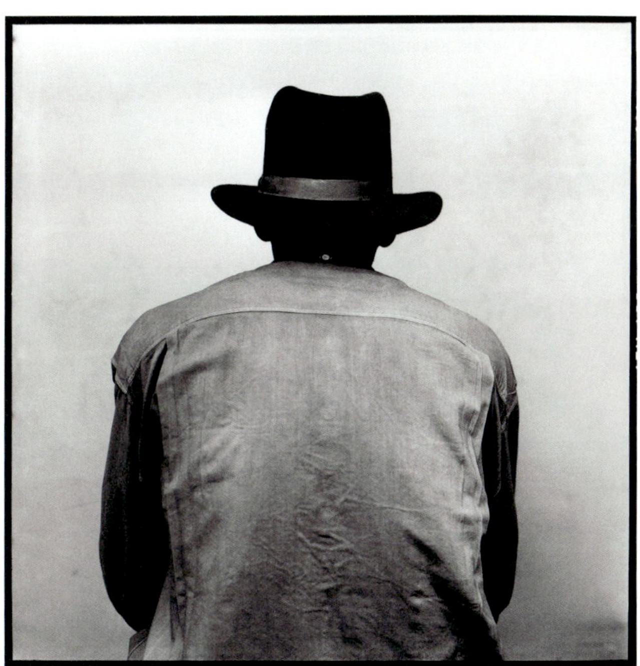


**4. PHANTOM - OLADÉLÉ AJIBOYÉ BAMGBOYÉ** When an object does not stay still in the field of vision long enough for the camera to capture a sharp shot of it, the blurred outline of the resulting image is called "a photographic phantom." It was a particularly common occurrence for most of the eighteen hundreds, when dark lenses and slow emulsions overly drew out the length of the pose. On the other hand, the very nature of photography shares a couple of essential attributes with phantoms. To begin with, both are apparitions, meaning a visual phenomenon which causes amazement. Secondly, both present themselves as a promise of eternity, foreshadowing an alternative kind of presence after death. This means one thing only: photography is the technological replacement and the expansion of the specter in the contemporary era. *Celebrate no. 2, 1994, c-print, cm 41.1 x 40.3*

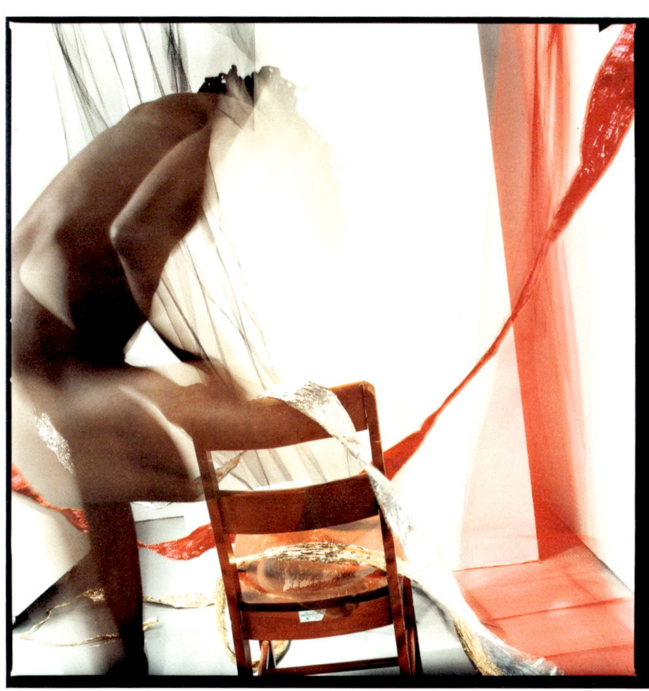

**5. TAMER - PIETER HUGO** The photographer, whether he be a professional, an artist or an amateur, always behaves like a tamer. He domesticates reality, overlaying it with his rules and the rules of his medium, thus transforming it into an image. *Mallam Galadima Ahmadu with Jamis, Nigeria, 2005, c-print, cm 152.4 x 152.4*

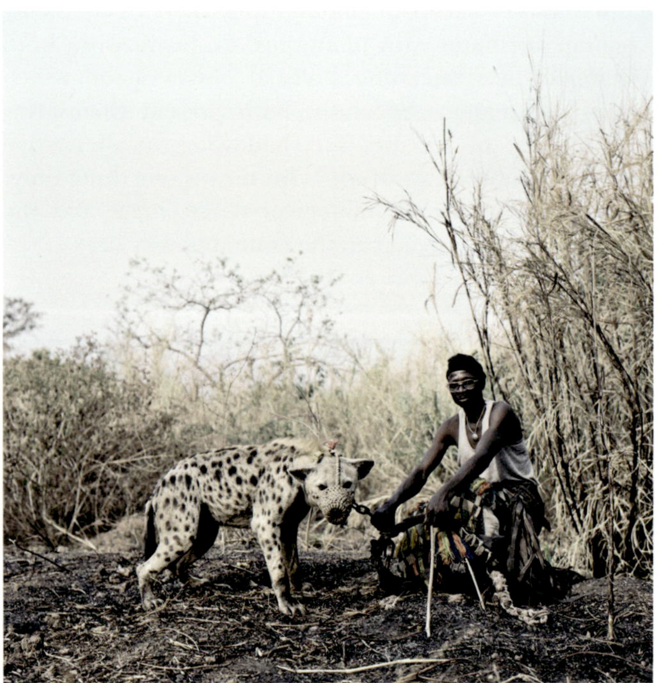

**6. THE HEADLESS MAN - JO RACTLIFFE** Until a few years ago the photographer lived like a headless man. Whatever equipment he used he could never manage to see his own face in the viewfinder of the camera. In front of a mirror, the camera usually concealed part of his face, forced him to bend over if he was framing using the waist-level system, or even concealed him under the black cloth in the case of a view camera. It was a prosthetic relationship. Man and machine had to be represented together: one on top of the other, one inside the other. Cyborg was at the gates. Then came the digital era, which freed the composition of the frame from the constraints of optics. Consider the web-cam or cameras equipped with 360° flip-out and twist LCDs: for the first time, after film, the photographer was able to see himself taking photographs. *Doll's Head, 2004, carbon print on cotton paper, cm 35 x 35*

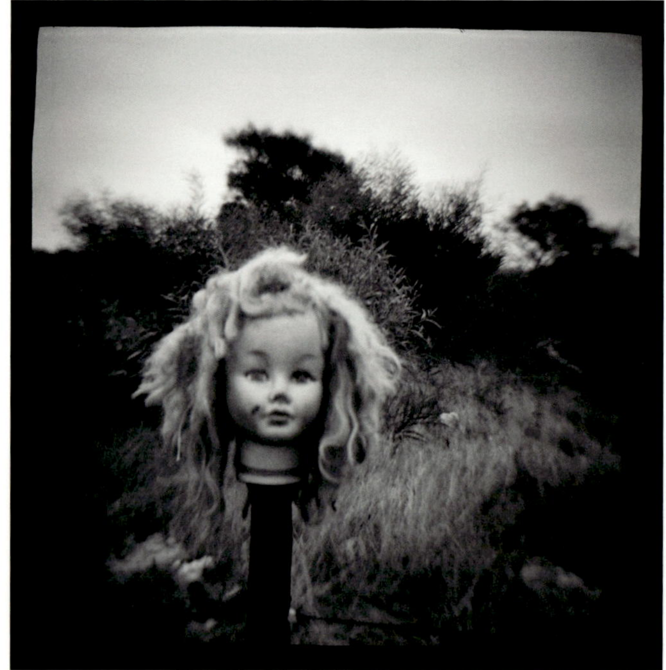

**7. PLACE - SANTU MOFOKENG** Every photograph is the portrayal of a place, regardless of whether it introduces environmental elements or whether it excludes them altogether. There is not a thing that can be done about it: the image captured by the lens is inevitably the result of a combination of time and, indeed, space. There is no photograph that is devoid of geographical coordinates, whether it shows the earth upon which the photographer placed his feet or whether it is abstracted from a completely white backdrop. *P.G. Mdebuka (original photograph by Aliwal North Location School, albumen print, circa 1900s)*

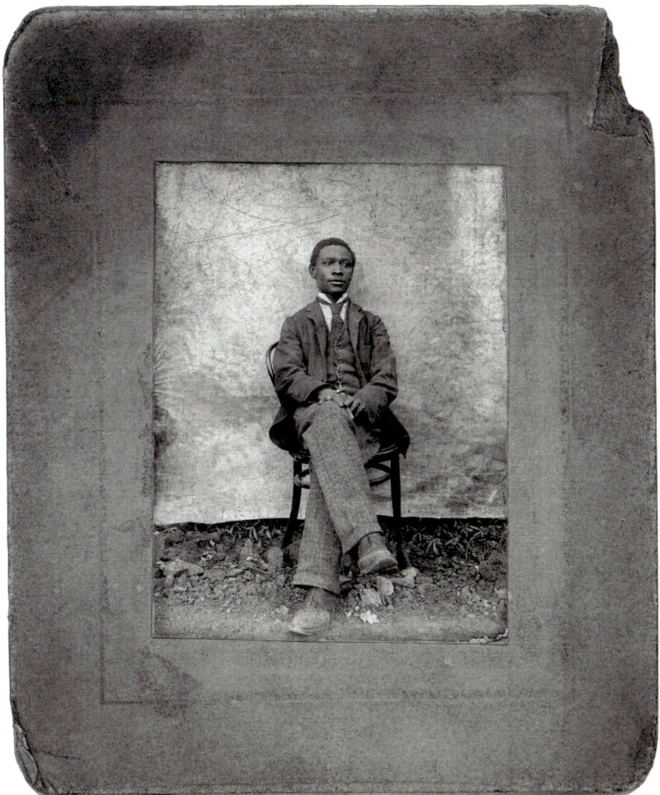

**8. ORIGINAL SIN - ROTIMI FANI-KAYODE** Photography is marked with original sin. The first to commit it and set a precedent were its very creators. Daguerre wrote at the beginning of the announcement he made in January 1839, in which he described the principal features of his invention: "It consists in the spontaneous reproduction of the images of nature received in the camera obscura..." Some years later Talbot prefaced the plates of his *The Pencil of Nature* with a note to the reader: "The plates of the present work are impressed by the agency of Light alone, without any aid whatever from the artist's pencil." Both, in publicizing the new discovery, focus the reader's attention on the presumed automatic nature of the process. They are perfectly aware of the pattern of this representative process and the centrality of the position held by the figure of man within it (both are artists and place their invention within this system), but simply fail to mention any of that. With the result that photography is forever trapped in the ambiguity of copy and duplication.
*Untitled, 1987-1988, digital c-print, cm 121 x 121.8*

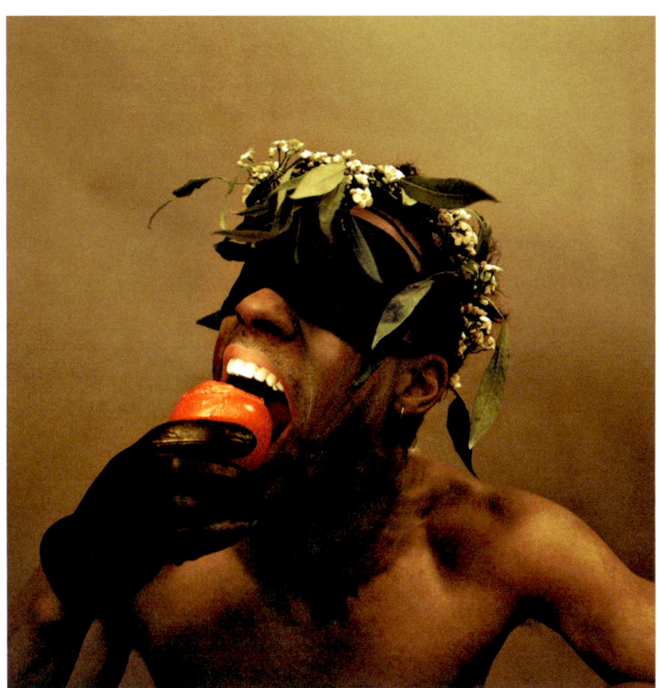

**9. HEART - GUY TILLIM** Drawing and photography are at opposite ends of the vast array of figurative arts. Drawing is the art of tracing the outline. The edges of each figure are delineated and remain the principal part of the composition. Instead, in photography, one begins with the substance of things, their mass, their heart. The perimeter of the subjects is the limit which halts their expansion, not a line which contains them. Its course is centrifugal. *Fiorinda Ngoma, her mother Rosalia Nahamba (holding baby Filomena Lasinda), and her sister Rosali Sindali, holding baby Guerra, 2002, pigment print on coated cotton paper, cm 60 x 76*

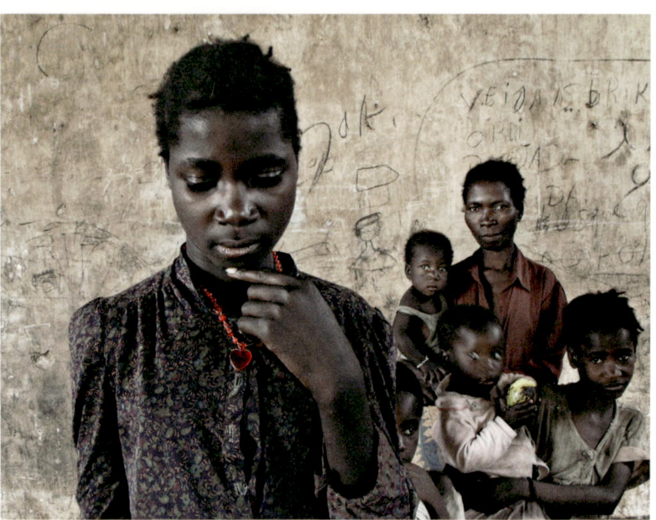

**10. THE DEEP - ALFRED MARTIN DUGGAN-CRONIN** Photographers can be divided into two macro-categories. There are those who use their medium to observe and describe how the world appears. For them, the camera works as a recording device. Others believe in its paradoxical ability to investigate the depth of the subject while only showing its surface. In this case, photography is an instrument which enables us to look inside what it represents (*The Anatomy Lesson of Dr. Nicolaes Tulp* painted by Rembrandt springs to mind) to the point where we are under the impression that we are entering it, turning it into a second skin. *The Late Chief Jonathan Molapo, from The Bantu Tribes of South Africa, Vol. II, Section III, The Suto-Chuana Tribes, Plate LVIII*

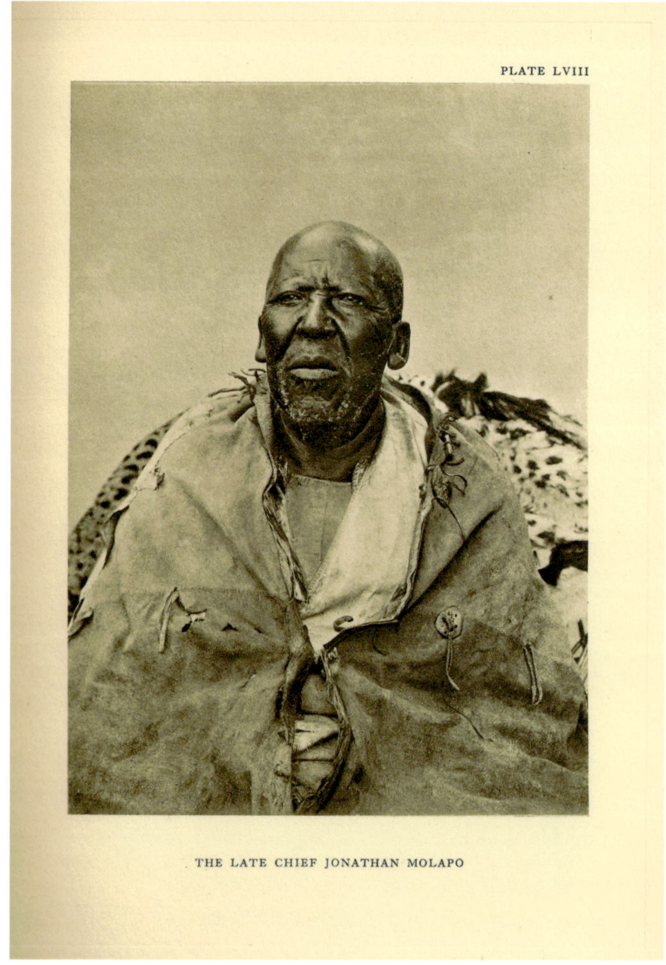

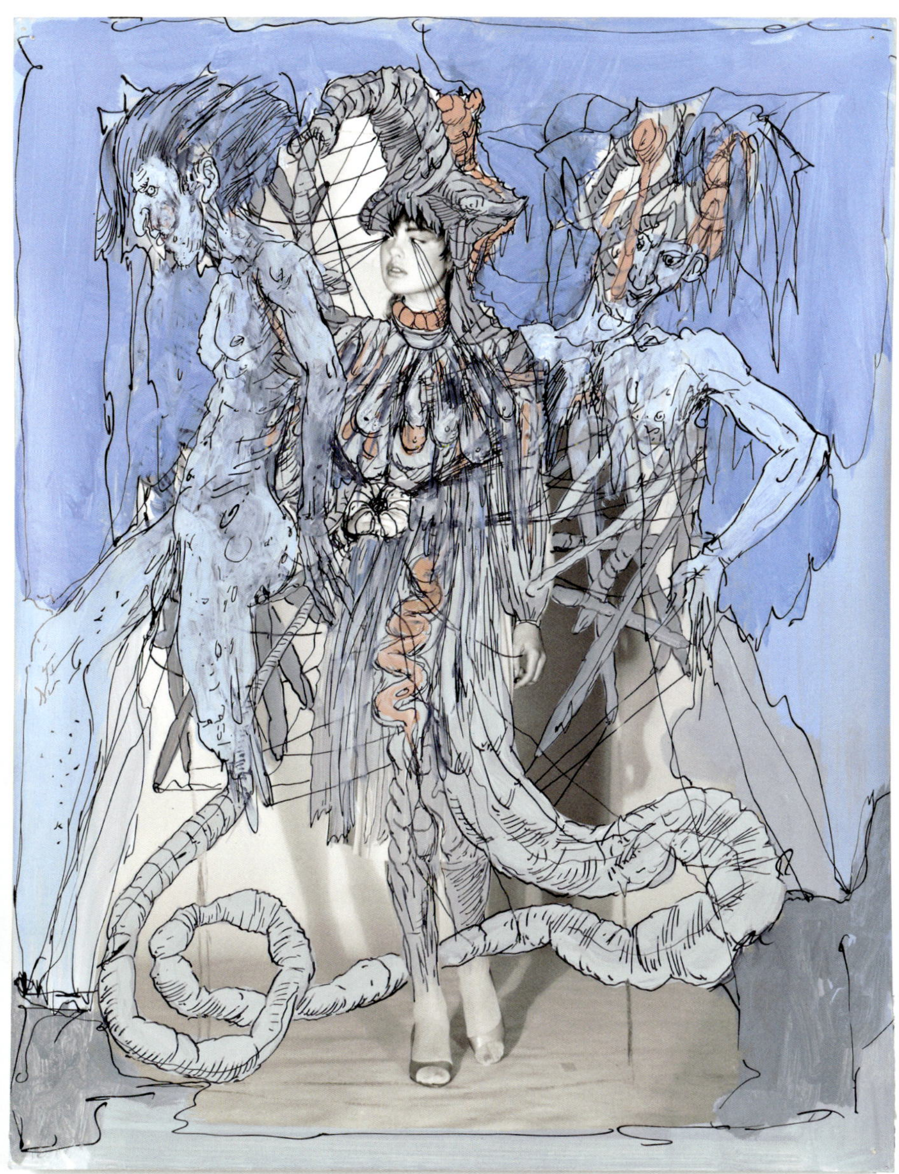

# KIM JONES

War drawings, rat sculptures, combat vehicles, performances: everything in the work of Kim Jones originates in his experiences, from his participation as a Vietnam War soldier, to the illness that kept him in a wheelchair between the ages of seven to ten. War permeates all of his work, as in the series of fashion photos he found in 1983, in the trash on 6th Avenue in New York. These elements are arranged with undertones of conflict and mutation, sexuality and violence: young men and women change into skeletons, androgynous figures and organisms. His works are shaped along the years, recycling materials and motifs, reworking figures, installations and performances. Limbs are extended and adapted, faces hidden and backgrounds transformed into even stranger creatures. These enigmatic figures also become studies for Jones' alter ego, Mudman, who he first embodied in the mid 1970s. Covering himself with sticks and mud, this compelling creature engaged with the streets of Los Angeles and, later, New York, conveying the material expression of an interior landscape. Born in California in 1944, he's currently based in New York.

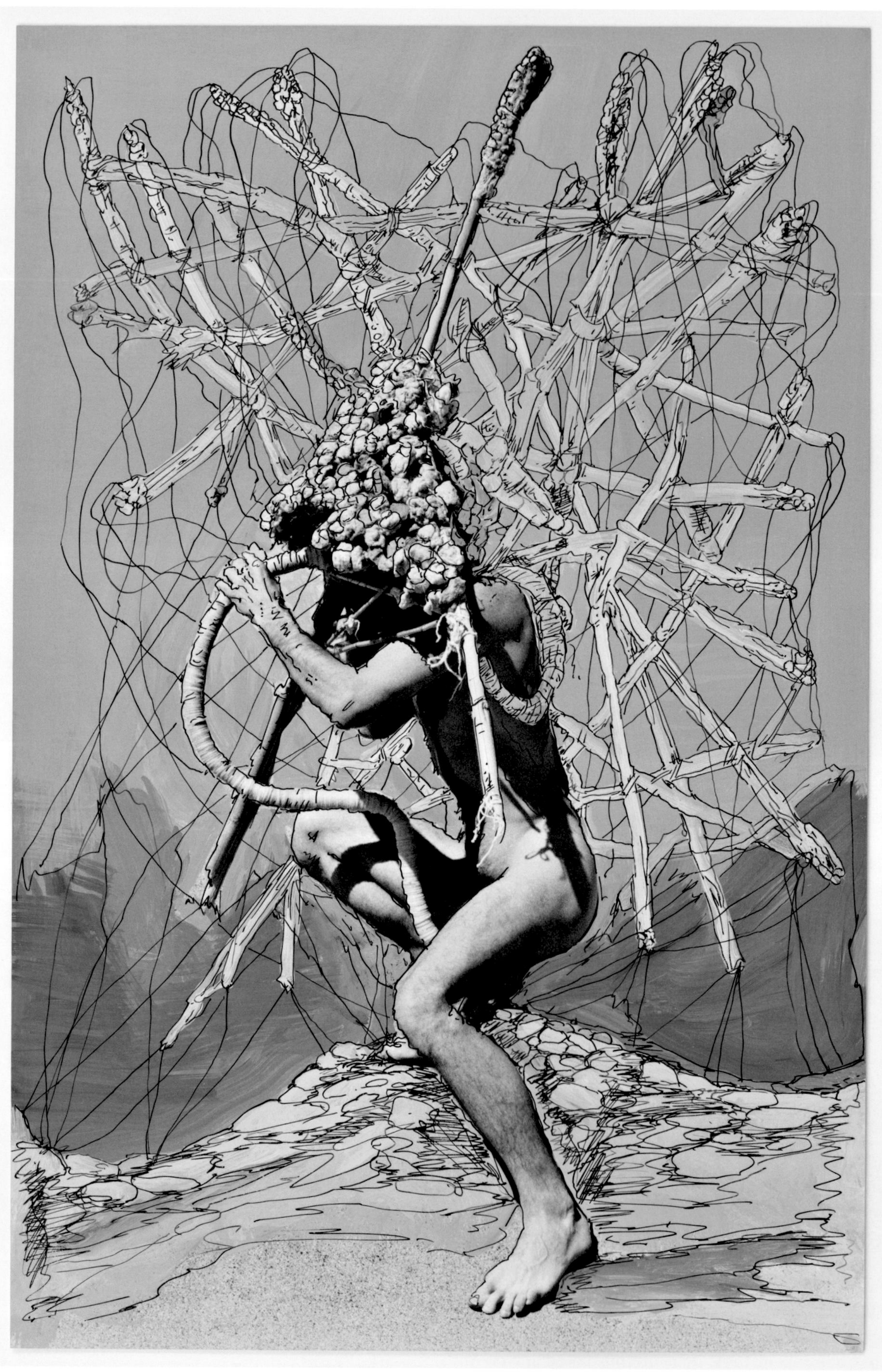

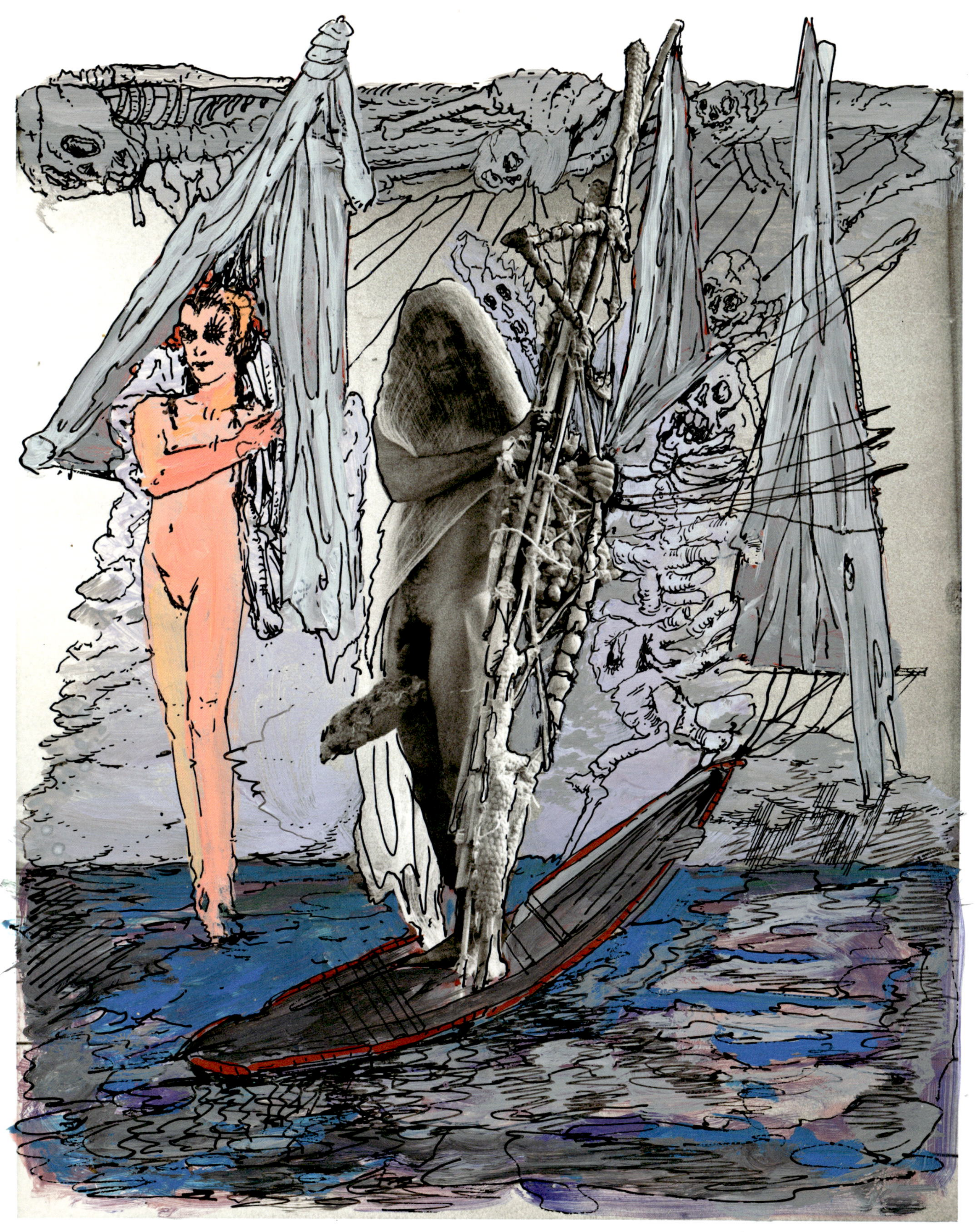

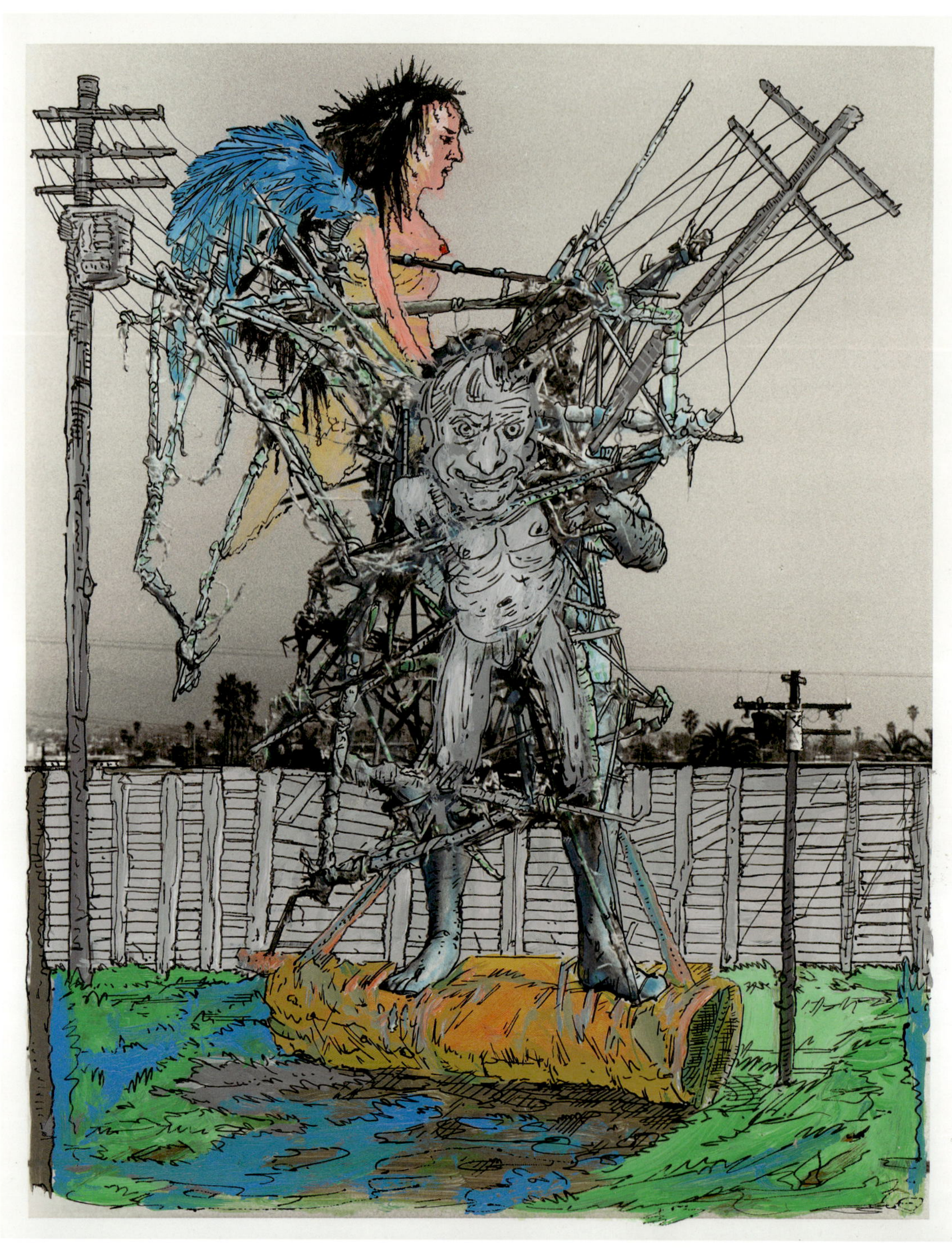

Page 61 Untitled, 1984-2004-2005, b/w photograph, acrylic and ink, cm 35.3 x 27.7. *Page 62* Untitled, 1974-2006, photograph, acrylic and ink, cm 45.6 x 30.4. *Page 63* Untitled, 1974-2006, photograph, acrylic and ink, cm 25.8 x 20.2. *Above* Untitled, 1974-2006, photograph, acrylic and ink, cm 25.8 x 20.2. *Right* Untitled, 1983-2006, photograph, acrylic and ink, cm 25.8 x 20.2. *All images © the artist, courtesy Zeno X Gallery, Antwerp*

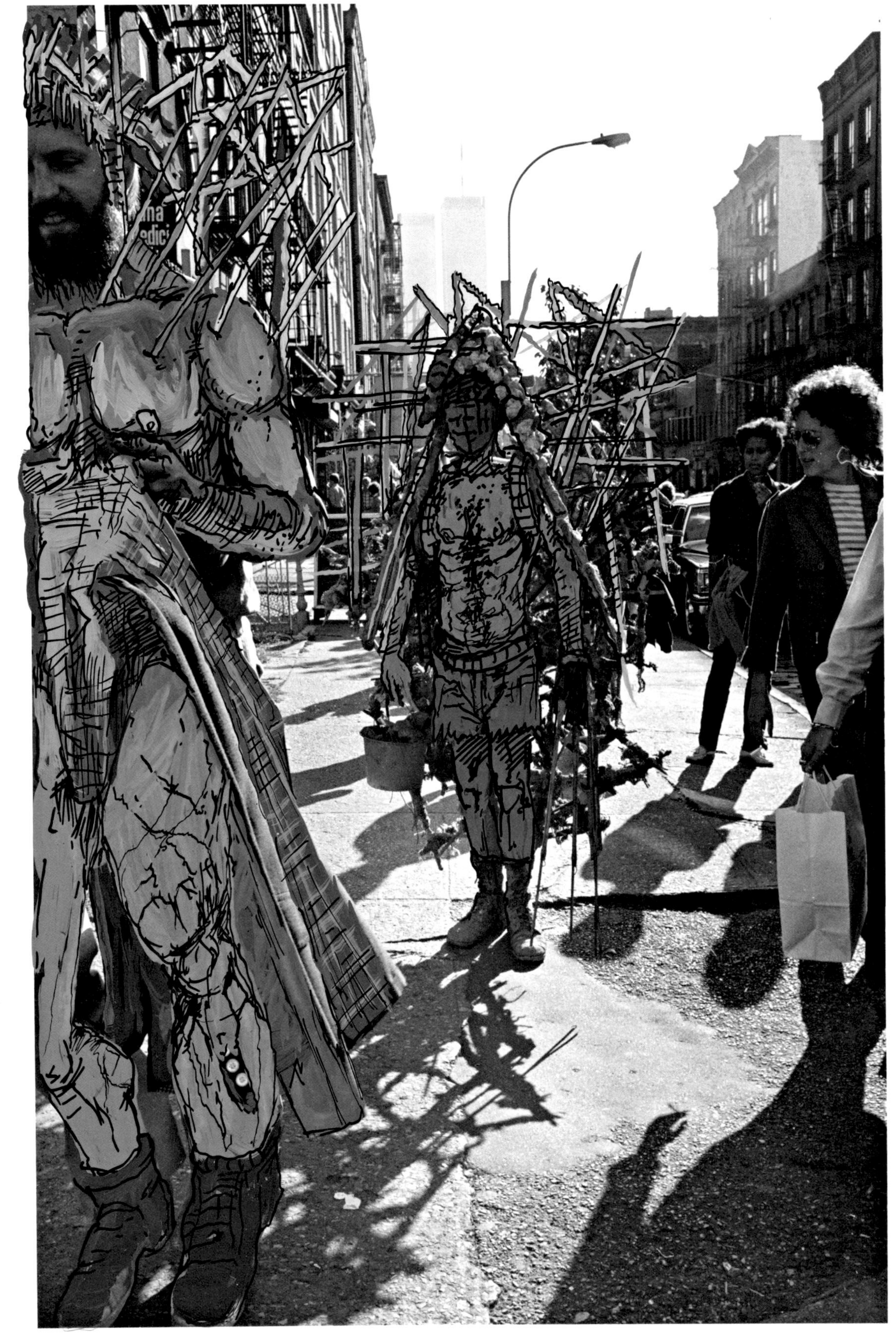

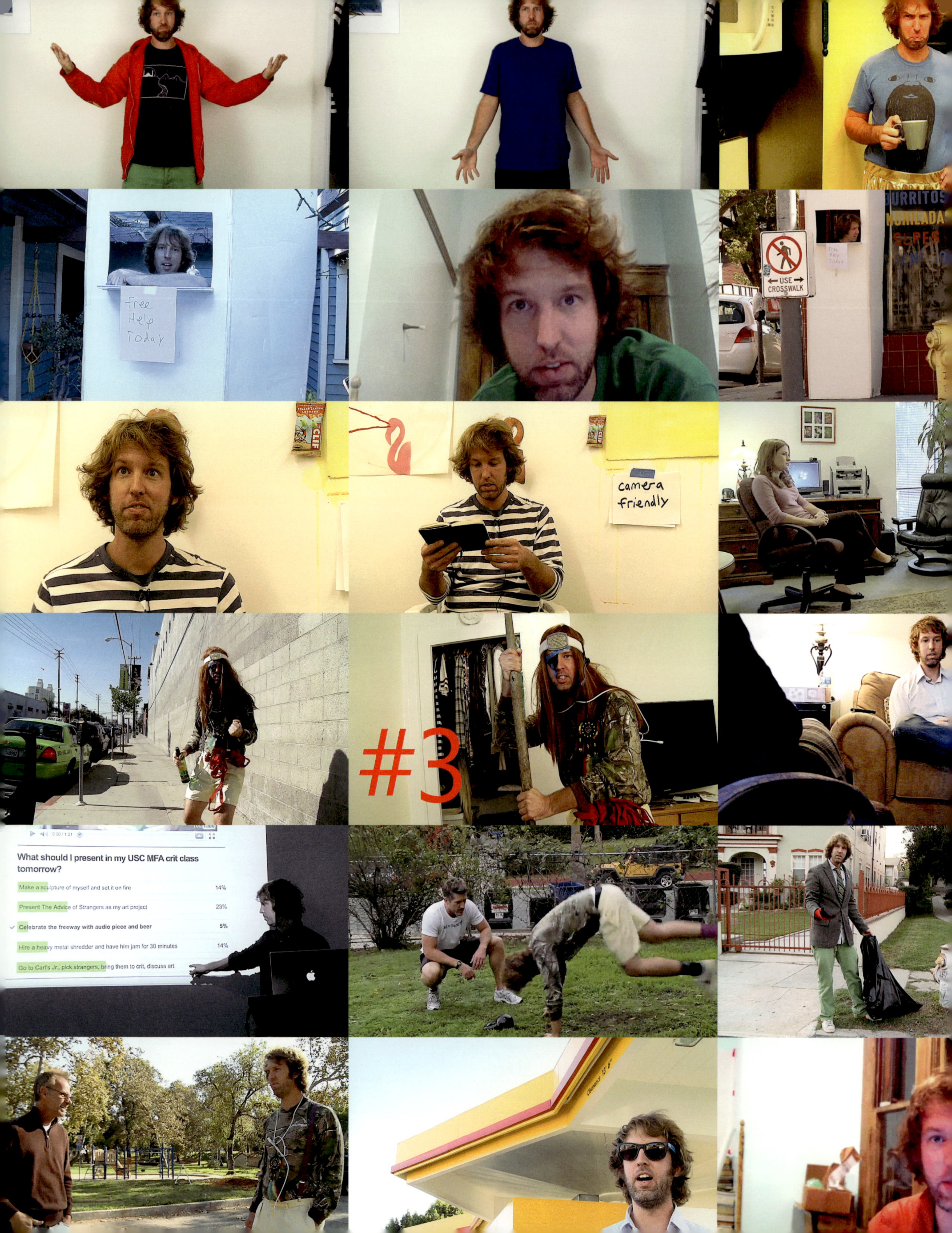
free Help Today
free Help Today
BURRITOS
ENCHILADA
SOPES
USE CROSSWALK
camera friendly
#3
What should I present in my USC MFA crit class tomorrow?
Make a sculpture of myself and set it on fire          14%
Present The Advice of Strangers as my art project      23%
Celebrate the freeway with audio piece and beer         5%
Hire a heavy metal shredder and have him jam for 30 minutes   14%
Go to Carl's Jr., pick strangers, bring them to crit, discuss art

# The Advice of Strangers
# MARC HOROWITZ
# by Alex Gartenfeld

For the first episode of *The Advice of Strangers*, Marc Horowitz's month-long project, the artist opens up questions in his life - some pressing, some trivial - to a registered online audience. Beginning with a characteristic sneer against privacy conventions, his first to-be-resolved question is a cliché of self-exposure: "I have a 10 AM appointment with my shrink… yes I have a shrink… What should I talk about with her?" As he would for the next month, Horowitz had pre-selected four options that he introduces in a video segment, which range in personal risk, banality, and humor: "embarrassing childhood moments," "my fears," "family drama," "people that I have wronged in the past." Thirty-nine percent of voters would lead him to discuss the latter, proof of which is posted in a second video. Over the course of the month, Horowitz put up for vote and videotape-recorded eighty-seven questions. That's a lot, for certain, and the artist covered such bases as his embarrassed pack-rat mother, and a girlfriend who refused to appear on-camera, but the sequences do not pretend to document his entire life. In fact, the starting point for Horowitz's project is ambivalence about the type of revelation offered by photography, video, and television, but with hopefulness that the traditionally auratic can temporarily puncture that skepticism. We follow his perambulatory, always jokey, often emotive stories without presuming them to be the artist's life story. Horowitz's careful editing suggests a performance with a beginning and end, and offers questions about what separates the staged event from life, and what kind of inter-subjective access we're getting as we watch the series unfold.

Horowitz extended his project by a week to include Art Basel Miami Beach 2010, during which time he gathered the results of poll #12, where the audience selected that he spend some time trying to locate his old friend, Greg. There's something anachronistic about him not being able to find the person instantly on Facebook, where one would have natively chosen or re-selected their constellation of friends. In the last episode, he, with an underhanded sense of melodrama, makes contact, after a month of trying. The conversation is edited to collapse it into a montage in which the audio favors the artist. Nonetheless, we hear what sounds like genuine excitement about shared memories, such as, "Don't prank call 911… Remember 'Eternal Dagger'?" and then an awkward necessity: "If there's any possibility you can come out to LA or I could go out there… " says Horowitz. "Give me a call back sometime, too…" suggests Greg, each considering how to extend the moment beyond the artificiality of the artist's premise. The native awkwardness of memory and maintenance is subsumed into the parameters of the project, and recorded on the reel of an ineffable document.

*Opening page: first row 1+2* Promostill; *3* Energy Drink and Coffee After. *Second row 1* Free Help Booth (In the Making); *2* Yapping; *3* Free Help Booth. *Third row 1+2 from* Meltdown Update; *3 from* My meeting with my shrink on the 1st day, 1st vote, voted to talk about people I've wronged. *Fourth row 1+2 from* My pirate audition, voted to wear this particular costume. I didn't get a call back btw; *3 from* My second appointment with my shrink where I was voted to have my new intern come with me and to discuss my insecurities. *Fifth row 1 from* My USC MFA crit where I was voted to bring somebody to the crit from neighboring Carl's Jr. to discuss contemporary art; *2* Personal trainer Jeremy Hovan came by and gave me the brutal workout people voted me to have; *3* Picking up trash around my neighborhood. *Sixth row 1* Talking to potential interns in my local Hermon Park. This particular gentleman thought it was a job and reneged; *2* Talking about Thanksgiving plans while voted to fill-up with no free car wash; *3* Talking about my new intern, Christian, who came all the way down from Portland to help out

*On the right: first to third row* Rafting on Echo Park lake with two marshmallows on chin and underwear on head (per a six-year old's request). *Third row 3 + fourth row 1* Seeing a psychic for the first time, Kate the Psychic, talking about my love life, getting my Tarot cards read. *Fourth row 2+3 + fifth row 1+2* Shoot my life as a B-movie. *Fifth row 3* The TAOS Nationwide intern search is on! *Below* Self portrait by Marc Horowitz. *All images © the artist and Creative Time, New York*

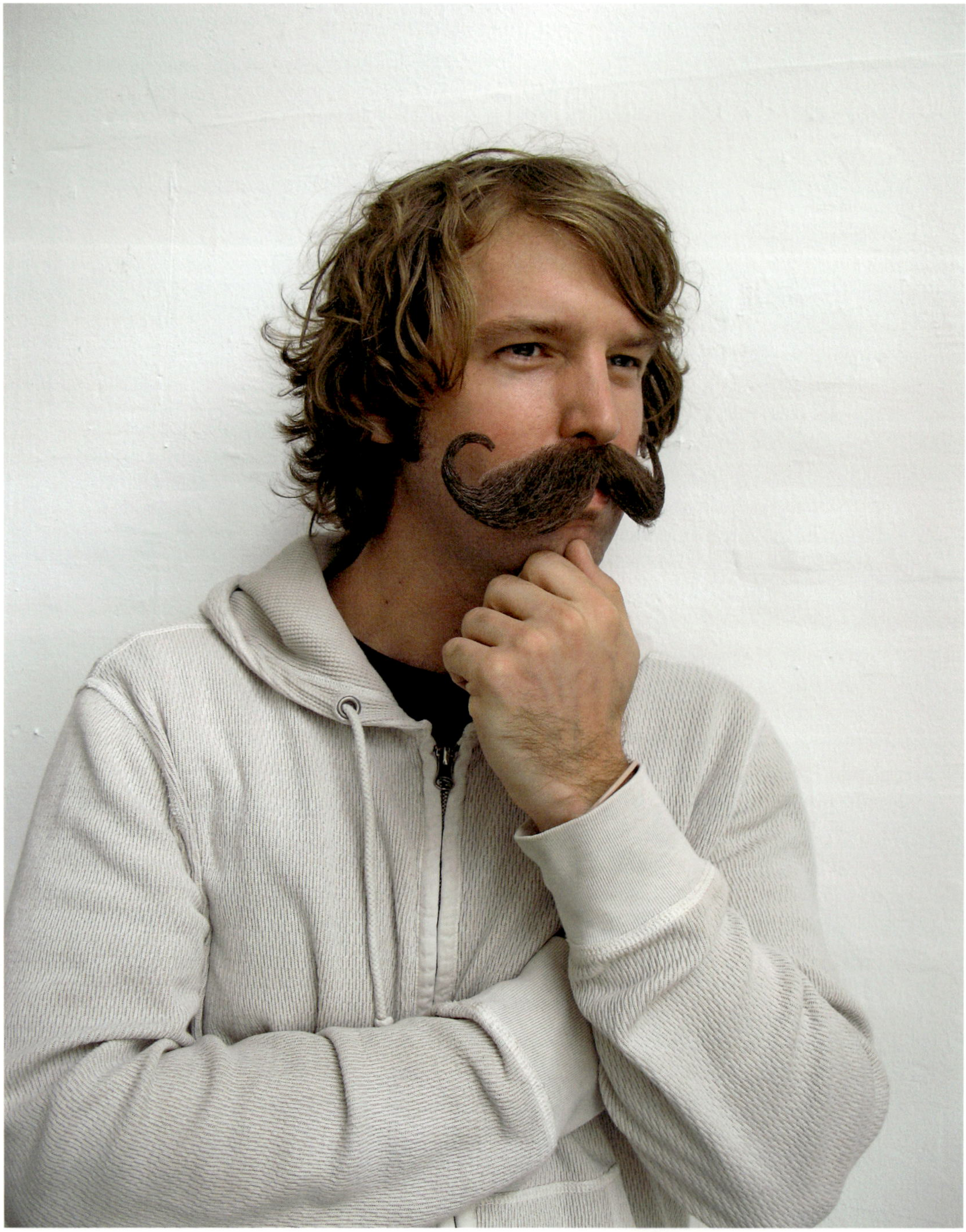

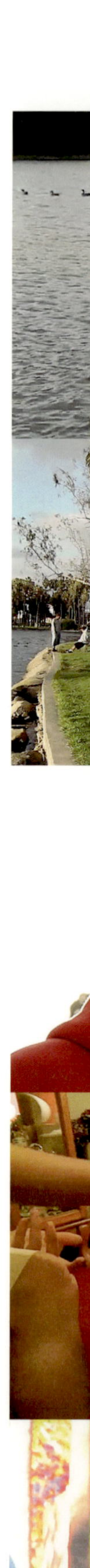

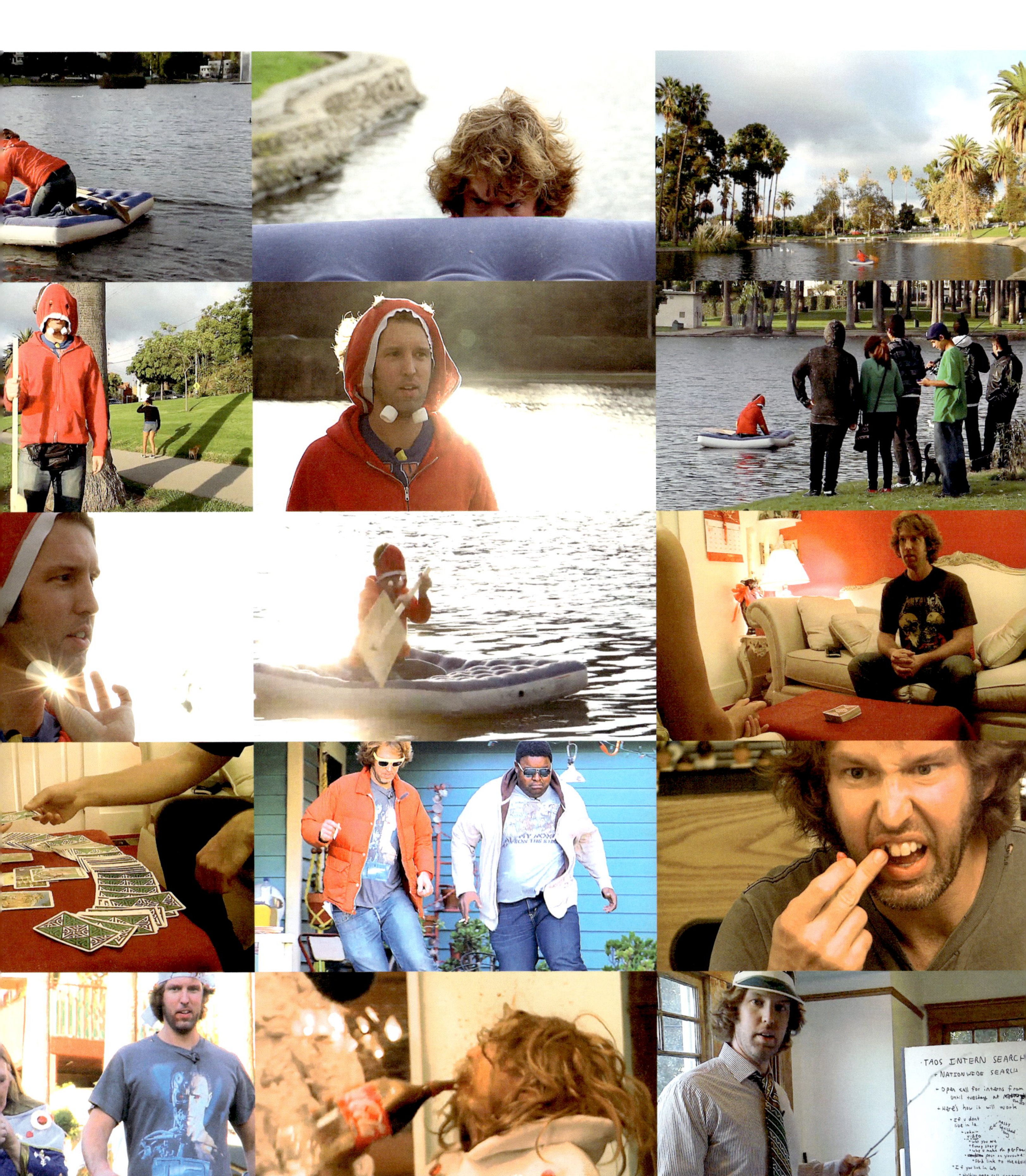
TAOS INTERN SEARCH
· NATIONWIDE SEARCH

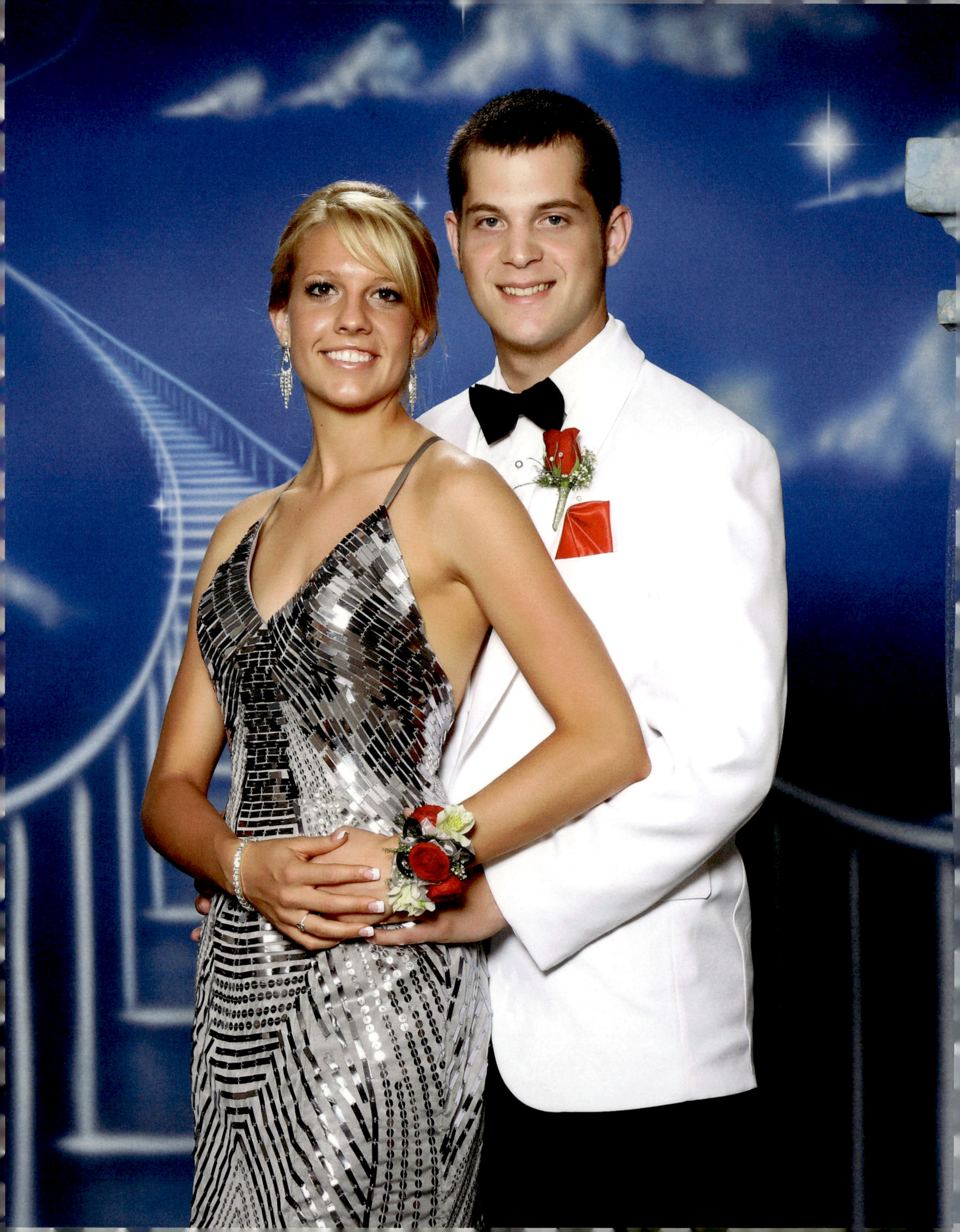

They have obtained iconic status in Western culture, with countless novels, magazines, movies and other narratives based on the event that seems to culminate the high school experience – Prom Night.

Popularized in the 1930s as a democratized version of the debutante ball, the prom offers female high-school students the opportunity to experience a 'coming out.' They also offer a site where social and romantic etiquette can be enforced, where adolescents can practice the rites and rituals hinged to adulthood. In essence, the prom has always been a contentious space, where youth identity politics are amplified by an aspirational consumer culture, and mediated by projections of 'becoming.' At first glance, the prom portraits appear jovial, even amusing. But more than simple records of experience, the prom portrait is a calculated and performative display of self, thus becoming prime territory to reveal larger preoccupations that are informed by class, race, gender and sexual orientation. Additionally, these images reference and reinforce another popular genre with widespread socio-political implications, namely, wedding or engagement portraiture.

The portraits are not a mandatory exercise; however, pre-prom, teens are provided the opportunity to customize picture packages and, in some cases, choose preferred backgrounds. Often backdrops are pre-selected, particularly when the organizing committee has set a theme. Students commonly have their images made outside of the dance itself, where they step into the prom portrait for a brief moment and then out again. Subsequently, the portrait is experienced once the physical object, the photograph, has been printed and obtained. The backdrop imagery is revealing; it often resembles honeymoon locations (Egypt, Hawaii), is fantastical (outer space, fairy tale castles), or aspirational in nature (a stately staircase, a luxury doorway, a red carpet in the center of Times Square.) The occurrence of the prom portrait can be exotic and exciting, or routine and obligatory. Regardless, the codes and conventions of such images confirm to the viewer, by way of a variety of signifiers, that this is a prom portrait.

In most of these, the composition is consistent and poses routinely directed; traditionally, males are positioned to the left, while females stand to the right, head tilted, and angled slightly frontward. Each with an arm behind the other, the couple mark a V formation with both their corsages in view. Commonly, behind the smile, faces appear stiff and limbs are tense; however, more often now photographers seem to encourage teens to 'act natural' in front of the camera. And for those willing, there is a space to express individuality: maybe a quirky pose before the shutter snaps, bold outfits or hairstyles.

Unlike many images captured during the night, which will undoubtedly end up on harddrives or social networking platforms to be shared and re-experienced, the prom photograph, in all its formality, is given elevated status - framed and placed in prime position upon a wall or mantle piece in the home, a confirmation of the individual's development from adolescent to (young) adult.

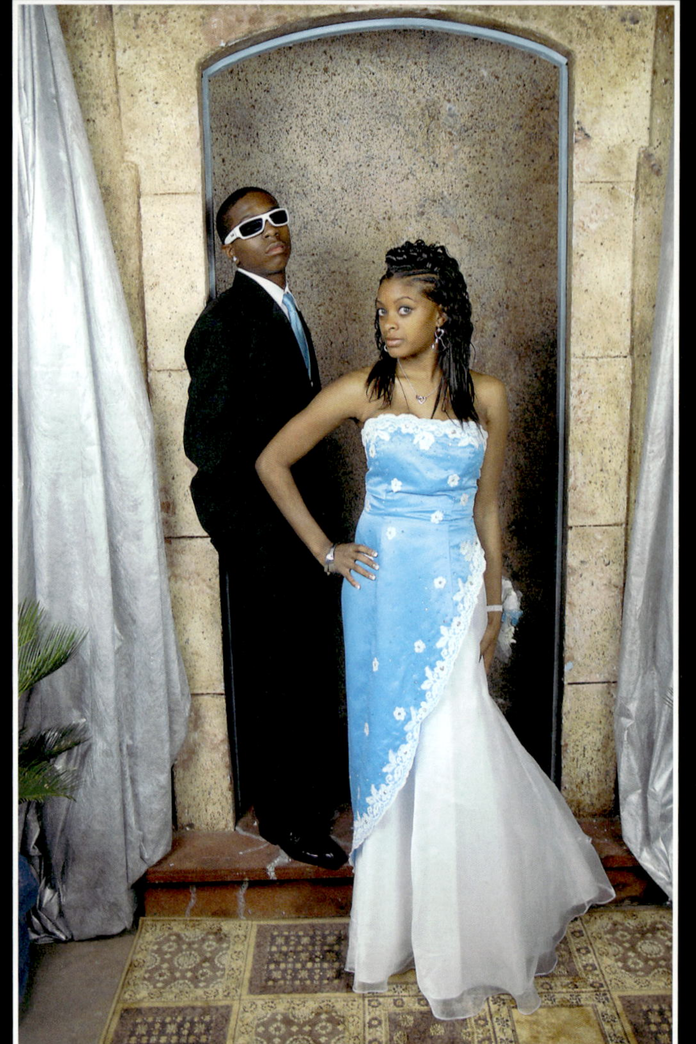

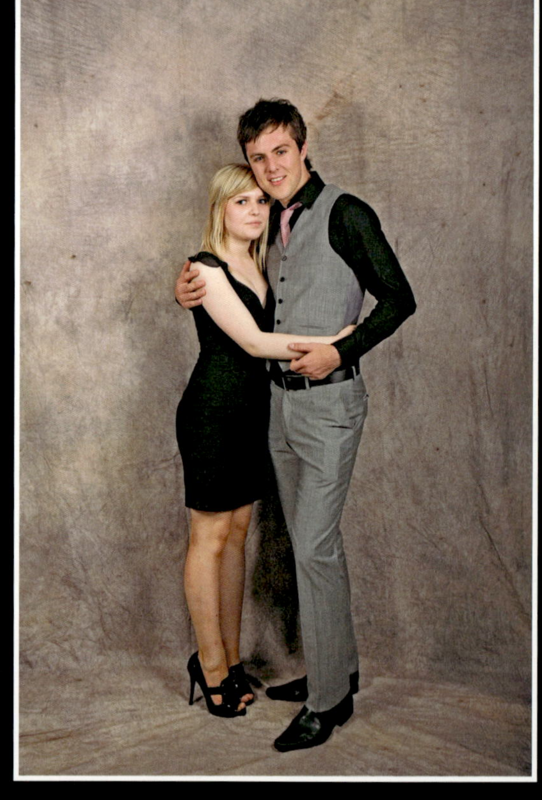

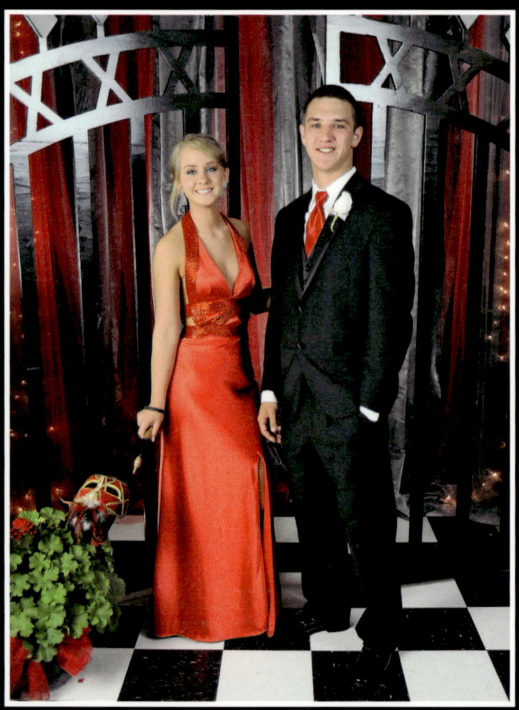

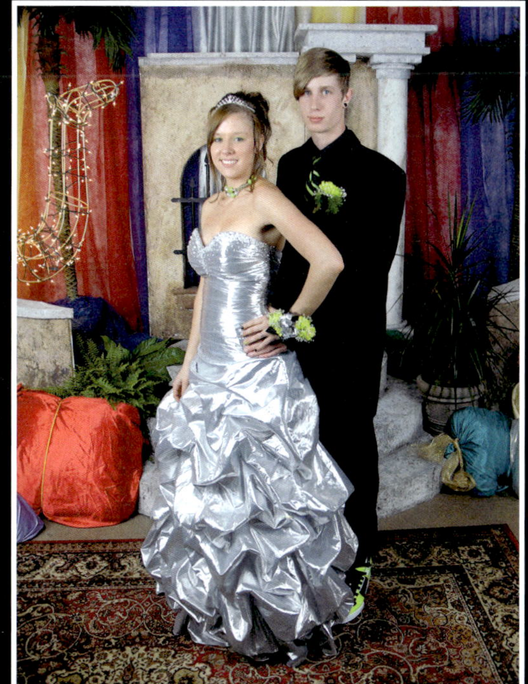

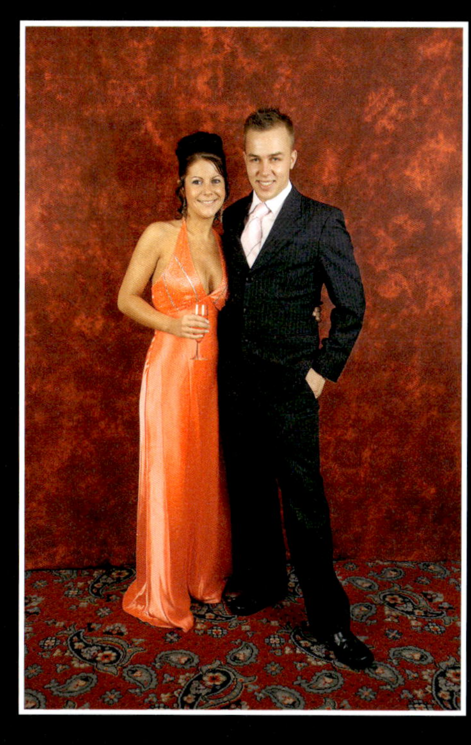

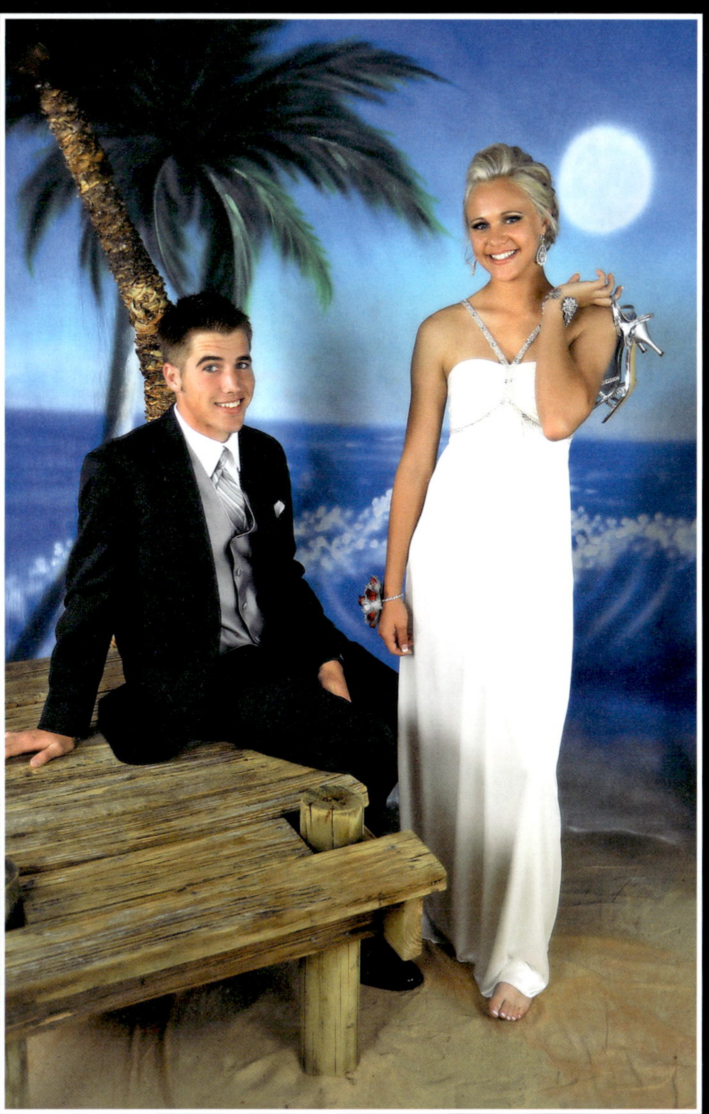

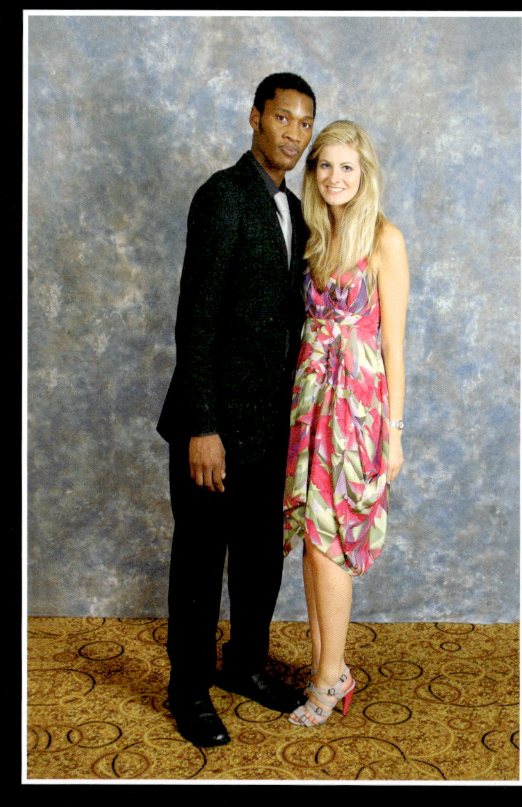

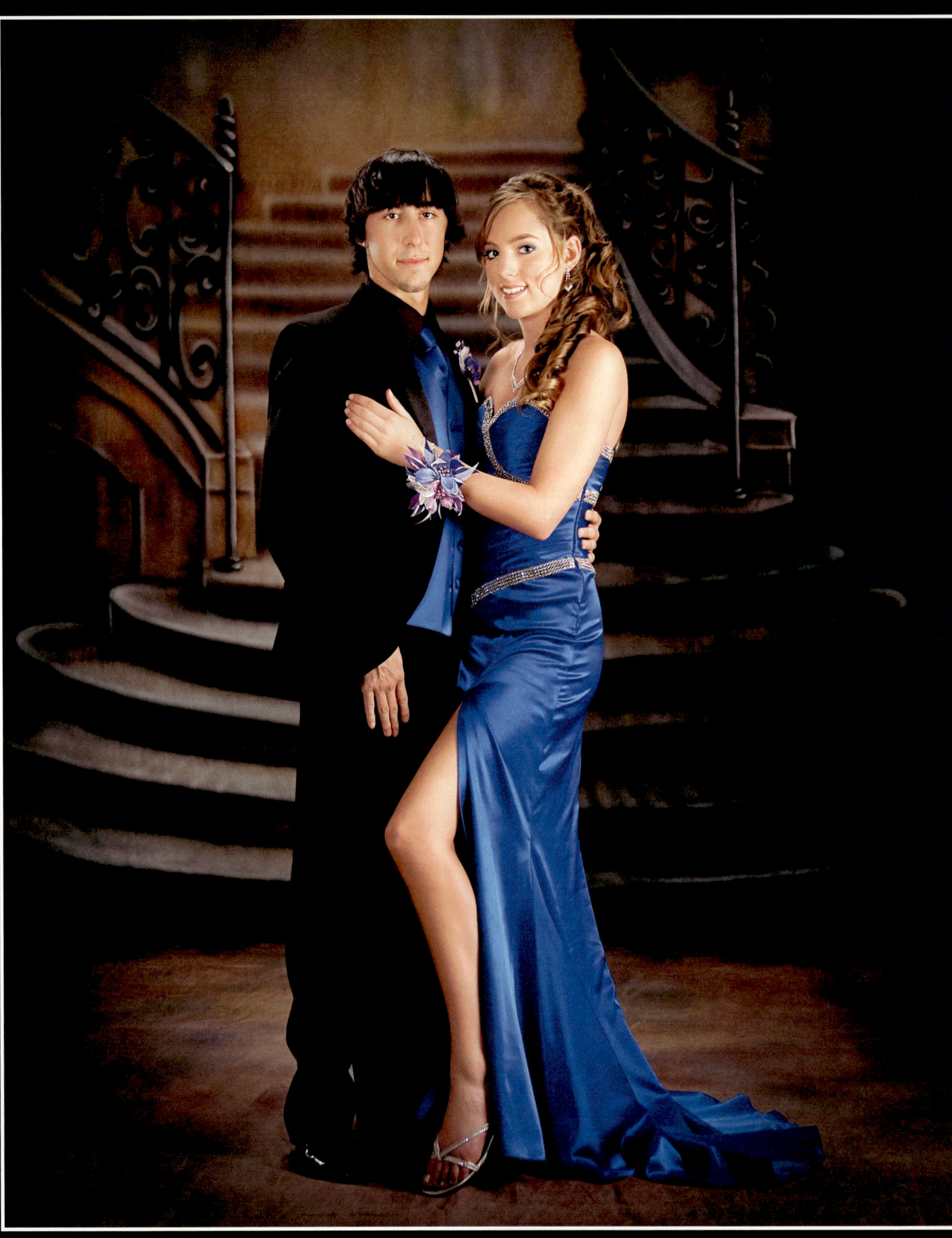

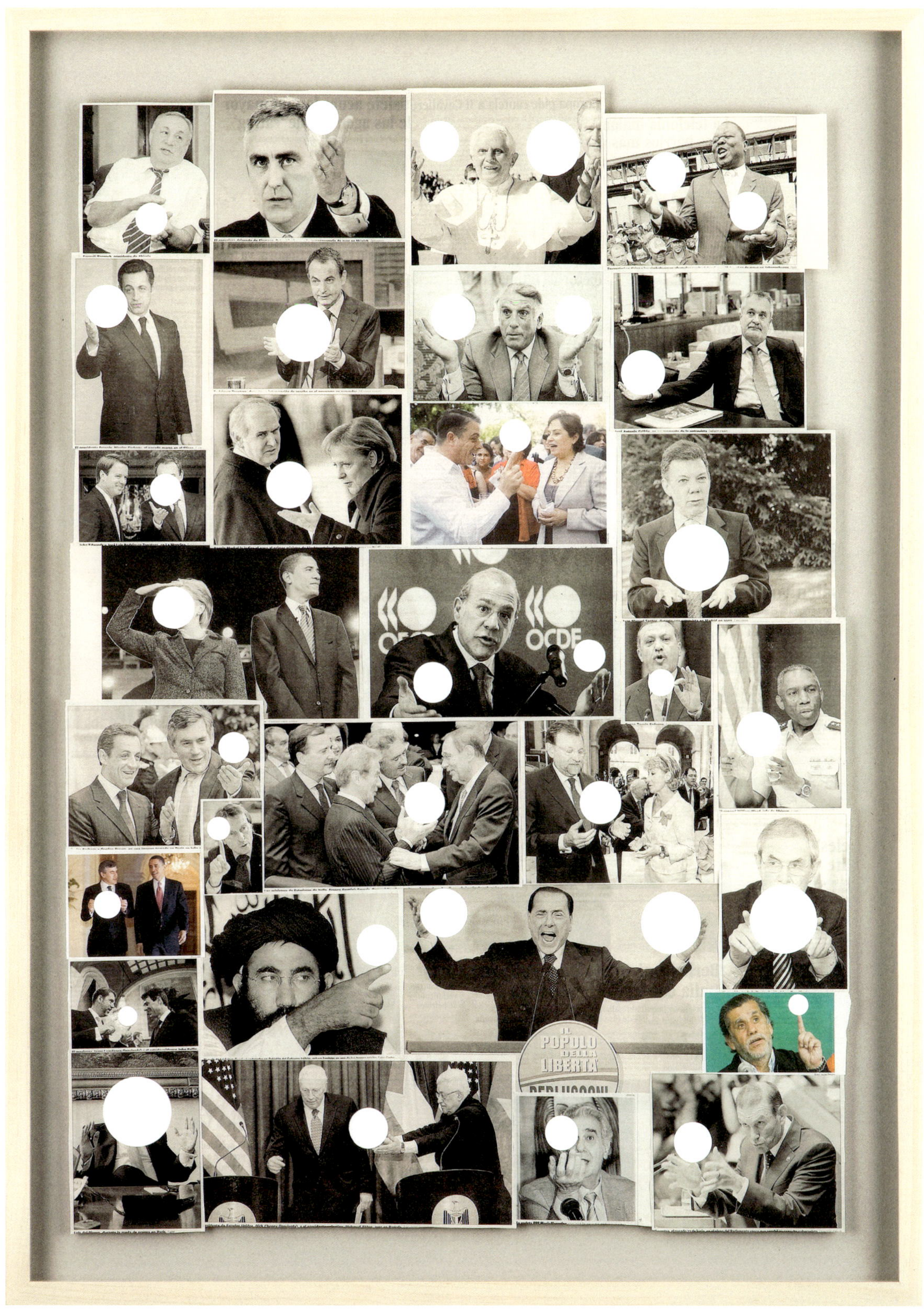

# JONATHAN HERNÁNDEZ
## From Mexico to Morgenpost

He is a native and local of Mexico City, but his artistic subjects and sources cover the world. In some cases, he spends months gathering fragments from newspapers for a collection, assisted appropriation or photocollage work. Once enough of one type of subject or action has been saved up, the artist may add a symbolic shape or mark as in the circular incisions of *Estado vacioso V*, 2009. This formal addition serves as an ironic form of graphic commentary leveled at the gathered group or situation. This artist's repetitive arrangements seem to suggest that what someone 'says' with their hands is as vacuous as the sphere that he adds to the composition. To emphasize the equivocal state of communication and action conveyed in the 'empty gestures' of his subjects, Hernández cobbles together unstable language for his titles - nonsense compound words and phrases that tease the viewer. Momentarily one thinks a title might convey something insightful, descriptive, or categorical about the picture but then suddenly it becomes apparent that these letters together amount to neither a conventional spelling nor even a meaningful malapropism. Nonetheless the term he assigns to designate his recent group of photocollaged compositions resembling totems, namely, Vulnerabilia is a clear indication of the uncertain state of affairs in the world. The term Vulnerabilia equally describes the shaky state of truth in the press and the unreliability of those persons featured in our papers. - Jonathan Hernández has mounted solo shows at galleries such as Kurimanzutto in Mexico and Krinzinger in Vienna. He has been featured in international museums such as Sala de Arte Público Siqueiros in Mexico (2006), Centro de Arte Contemporáneo de Málaga in Spain (2003), and the New Museum in New York (2008).

*Page 75* Estado vacioso V, 2009, newspaper cuttings with a singular incision each. *Right* Rongwrong XX, 2008. *Pages 78-79 from* Pofupoji, 2005-2006, a series of 27 postcards. *Pages 80-81* Vulnerabilia (Volare), 2005-2008, 63 newspaper cuttings on cardboard. Photos of the works by Estudio Michel Zabé.
*All images © and courtesy Kurimanzutto, Mexico City*

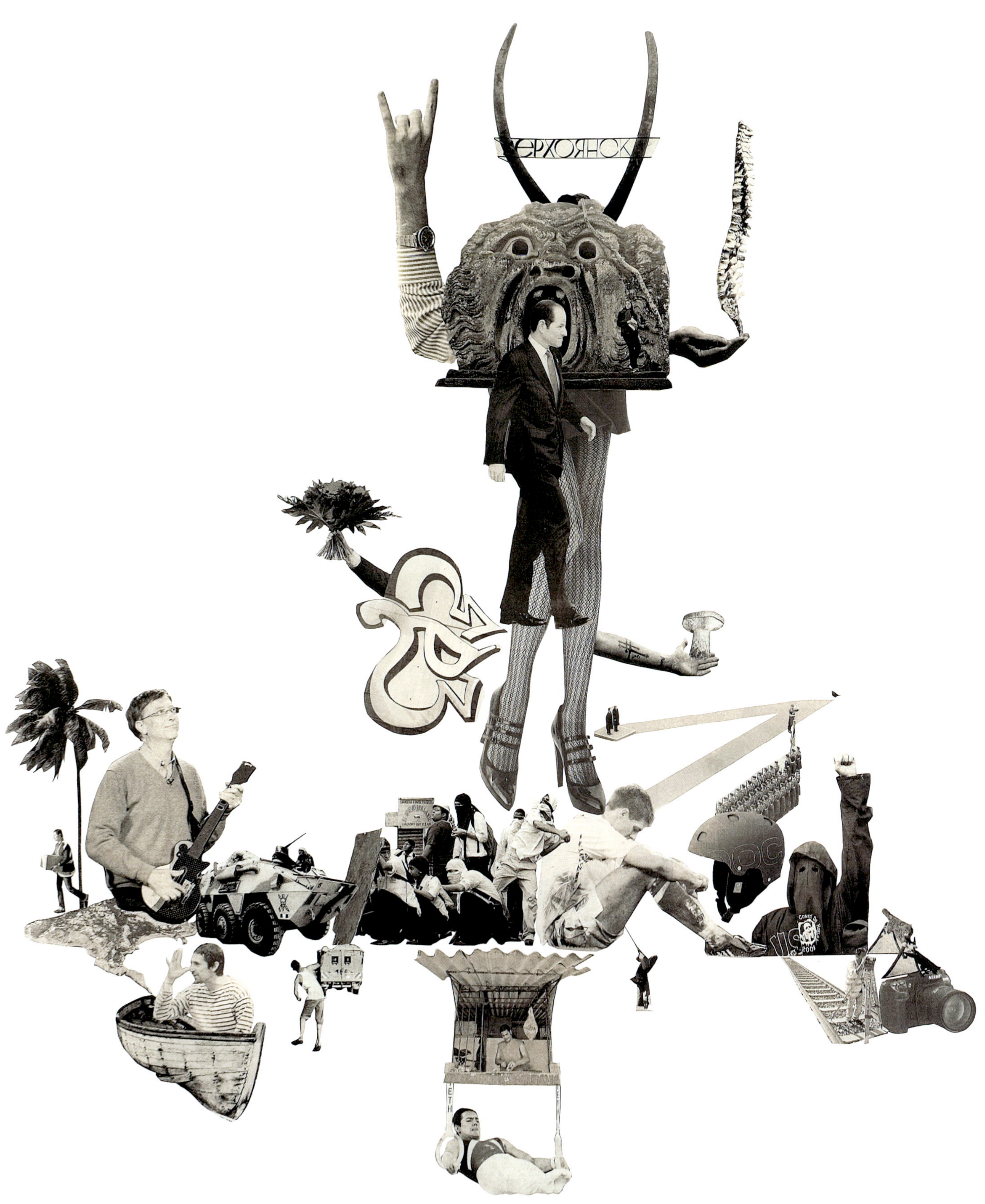

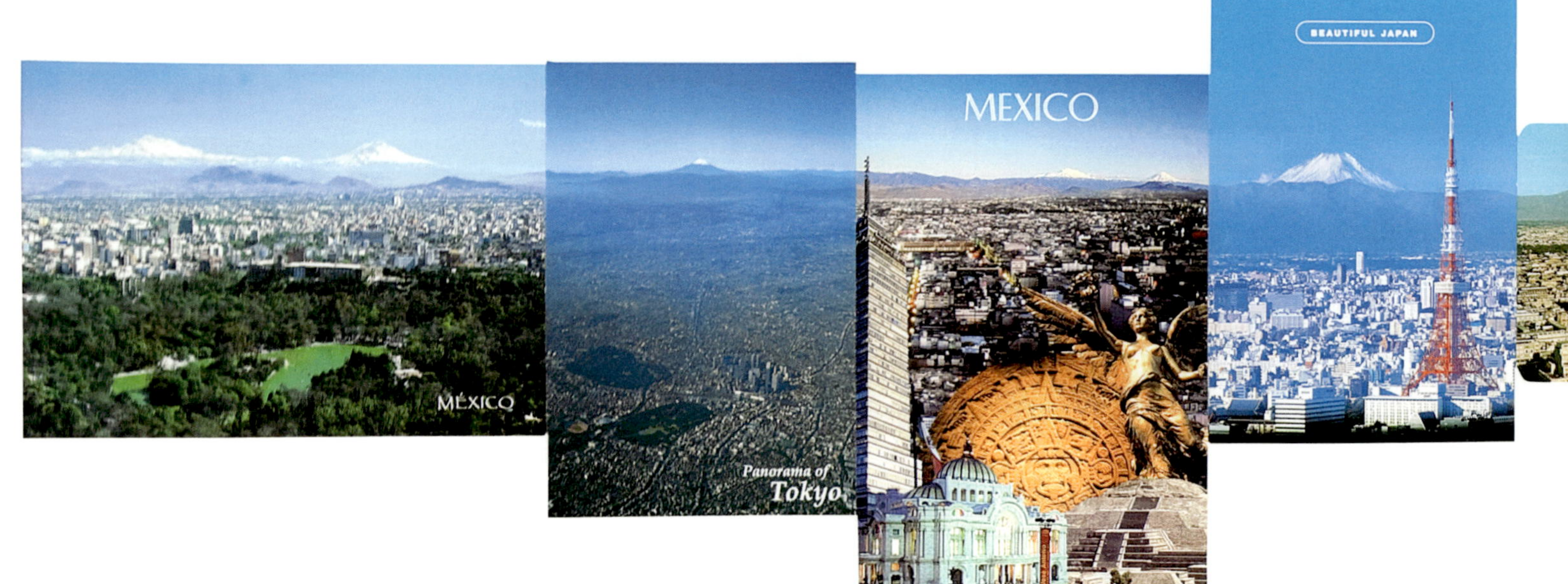
MÉXICO
Panorama of Tokyo
MEXICO
BEAUTIFUL JAPAN

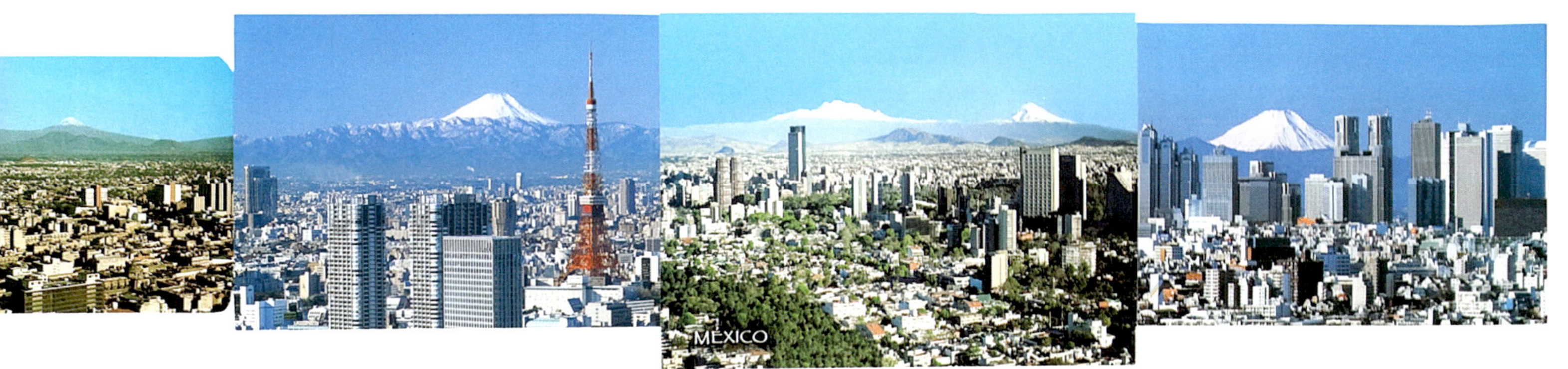

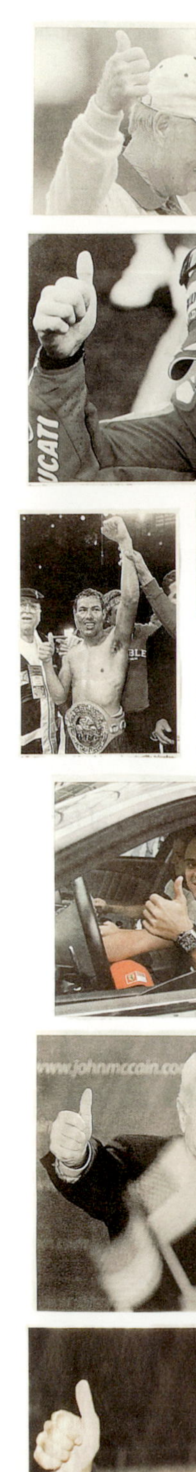
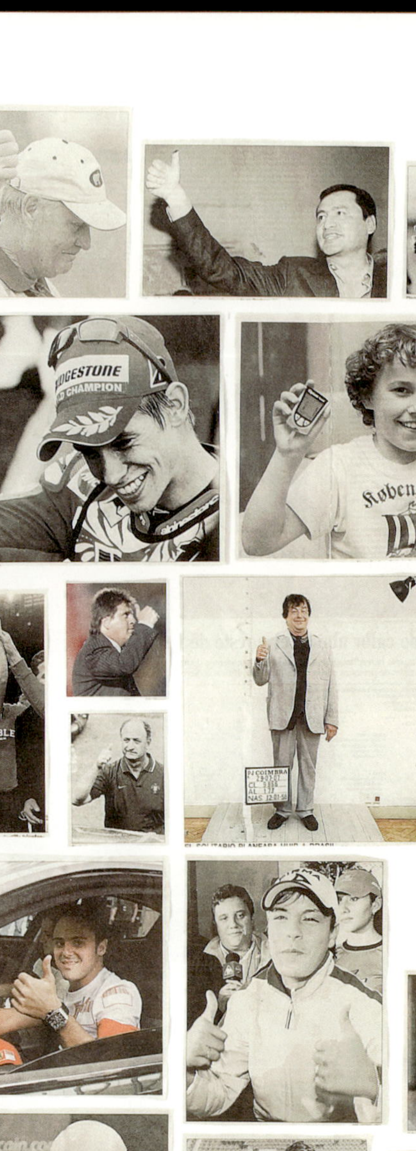
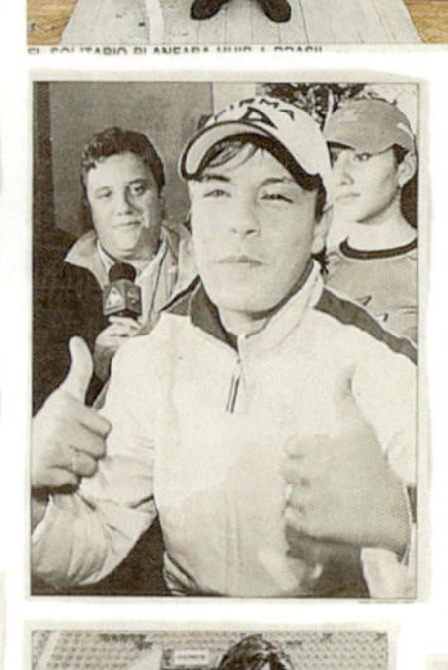
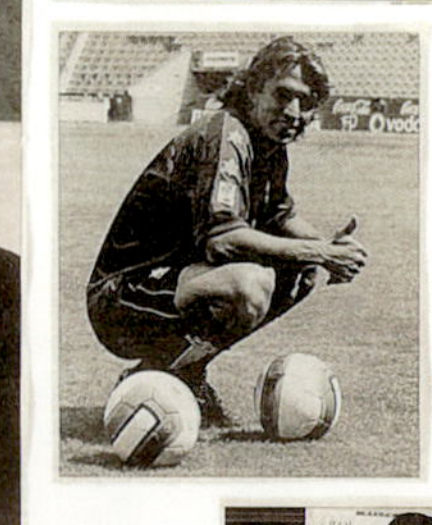
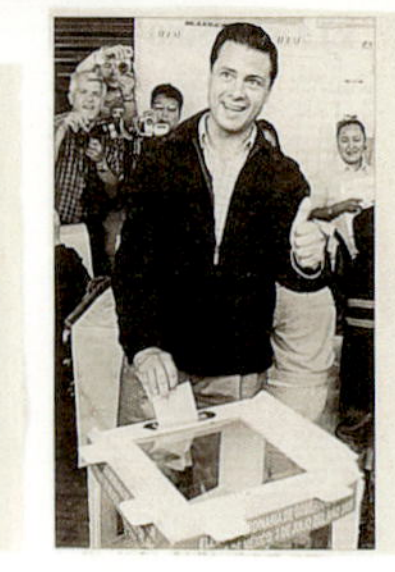
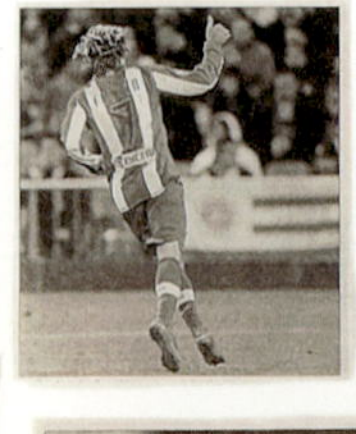
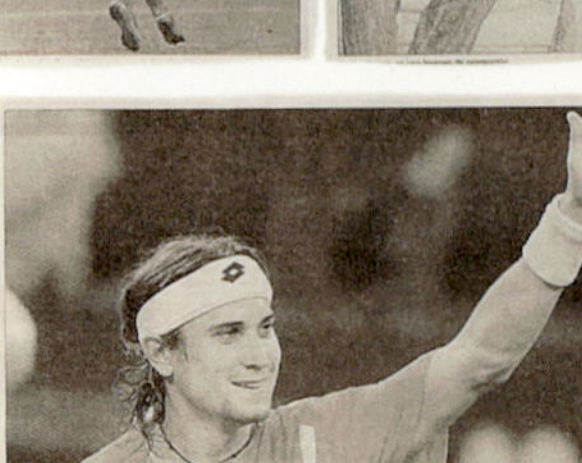
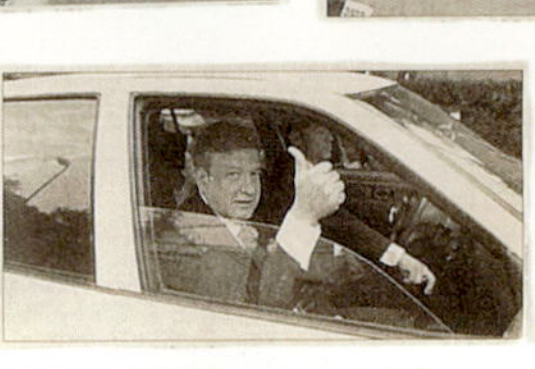
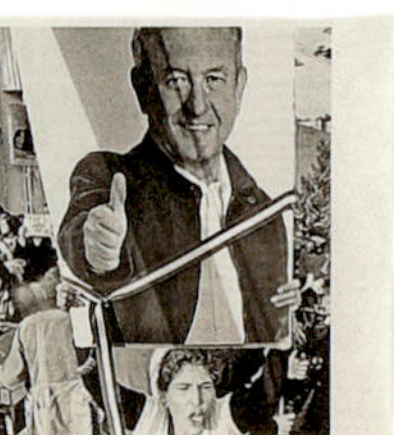
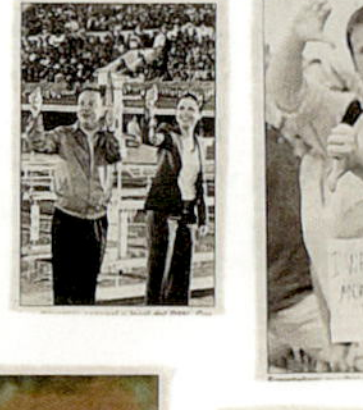
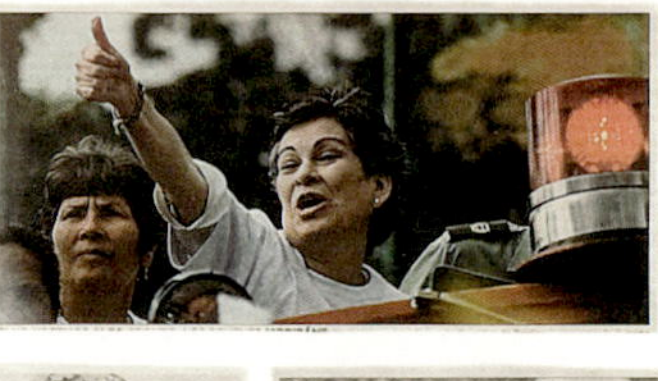
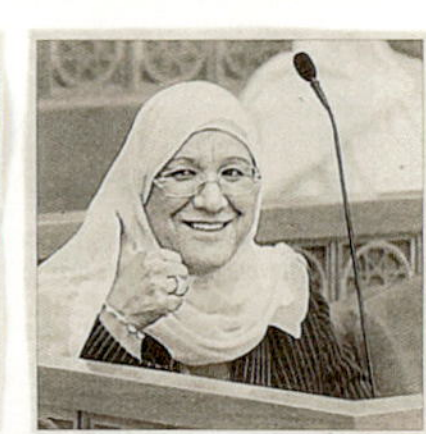
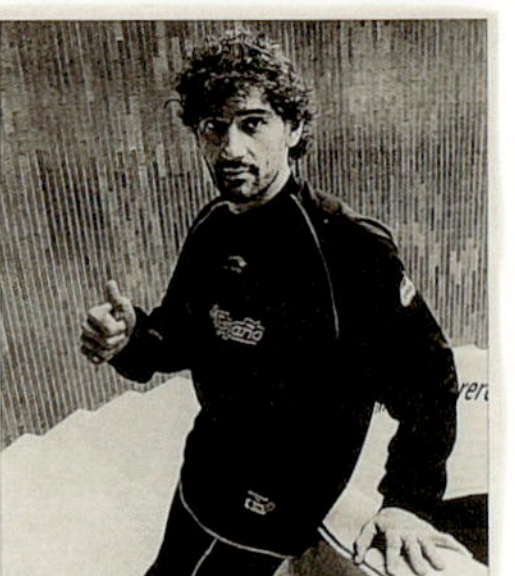
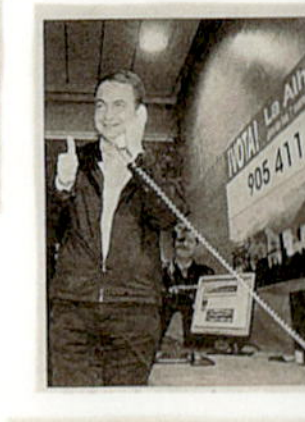
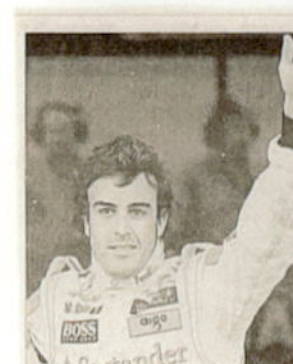

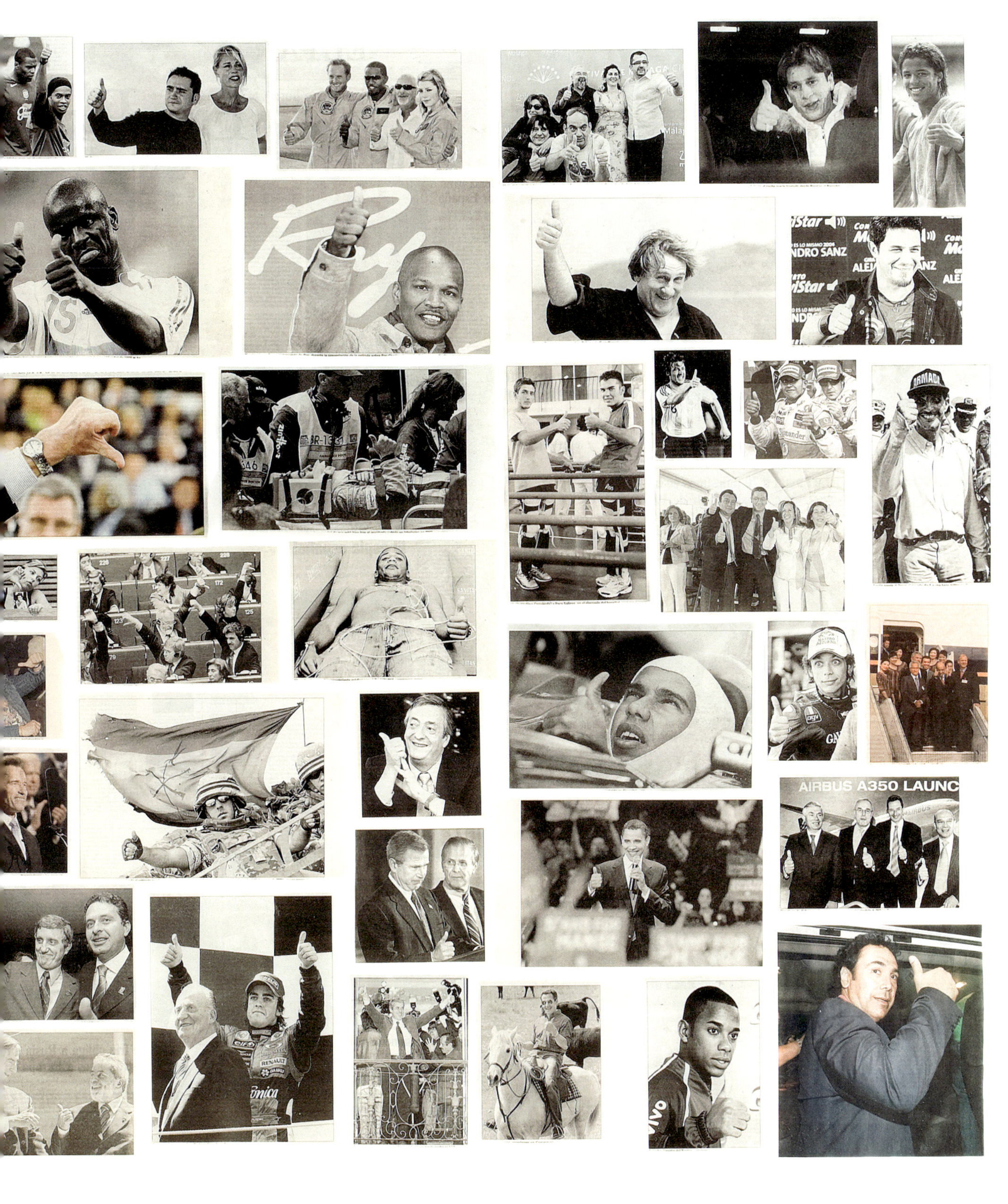

# SUPERHEROES
## sampled by Francesco Jodice

Matt Murdock is blind. Donald Blake has a limp. Charles Xavier is paralyzed. Steve Rogers is an old man. Rick Jones has a tumour. Tony Stark is an alcoholic. Luke Cage is black. Bruce Banner is a monster. These men are better known for their alter egos: Daredevil, Thor, X-men, Captain America, Iron Man, Power Man, Hulk. They are superheroes.

Stanley Martin Lieber is a Jew of Romanian decent. He landed in Brooklyn at the beginning of the twentieth century and is better known by the name of his alter ego, Stan Lee. Between 1961 and 1964, Stan Lee and his fellow cartoonist Jack Kirby (a.k.a. Jacob Kurtzberg), created Marvel Universe, an endless crossover between a soap opera that has been running for half a century and a cosmogony of Homeric proportions. Marvel Comics superheroes became the modern epic.

In America, superheroes were already a dime a dozen. There was Superman, who was an alien god raised on white bread and traditional values in Kentucky, and Batman, a millionaire devoted to charity but ready to punish petty street thieves, and Wonder Woman, who appeared to be the product of a puritan Miss America contest. After 1961 Stan Lee introduced his personal den of fools: black men, drunkards, cripples, paralytics and so on and so forth. Rather than achieving hero status due to divine right or birth, his characters seem to be outcasts driven by strange sentiments of humanity and tolerance, sharing ordinary people's everyday problems: overdue bills and broken hearts.

Years ago, a reader of Marvel comics complained to its publishers in the letters page when Steve Rogers, alias Captain America, moved from Brooklyn to Queens. The reader wrote to Marvel that, over the years, he had put up with all kinds of dangers with Captain America as a neighbour and had kept quiet about the hero's secret identity and that now, without any forewarning, Marvel was sending him far away, to Queens. "It isn't right," said the neighbour bitterly.

*Right advertisement page from* Hulk n.7. *Page 84 left* Iron Man n.128; *right* I Fantastici Quattro n.34. *Page 85 left* Daredevil n.32; *right from* Cage n.1

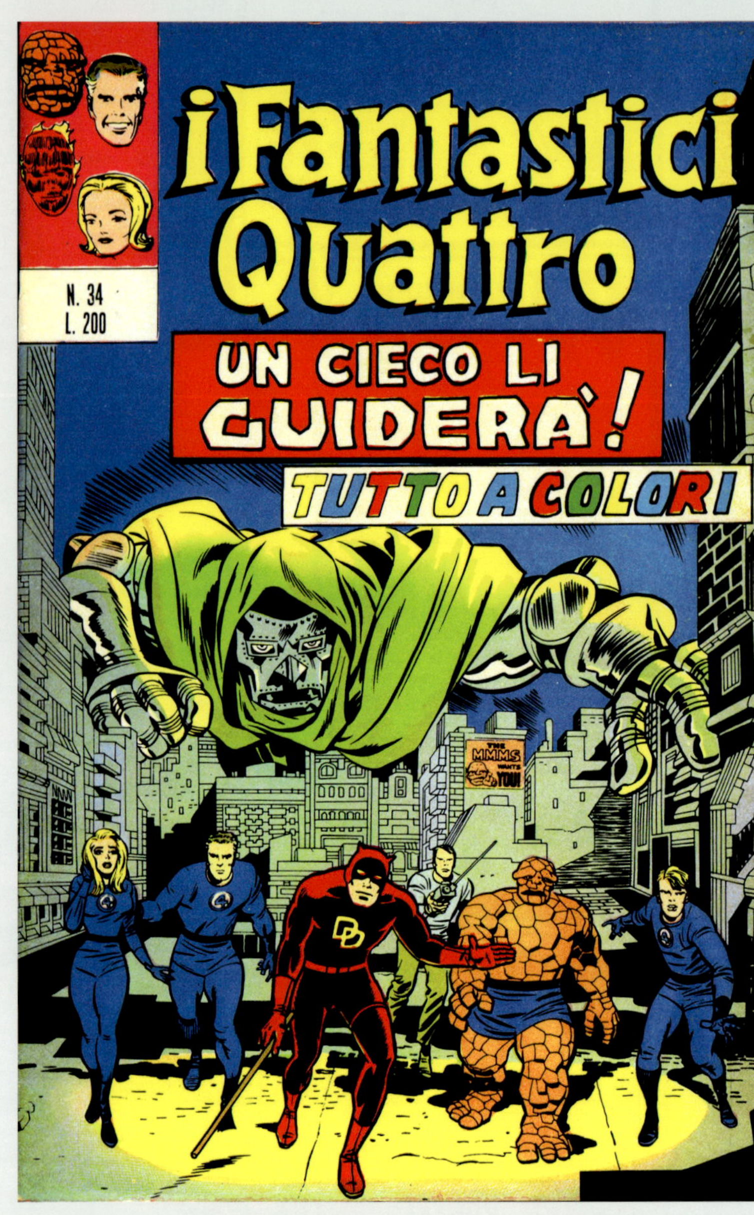
i Fantastici Quattro
N. 34
L. 200
UN CIECO LI GUIDERÀ!
TUTTO A COLORI

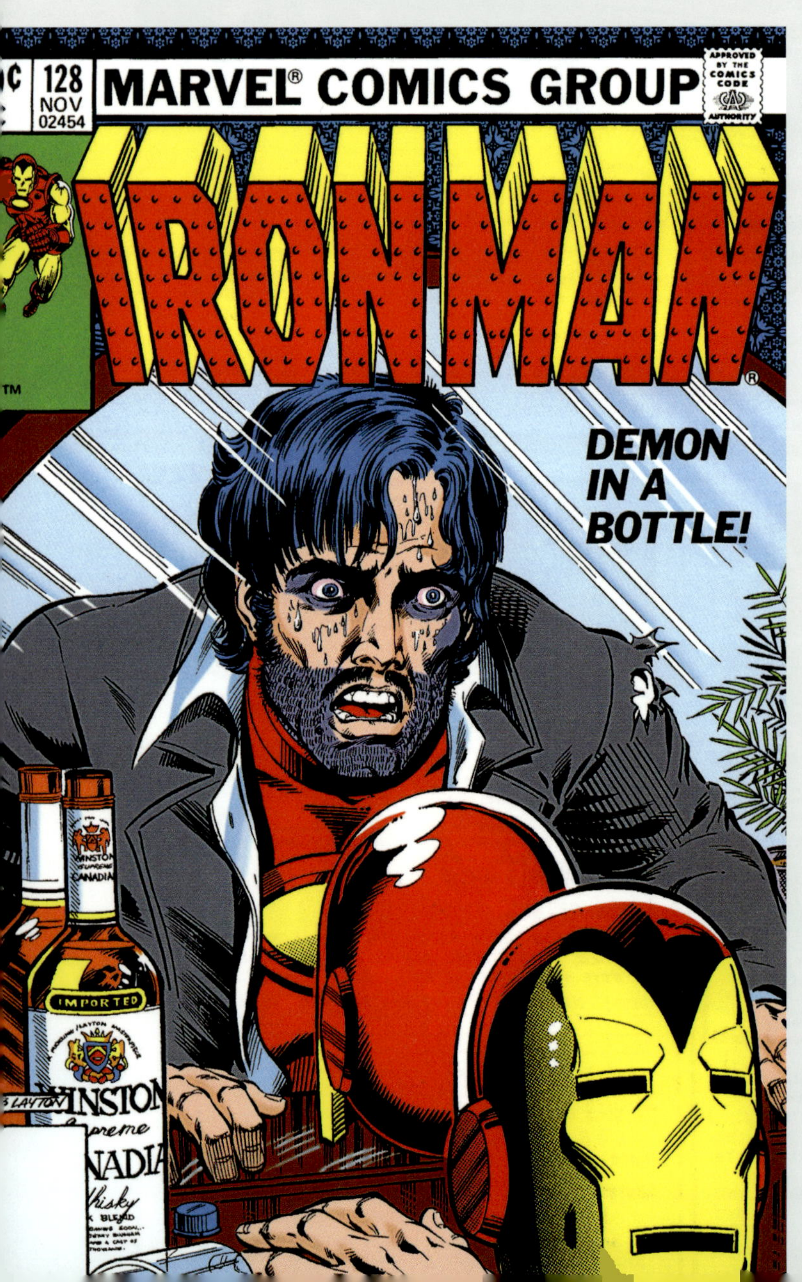
128
NOV
02454
MARVEL® COMICS GROUP
APPROVED BY THE COMICS CODE AUTHORITY
IRON MAN
DEMON IN A BOTTLE!

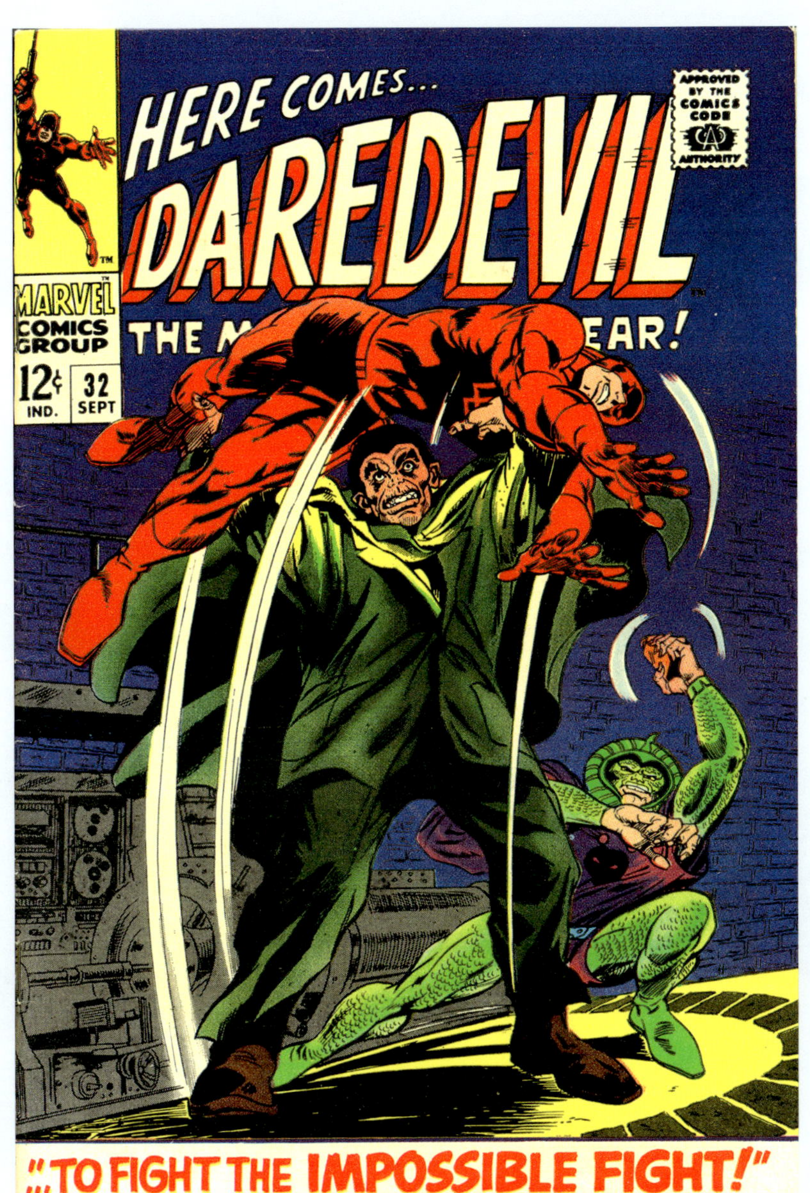
HERE COMES...
DAREDEVIL
THE MAN WITHOUT FEAR!
MARVEL COMICS GROUP
12¢ IND. 32 SEPT
APPROVED BY THE COMICS CODE AUTHORITY
"...TO FIGHT THE IMPOSSIBLE FIGHT!"

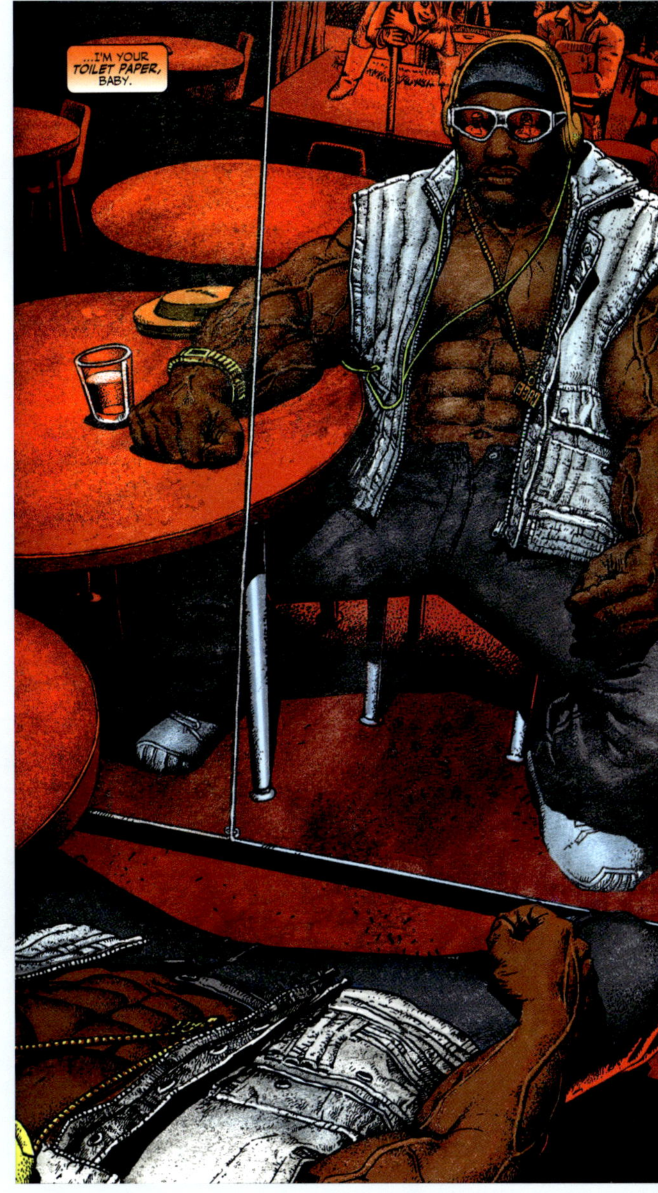
...I'M YOUR TOILET PAPER, BABY.

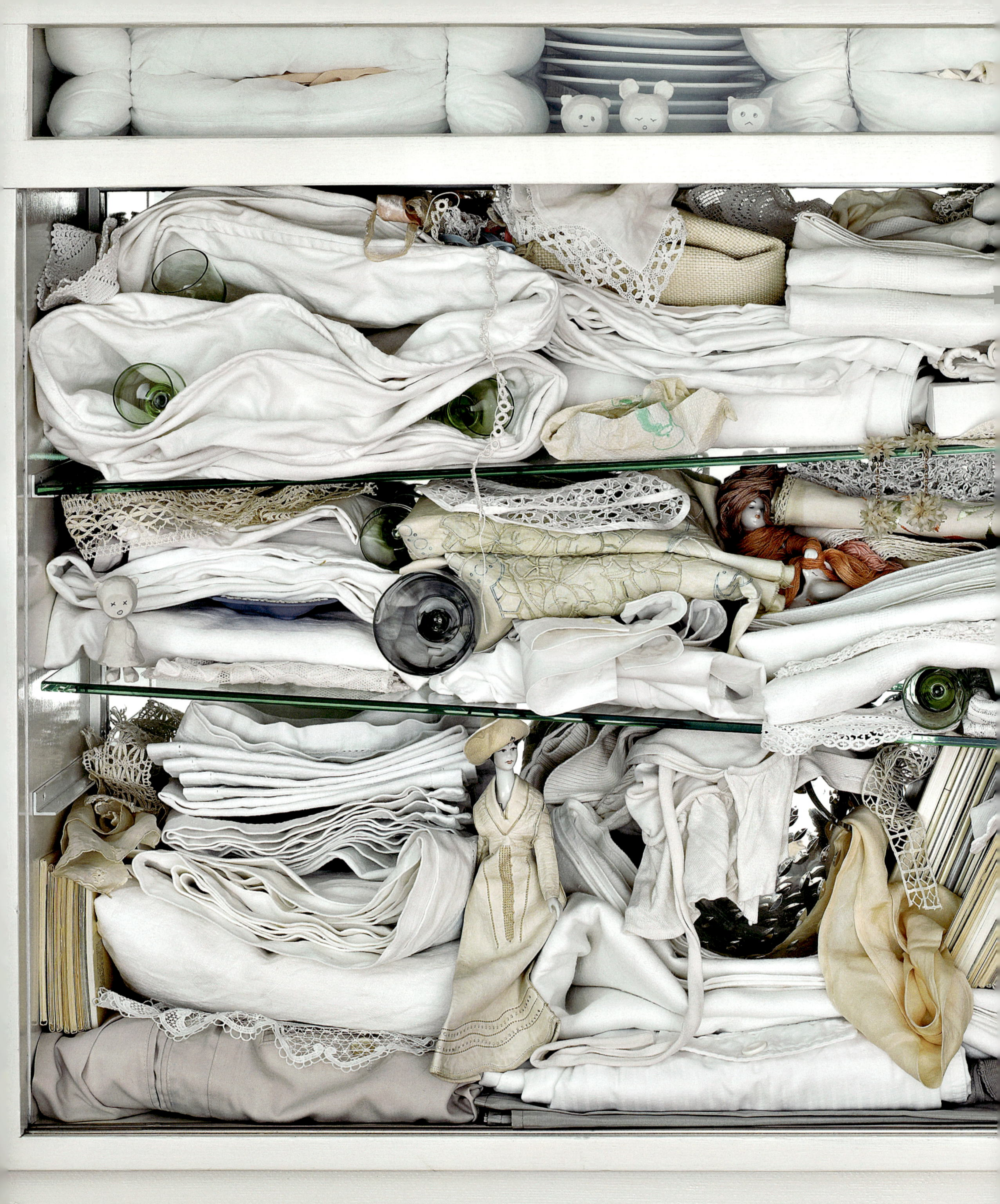

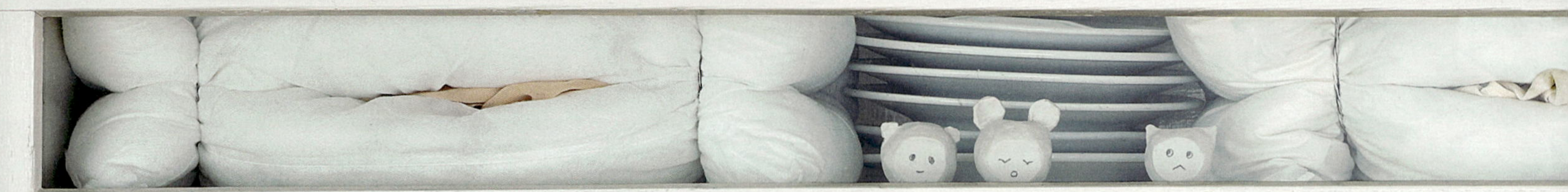

White Things *from the* Show-Cases *series*, 2009, pigment print, cm 100 x 143. *Image © and courtesy the artist*

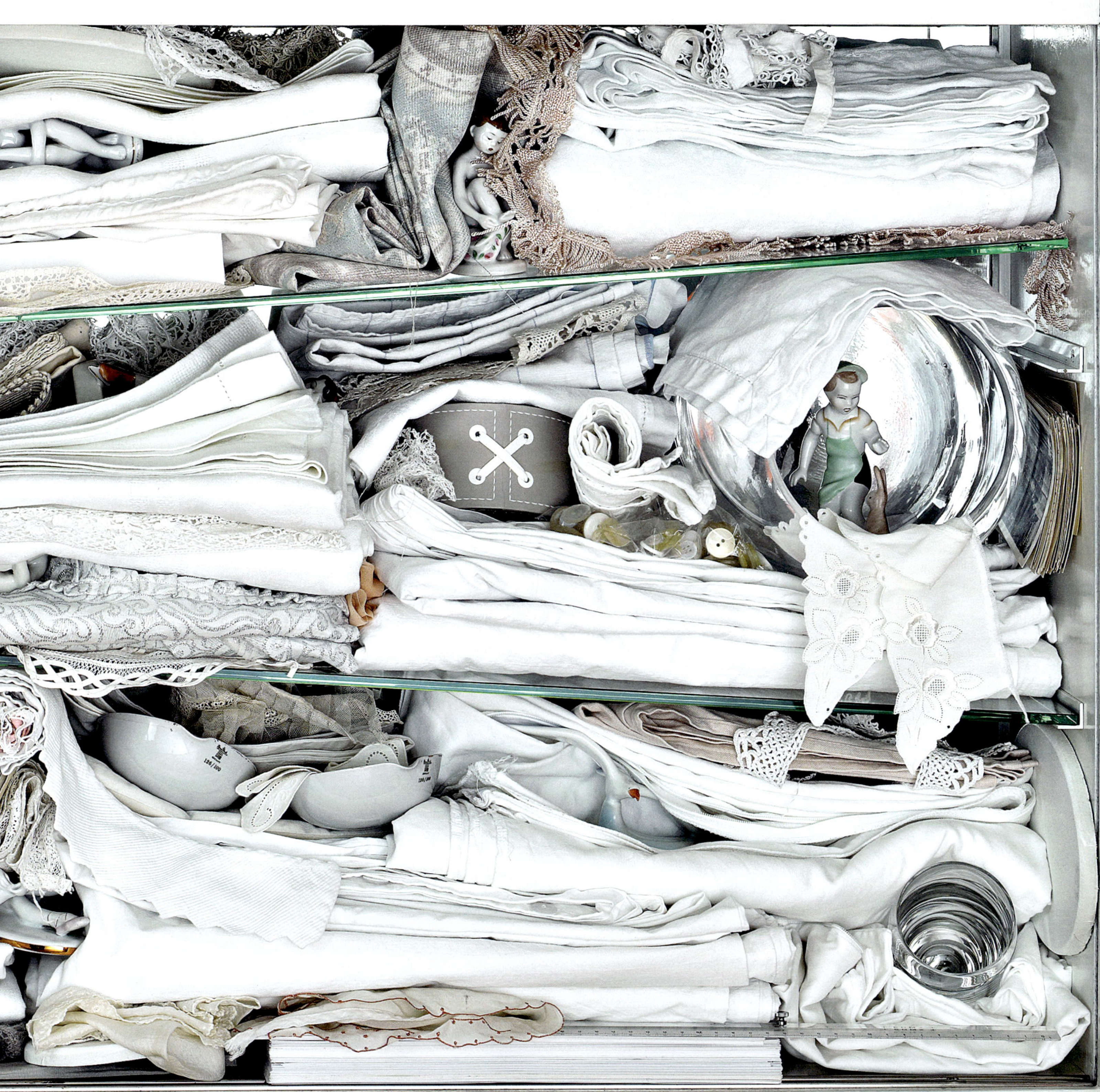

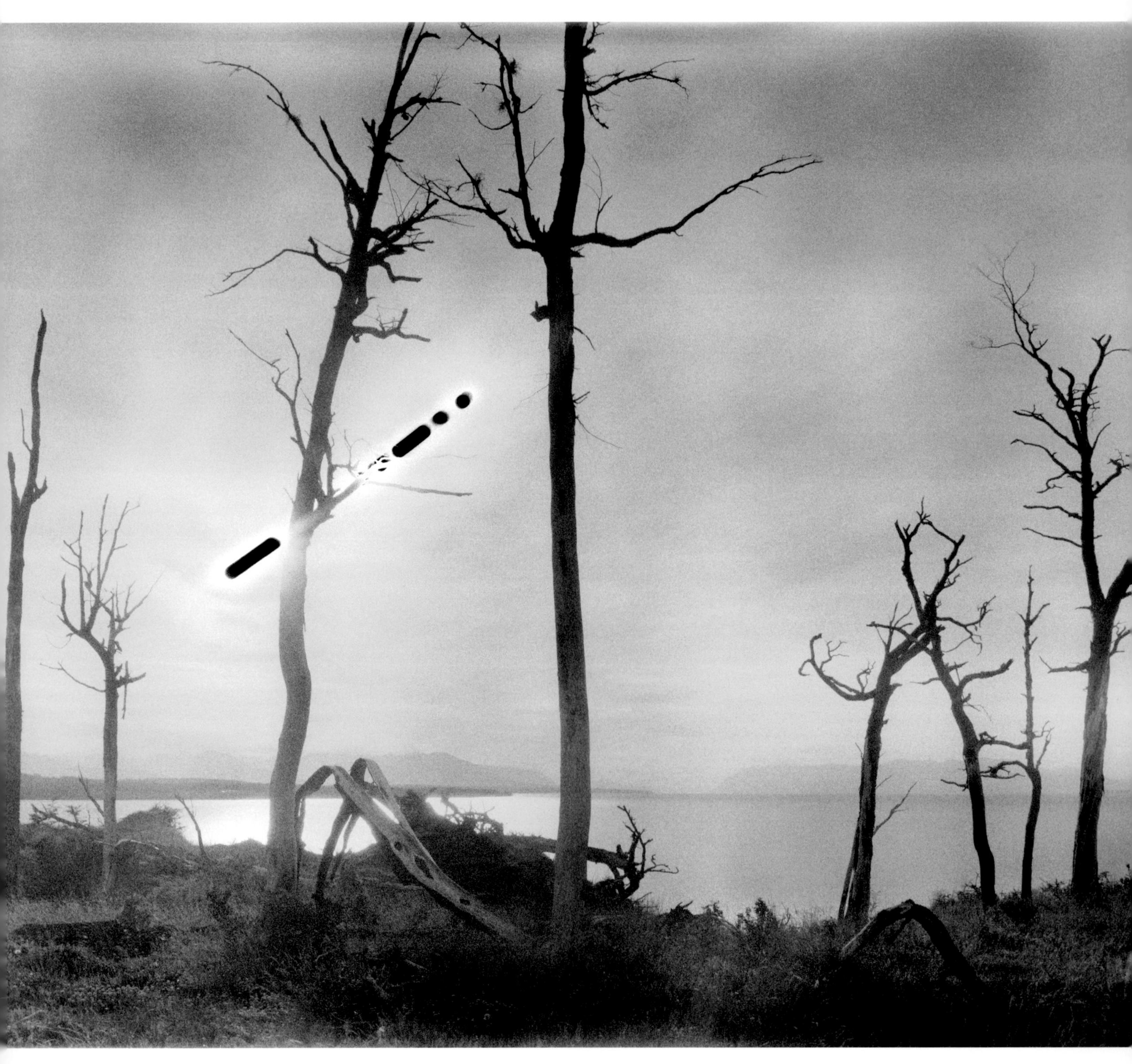

# *One Hour*
# Marc Feustel in conversation with
# HANS-CHRISTIAN SCHINK

**Born in Erfurt, Germany, in 1961, Hans-Christian Schink studied at the Academy of Visual Arts in Leipzig, where he received his BFA and MFA. For *Fantom*, he talks with Marc Feustel about his project, *1h*: a haunting collection of solarized photographic experiments that amalgamate a broad scope of aesthetic, mechanical, and theoretical disciplines. Though initiated in 2003, the images featured here are extracted from his most recent development of the series, the Southern Hemisphere, which were taken mostly in 2010.**

**MARC FEUSTEL** *I'd like to start by asking you how the idea for this project first came about? It seems to be a significant departure from your previous work in terms of your visual approach.*

**HANS-CHRISTIAN SCHINK** I first used solarization in one of my works in 1999 when I was invited to submit a work to the Department of Physics and Astronomy at the University of Jena. I submitted a piece made up of three panels with abstract color gradations of a sky during the day, a sky at night, and the path of the sun, which appears as a solarized, black line on a white background. Initially, I got the idea from a Hermann Krone photograph from 1888. Unlike Krone, I pointed my camera straight at the sky in order to get a clean, linear image of the sun. Later, on a trip to the Mojave Desert in California in 2003, I was so fascinated by the landscape and the blazing light that I wanted to find a way of reproducing this almost unreal impression. I remembered Minor White's photograph, *Black Sun*, of a winter landscape where the sun appears as a solarized black dot - an accidental effect created when the camera shutter briefly froze. I wanted to try to use this effect with a longer exposure, but I wasn't sure if any of the landscape would be recognizable at all. I wasn't sure that it was possible to construct a solid concept from what was quite an atypical approach for me. Mostly, I wasn't sure that the project could become something more than a technical game.

*What was it that convinced you that you could turn the project into something more than a technical exercise?*
It was a question of the atmospheric power of the image. To me, the Hermann Krone picture was the document of an experiment: it only contains the line of the sun and a faded rooftop silhouette. My first test photos didn't look very different. But when I found a way to balance out the aesthetic power of the landscape with the dominating phenomenon of this mystical black line, I knew it would work.

*The project seems to deal with the very essence of photography: drawing with light. These sun traces seem like the most primitive manifestation possible of this. Was this project a way for you to explore the basic components of photography, light and time?*
Yes, absolutely. And in a very unusual, almost abstract way. I was able to reproduce the light of the sun and the passage of time without them being recognizable as such at first glance. The pictures show a completely different reality of their own that can only be perceived through photography. This touches on one of the key issues of the medium: the ability to depict reality.

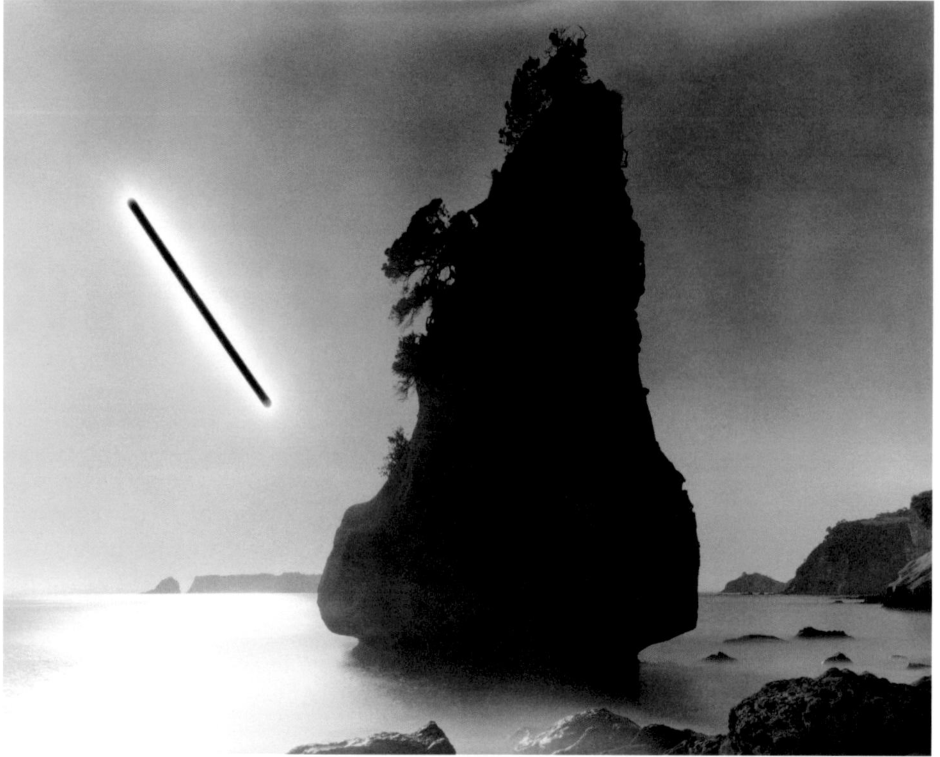

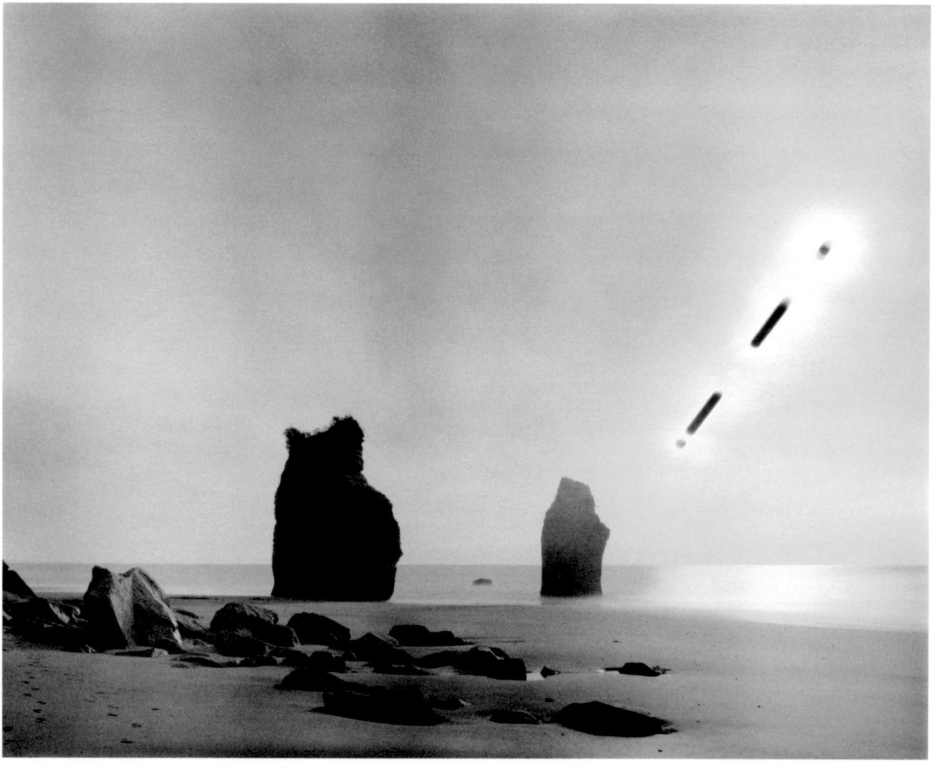

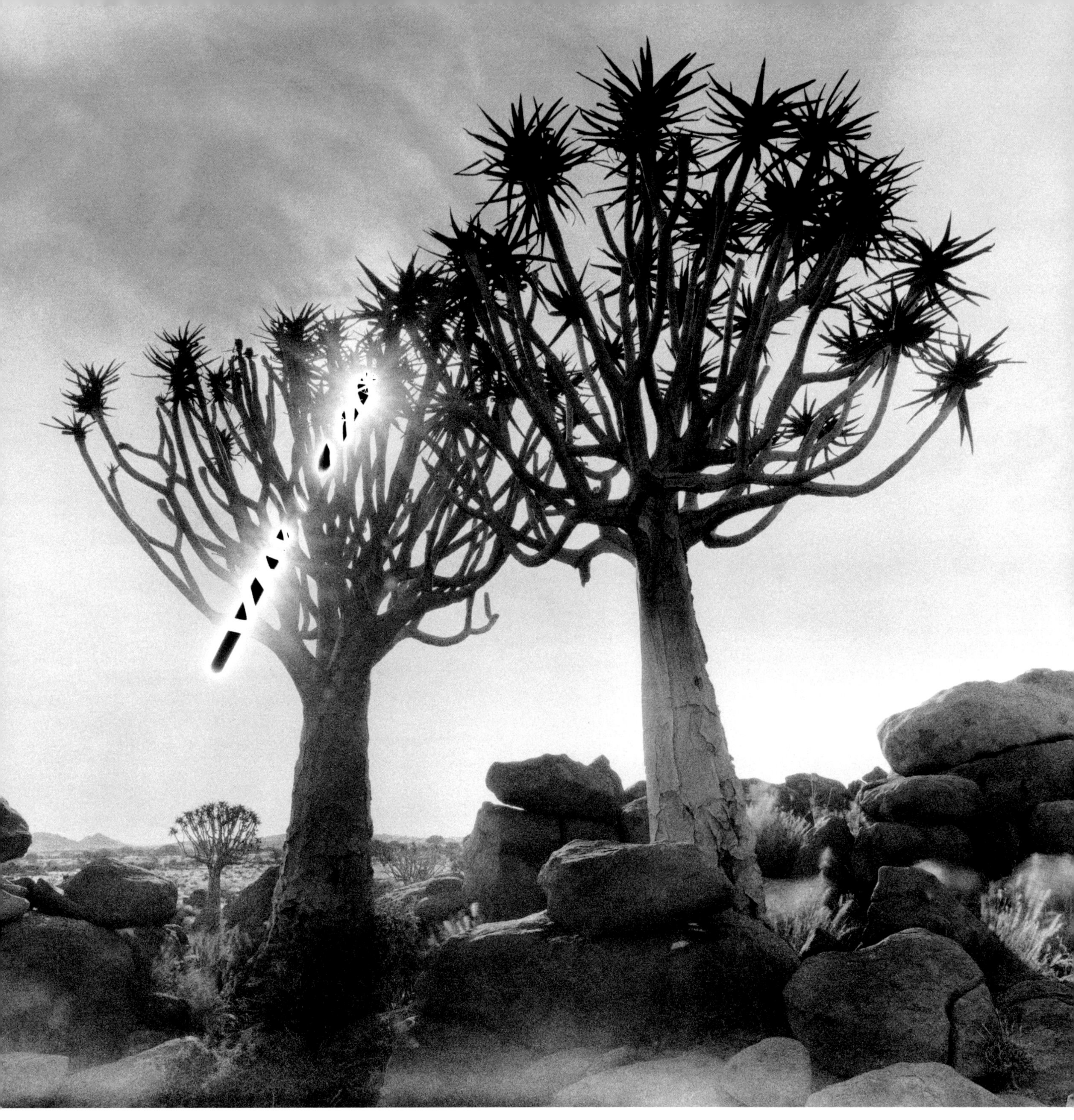

*Opening page* 2/04/2010, 7:22 pm-8:22 pm, S 54°35.873' W 067°22.541'. *Left page top* 2/26/2010, 7:54 am-8:54 am, S 36°49.622' E 175°47.340'; *bottom* 2/21/2010, 6:43 pm-7:43 pm, S 38°49.086' E 174°34.936'. *Above* 4/10/2009, 4:11 pm-5:11 pm, S 26°28.034' E 018°16.142'

*The relationship to reality is a very interesting component of these photographs. Although the landscapes are real, the black trace of the sun makes us question the reality of these images. In general, it seems that photography's link to reality has become more and more hazy with technological developments in recent years. Do you think that people would still be as attached to photography if it were no longer perceived as a document of reality?*

I don't think of photographs as documents of reality. Even if they are taken from reality, to me photographs are beyond reality, in either a positive or negative sense. Looking at hundreds of holiday snapshots taken with enthusiasm during a trip to an exotic location, you will most likely realize that these images do not translate the atmosphere of that place at all. Your own experience of reality is far from what's depicted in a photograph. On the other hand, in a photograph as a work of art you will always find more than you can actually see in the picture. It will create its own kind of reality. Of course, the presumed link to reality is still one of the most important aspects in photography. Even if we know that a "photographic" image is completely digitally composed, it somehow appears to be a document of reality. It's a matter of perception versus knowledge and I don't think this tension is going to weaken.

*I'm interested in the specific aesthetic of the images. The long exposures give the pictures a very particular feel, like faded nineteenth century travel photographs where the chemistry has changed over time. Did you have something specific in mind when you started, or was this just the result of the complicated long exposure process?*

It was a result of the process. I just needed to understand that this particular aesthetic is essential to the work. I realized that the technical imperfection was a benefit, not a drawback, that it gives a certain 'back-to-basics' impression. The whole project was about accepting conditions that were completely different from my previous projects.

*The black trace of the sun has a great democratizing power. All of the landscapes, no matter how dramatic, beautiful or iconic appear to be dwarfed by this primitive trace or scar in the sky. The chemical inversion of sunlight from white to black also seems to reverse the properties of the sun. It is no longer life-giving, warm or nourishing, but rather becomes brutal, stark, and even creates a sense of melancholy.*

I agree and I'm quite happy that the results turned out that way because that was what I was hoping for. Though, one of the many ambiguous aspects of this project is that the atmosphere of the image is so different from the one when taking the picture. The hours I spent waiting next to the camera, often just observing the landscape while the sun did its job, were fascinatingly intense, sometimes unforgettable experiences… among the best experiences I've had in my work up to now.

*How did you decide on the 1h timeframe for the exposures?*
I started with timeframes of 10, 20 and 30 minutes, always curious as to the effect this extreme overexposure would have on the visibility of the landscape in the picture. I was surprised by the results and so I finally settled on an

exposure time of one hour, since it's the most commonly used unit of time. Dividing time is the human way to deal with eternity.

*I'm interested in the disconnect between these photographs and your experience when capturing these images. Of course you cannot look directly at the sun, let alone watch it inscribe its path in the sky over one hour. Can you describe your experience observing these landscapes while waiting for your camera to capture the trace of the sun?*
At the early stage of the project I always felt a little nervous during the one hour of exposure time, concerned about the result. Over time I learned to accept that once the cameras are set, the result would be beyond my power anyway. Given this, I became much more relaxed. I developed a kind of laid-back stoicism and was able to enjoy the situation, to enjoy the sunlight, which was of course warm and nourishing then. Even at locations in L.A. or Tokyo for me there was this atmosphere of calm and quietness. And in some particular places, like in the Algerian or Namibian desert, this experience became really amazing. There were moments of contemplation when I started to sympathize with the idea of worshipping the sun.

*When you began the project in the Mojave Desert I believe that you initially intended to shoot it in a single location. What made you decide to extend the project across the globe?*
One of the most fascinating aspects of the experimental phase before I actually started the project was exploring how the angles of the sun line varied according to the latitude of each location. As a result of this variation, I decided to expand the project to cover the whole world and therefore began checking to see if the destinations I had already selected would be suitable locations for this series. At the same time I also started looking for places that fulfilled certain criteria, for example I wanted a photo from the northernmost and southernmost points that could be reached with a reasonable amount of effort. I also wanted a picture of the midnight sun, photos from places along the Tropic of Cancer and Tropic of Capricorn taken during the solstice, a picture shot from as close to the equator as I could get, and one taken along the International Date Line.

*The sun is a universal symbol that has deep cultural and religious connotations that differ around the world. Was this something that you considered in choosing the different locations?*
Yes, in the beginning. Actually, I was thinking of going to Egypt, for example, but then it would have been almost impossible to avoid photographing at locations related to the sun as a religious symbol. The next question would have been why choosing only one specific location since there are so many other sun-related places all over the world. The focus would have turned too much to human culture and religion.

*You chose to focus not only on natural landscapes but also on some urban locations. What made you decide to include these cityscapes alongside the more dramatic natural landscapes in the series?*
It was important for me to show that this phenomenon

occurs everywhere, not only in landscapes far from civilization. The power of the sun is present all over the globe. However, it was extremely difficult to find urban settings with no visible 'life,' with no or few people, no cars going by in front of the camera causing reflections that would have distracted the viewer's eyes from the line of the sun. In the beginning, I also photographed in places that were easily recognizable, such as Downtown L.A. or the Reichstag in Berlin, but I finally decided not to use them, for the same reason.

*You have referred to the connection of this project to nineteenth century travel photography. Today it seems that the sense of discovery in travel has all but disappeared, there are virtually no places left to discover. I was struck by the fact that your series revives the sense of discovery by showing us the world in a way that cannot be seen by the naked eye.*
It's a different kind of discovery. I like the idea that this discovery can take place everywhere; you don't even have to travel to experience it. But I did, and it was my goal to show the world in a way that cannot be seen by human eyes.

*In the book, you include a map detailing the itinerary that you took to shoot the series. I was interested in the fragmented nature of this journey: it is not an around the world trip but a series of individual trips which extend out over time from your home in Germany. How important was the journey process for you in making this series?*
The final journey I made to complete the project was actually a three-month around the world trip. After all the single trips undertaken to get to a particular destination, I

thought it would make sense for the final journey to literally follow the sun on its way around the earth. Knowing the facts of modern astronomy, I think this geocentric perspective is still the way we look at this phenomenon up in the sky.

*The captions to your images provide details of the date, exposure time and coordinates where the image was taken. This information is at once very specific, scientific even, and yet it reveals nothing to us about the subject or location of the photographs. Why did you decide to use this information for the captions and to omit the names of the places where you were taking these photographs?*
Since the photos are not about the individual locations per se, I decided not to mention the places in the title, because they would always evoke some sort of visual association. I also like the contradiction between the fact that the title of each work gives the most precise information possible about the location but nobody knows where it is. We still rely on names to imagine a place, even if our imaginations don't reflect the reality of that place. I also enjoy the contradiction between the fact that the images seem to show something completely beyond human control, something out of this world, but if you check the coordinates with Google Earth, within a few seconds you're looking down from above like a god on the exact place where the picture was taken.

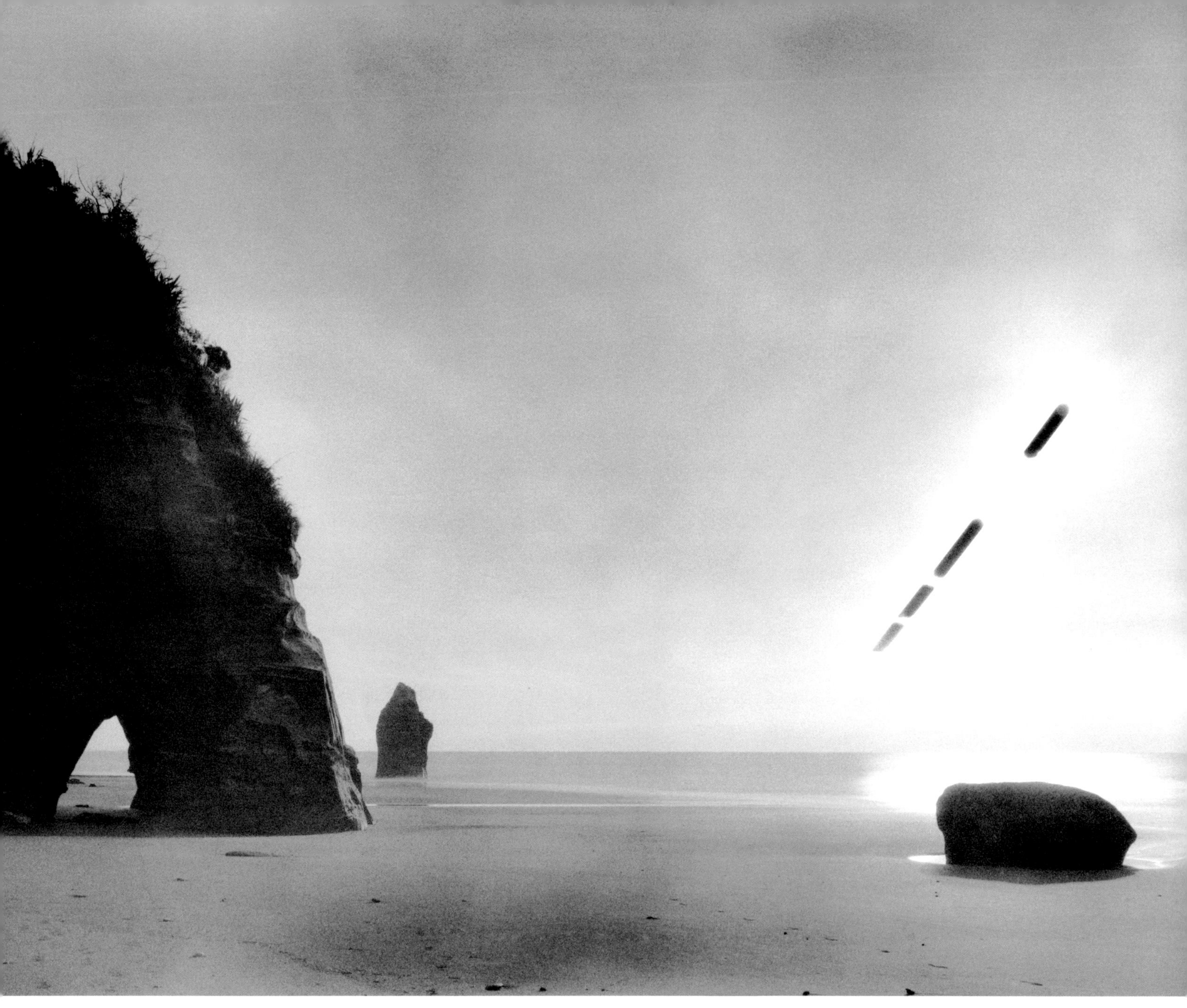

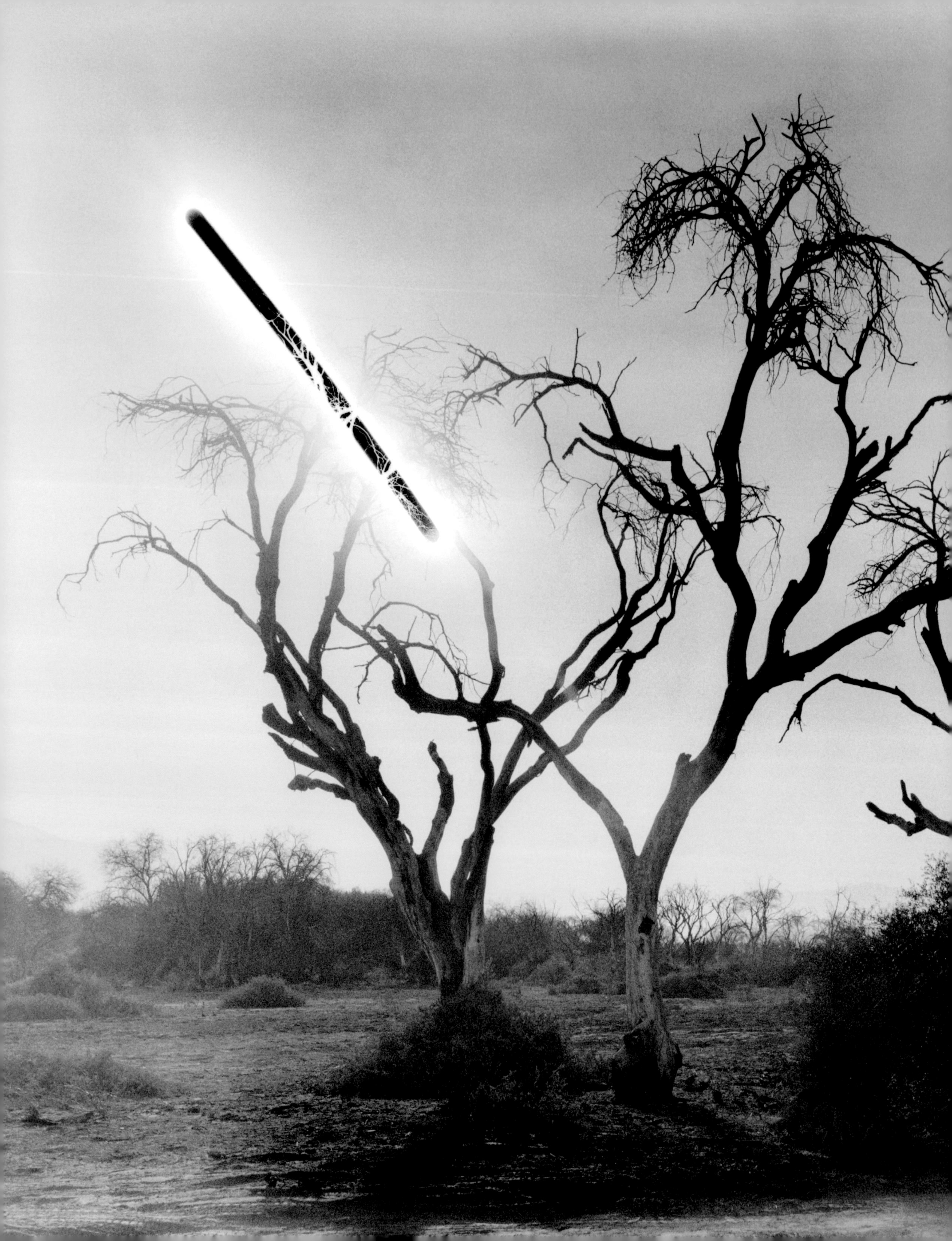

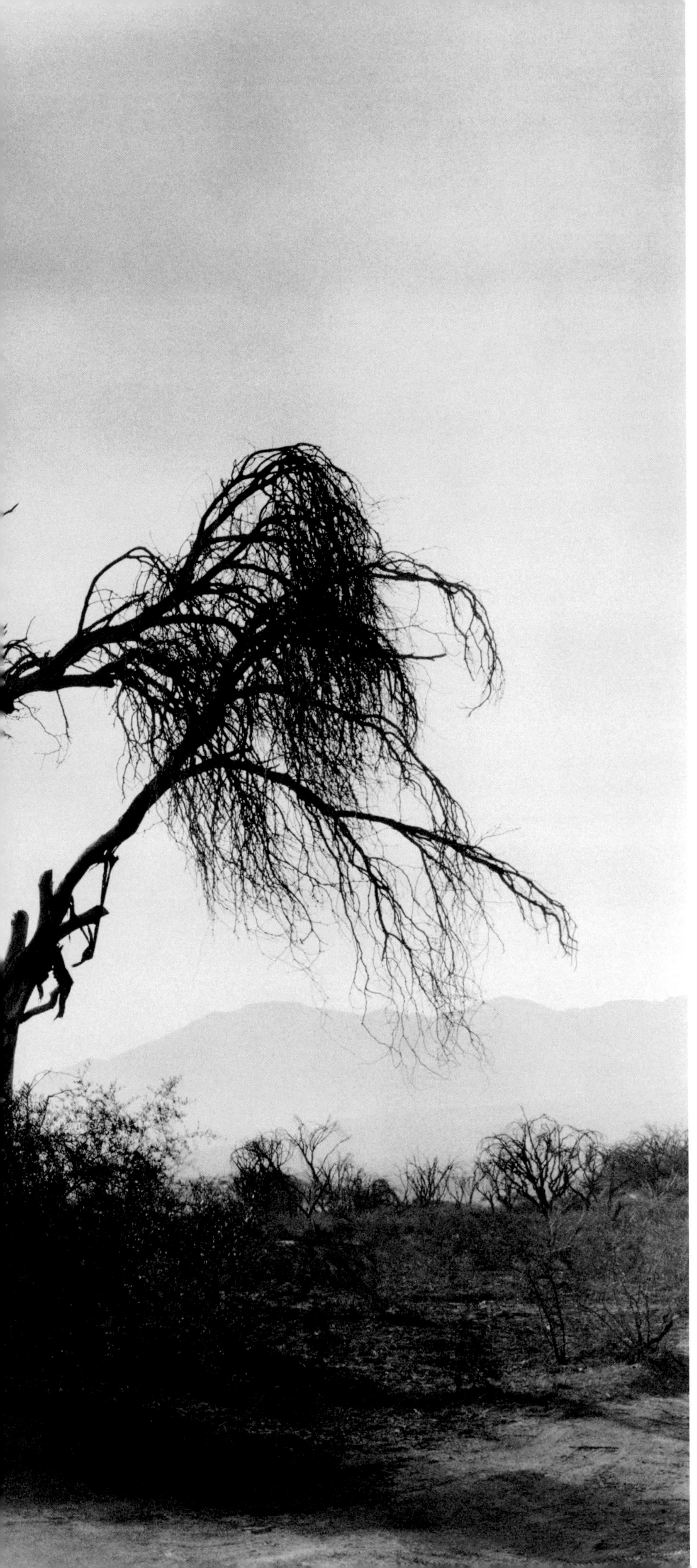

*Page 95* 2/21/2010, 7:00 pm-8:00 pm, S 38°49.042'
E 174°34.976'. *Left* 6/01/2008, 9:18 am-10:18 am,
S 26°03.817' W 065°54.723'

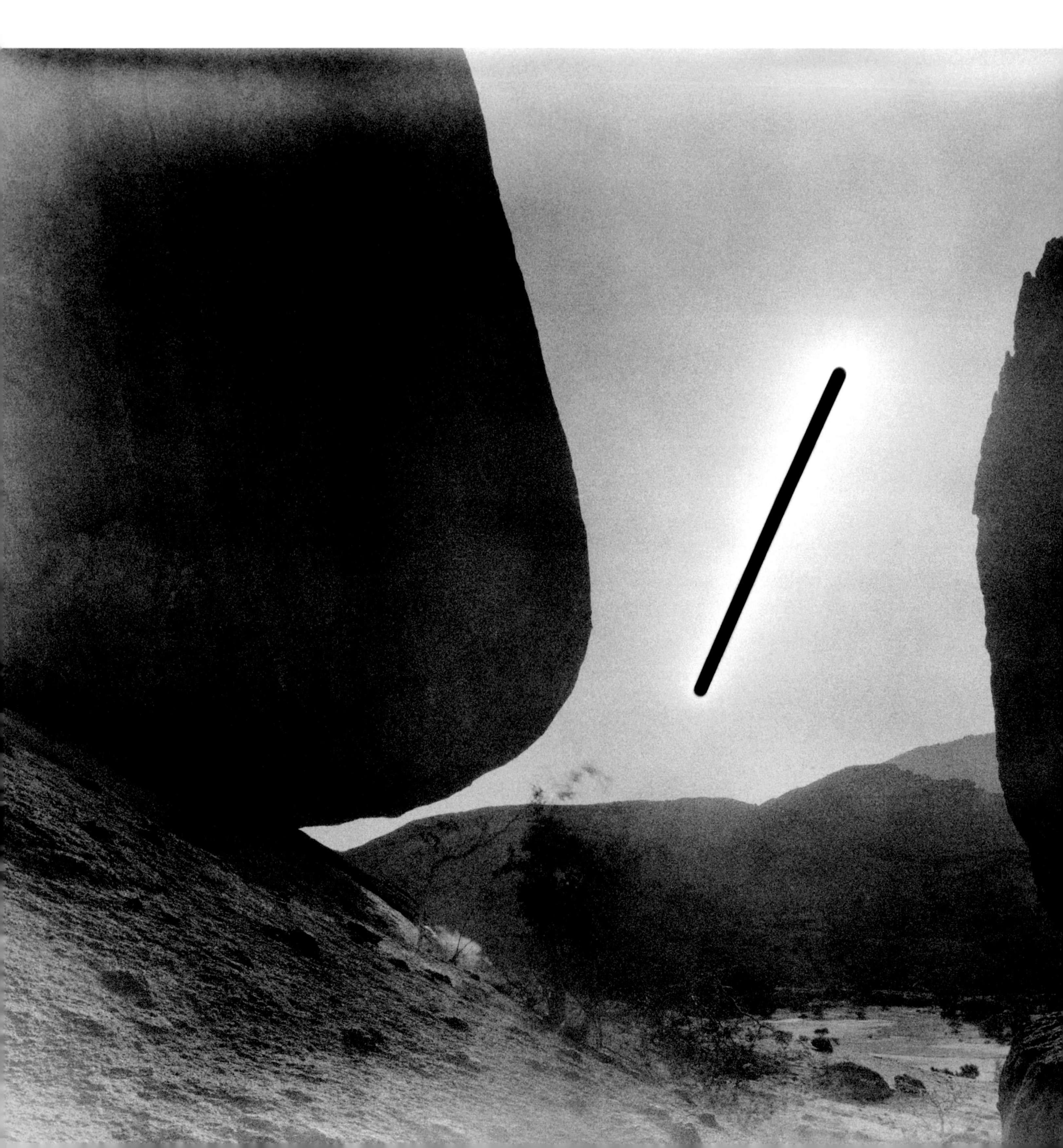

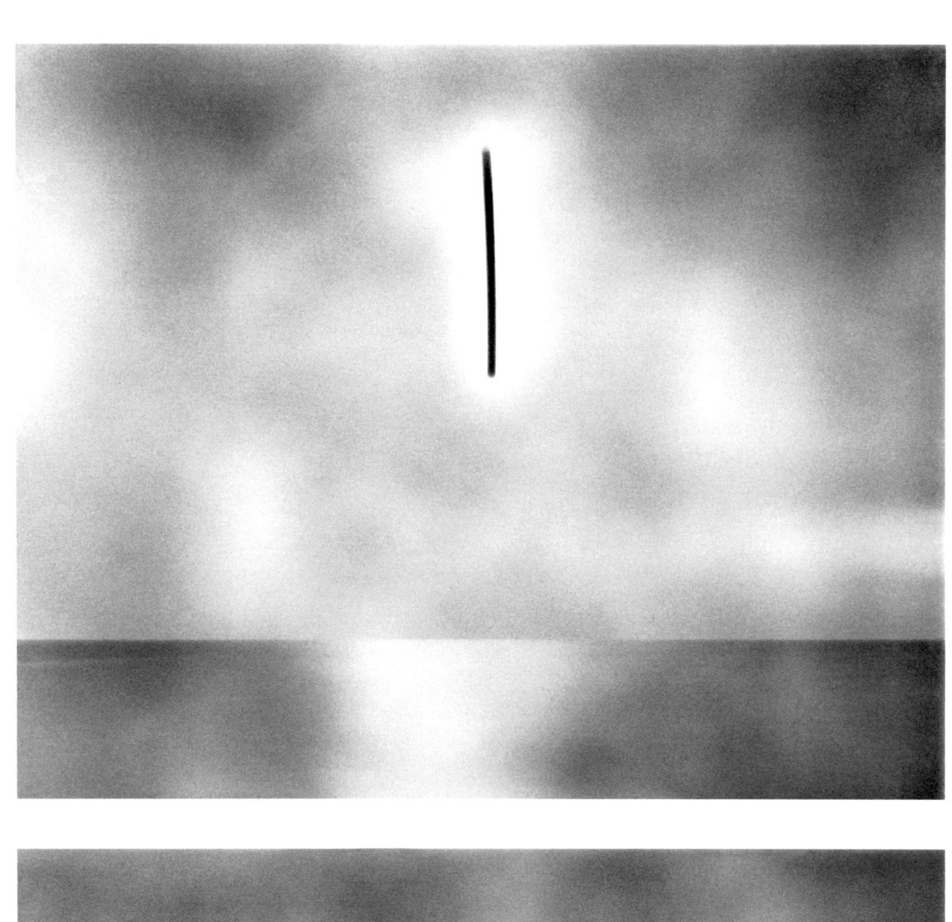

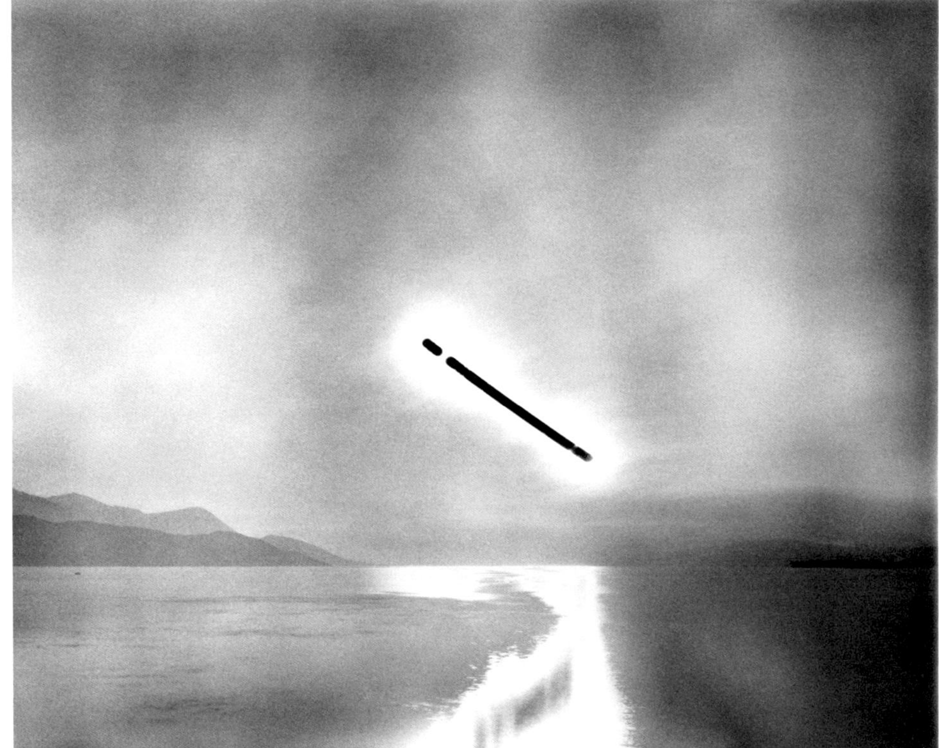

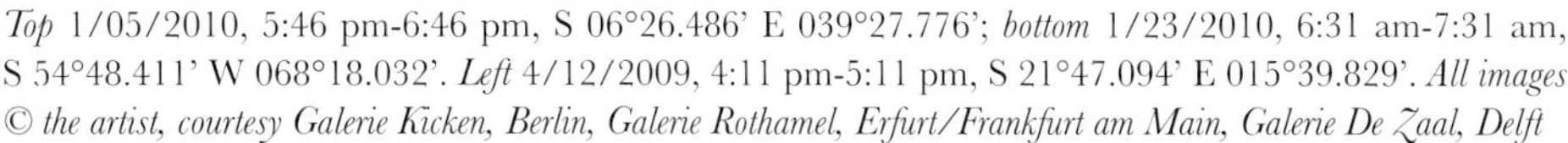

*Top* 1/05/2010, 5:46 pm-6:46 pm, S 06°26.486' E 039°27.776'; *bottom* 1/23/2010, 6:31 am-7:31 am, S 54°48.411' W 068°18.032'. *Left* 4/12/2009, 4:11 pm-5:11 pm, S 21°47.094' E 015°39.829'. *All images © the artist, courtesy Galerie Kicken, Berlin, Galerie Rothamel, Erfurt/Frankfurt am Main, Galerie De Zaal, Delft*

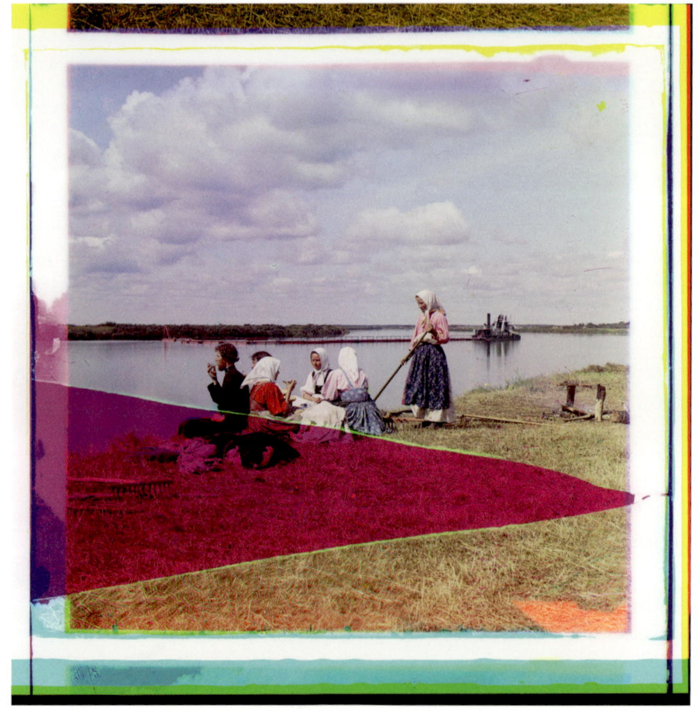

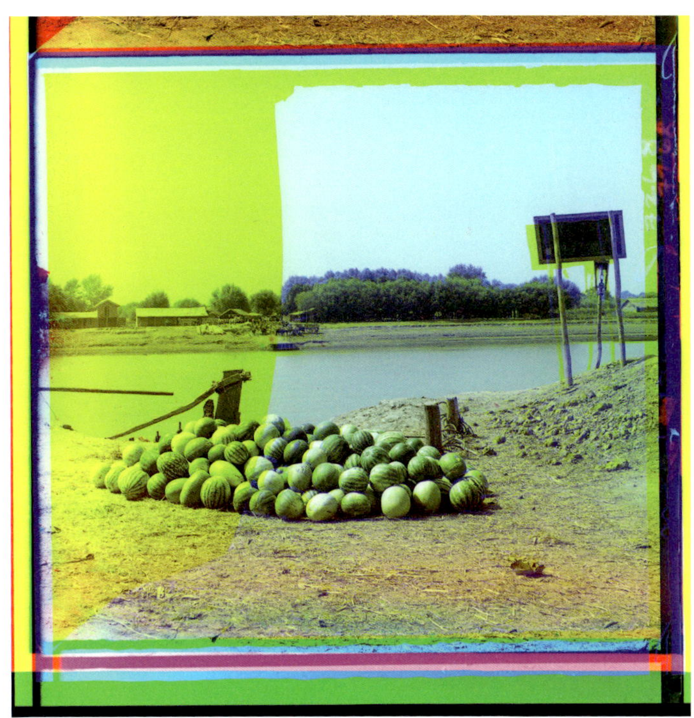

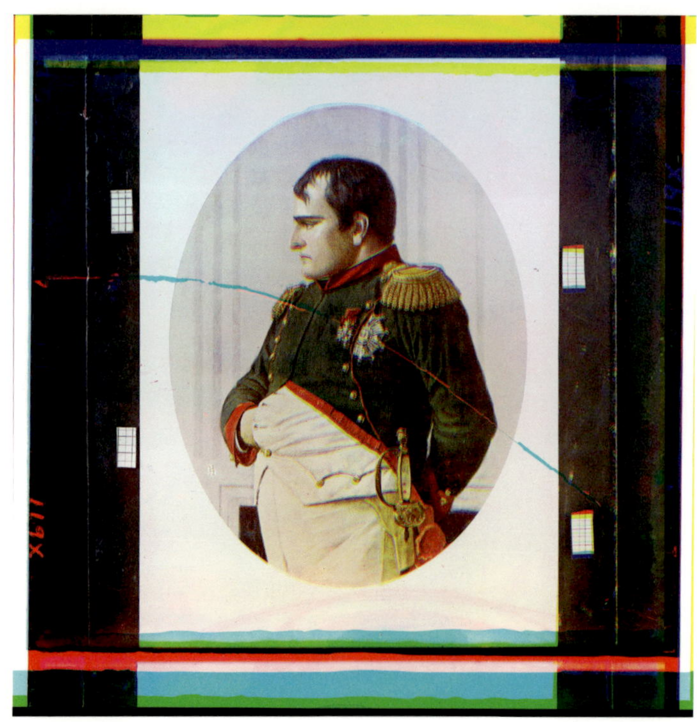

# BETWEEN COLORS
# Prokudin-Gorskii told by Natalie Marie Gehrels

**"Your Majesty might also be interested, perhaps, in seeing from time to time the true Russia and her ancient monuments, and in the same way also the beauties of the diverse nature of our great Motherland."**

*(Sergei Mikhailovich Prokudin-Gorskii)*

It was 1908 when Prokudin-Gorskii, an internationally renowned scientist and photographer, contacted Tsar Nicholas II to propose a photographic expedition of the Russian Empire from Finland to the Pacific Ocean. He promised to return from the journey with images that would "capture all the splendors of our far flung native land in natural colors." The offer was so intriguing to the Tsar that he agreed to support the project by granting Prokudin-Gorskii access to all areas of the vast turbulent country and equipping him with a steamship, motorized boat and motorcar.

While on this quest to convey the richness of the Tsar's realm Prokudin-Gorskii was challenged by a veil of great instability in the land. From 1909-1915, his life was dedicated to this photographic journey, during which he witnessed the start of a revolution as "The War of Wars" was forging ahead and the landscape and people of the Russian Empire were dramatically changing before him. These difficult conditions were also combined with a rigorous travel schedule, which forced him to develop using an improvised laboratory while on the road.

The meticulous process began with the design of a custom camera that shot three consecutive black and white negatives over a period of several seconds. The three exposures then developed were tediously aligned and layered with different color filters: red, green and blue. To create the final color image, Prokudin-Gorskii would compile the plates and then present them using a light projection system. Although he dedicated a great portion of his studies to developing a method of re-producing his imagery through printing, the majority of the images were viewed in the form of projections.

Prokudin-Gorskii proclaimed his vision to "leave an exact document for the future" and throughout his career strived to create a technically perfect archive that would accurately preserve Russia's rich history and serve to educate the land's youth. Until now, nearly all of his published work has successfully reached this goal and the images as a result have been showcased for the fascinatingly advanced technique that challenged many of the undiscovered areas of color photography at the time of their creation.

The images featured in this story are printed from digital color composites that were commissioned by the Library of Congress in 2004, all of which have been adjusted overall to match Prokudin-Gorskii's original glass plates. They have been selected because they illustrate his genuine struggle with a "complex and capricious process" and reveal many of the trials he faced when attempting to achieve an idealized precision. He undoubtedly would not have wanted the world to see this "flawed" work, but it serves us now by allowing the viewer to connect intimately with the delicate nature of his process. These images uniquely evolve from the effects caused by misaligned negatives, aged emulsion and cracked glass plates, and they highlight the true instability of an epoch through indifferently distorted perspectives and awkwardly distributed vibrant panels of colors. These defects become a commentary on the intricate instant of the image's conception where the real voyage is no longer in the original scene, but is instead in the effects of the physical process itself.

*Page 100* Dinner during Haying, 1909. *Page 101* Watermelons, an import along the Kura River in Petropavlovskoe, 1905-1919. *Left* Painting of Napoleon, 1905-1919. *Page 104* Bananas and trunk of a date palm after winter, 1910. *Page 105* View of the fortress wall from Veselukha Tower, Smolensk, 1912. *All images © and courtesy of the Library of Congress*

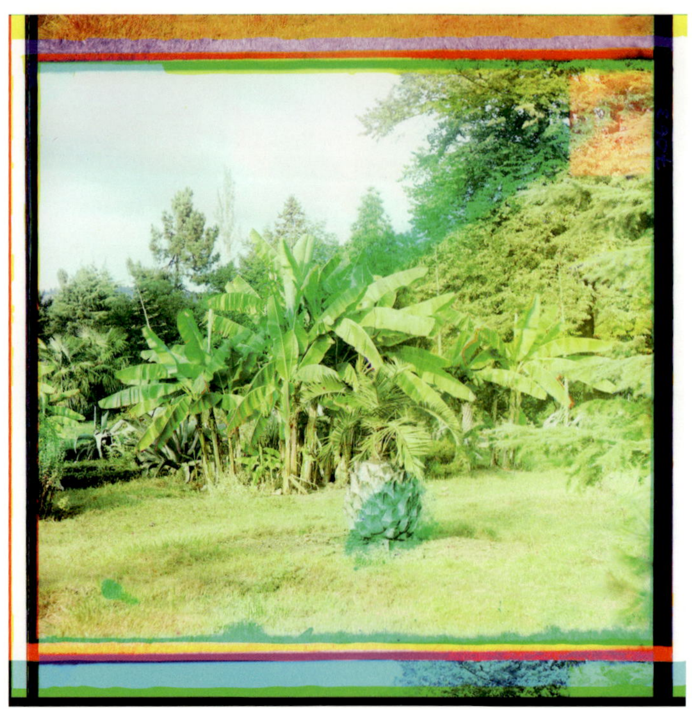

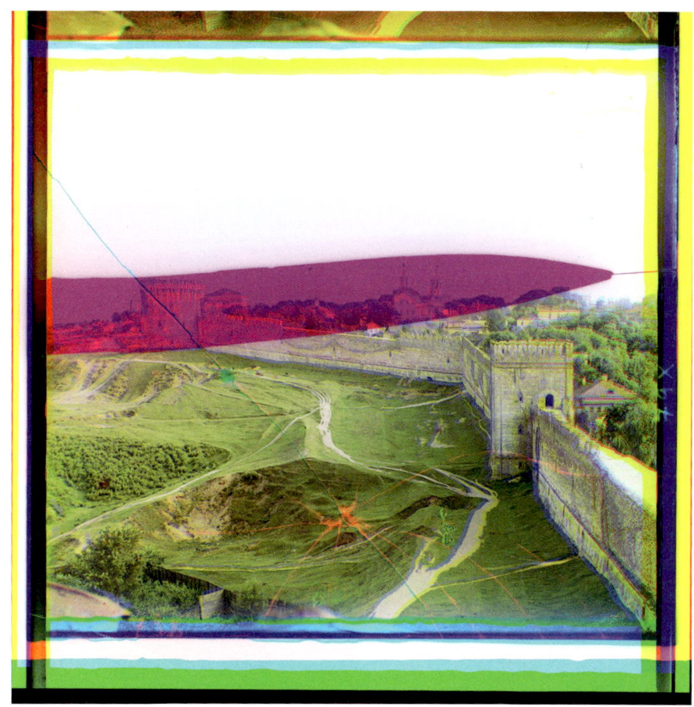

*This page* Guide to the Wastelands of the Lea Valley: 12 Empty Spaces Await the London Olympics:
Channelsea Island, Canning Road, West Ham

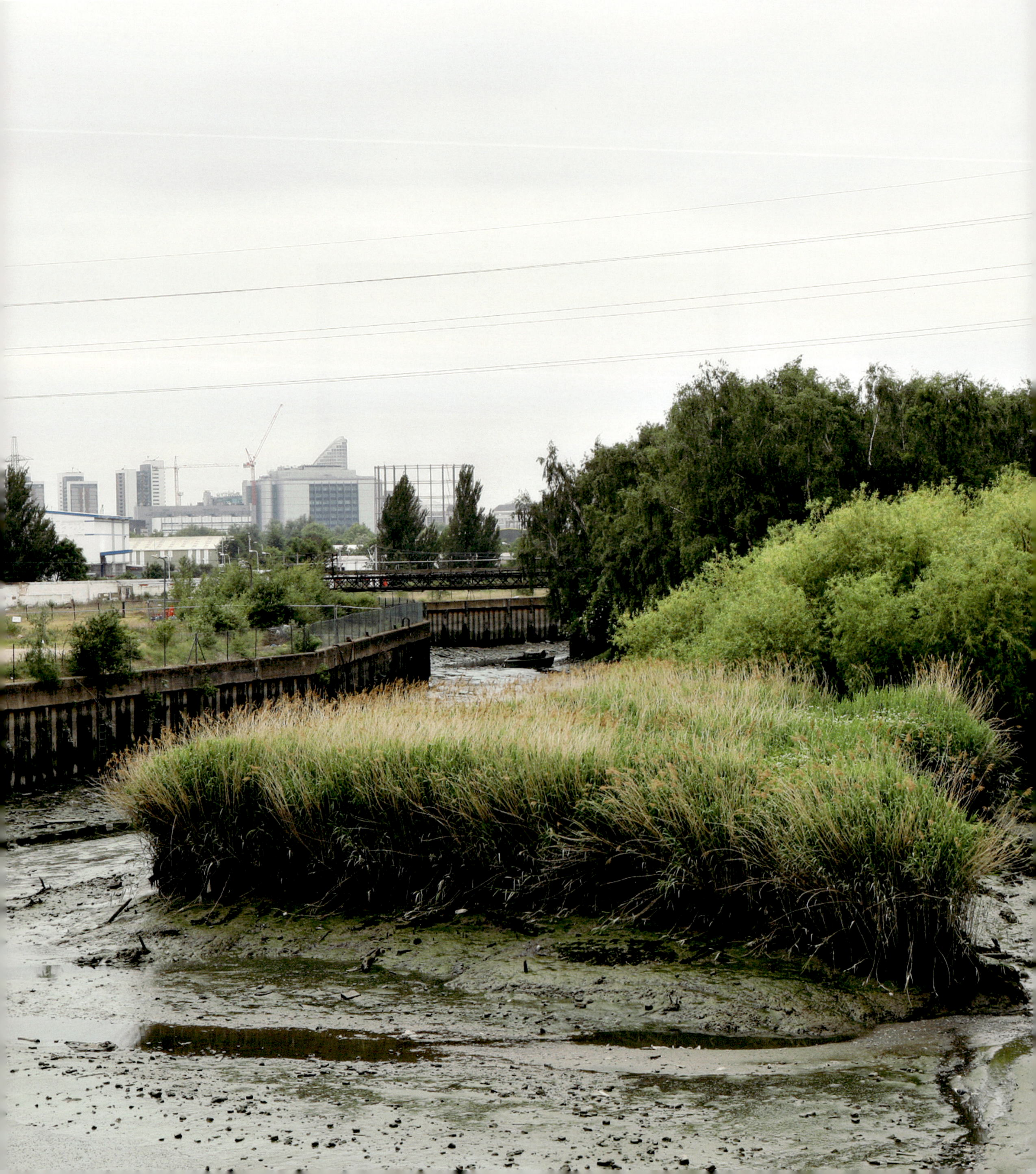

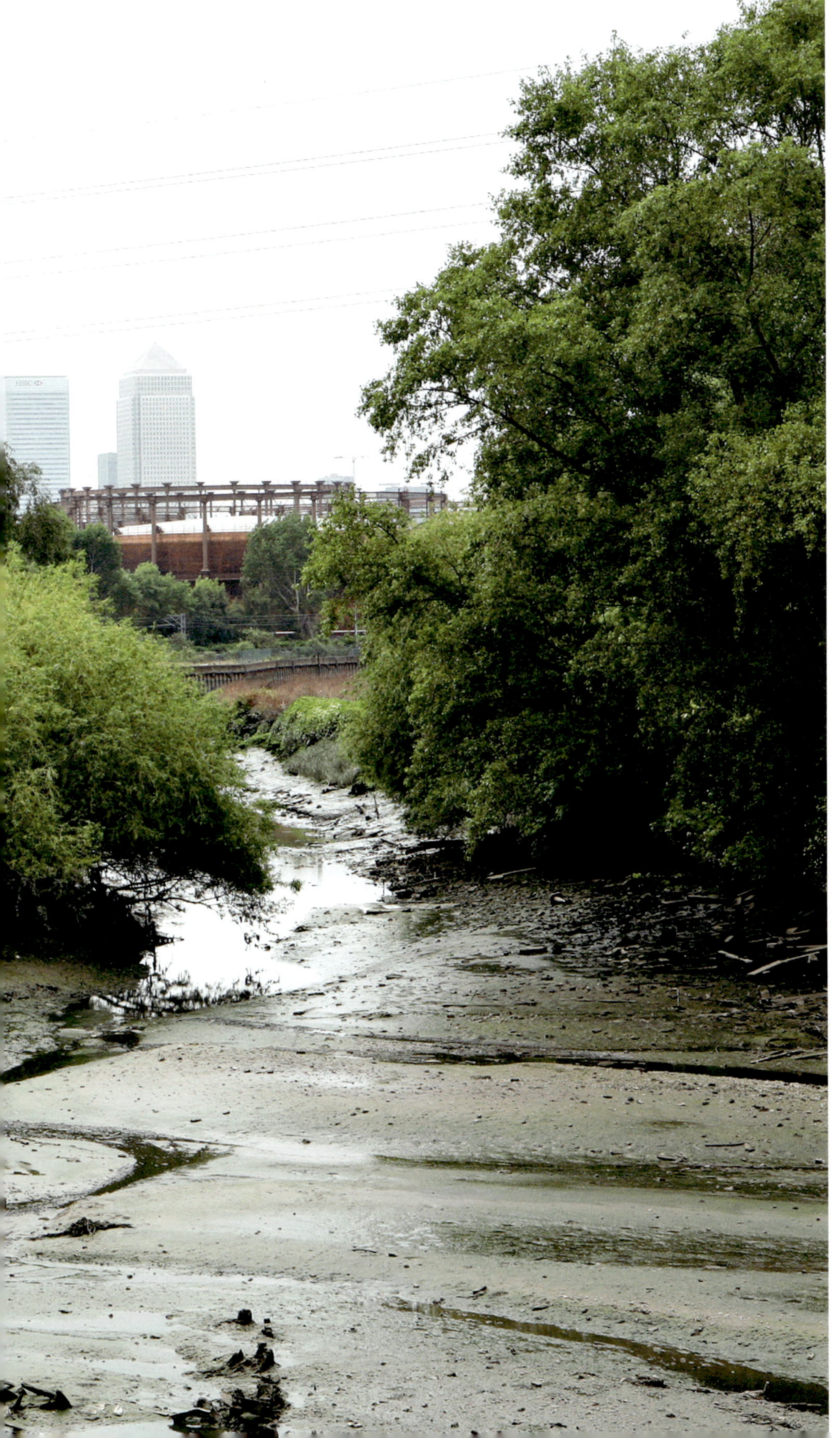

# LARA ALMARCEGUI
## GUIDE TO THE WASTELANDS OF THE LEA VALLEY

Lea Valley is situated to the north of London and takes its name from the Lea River, which runs through it before flowing into the Thames after its short course of approximately 68 kilometres. An ancient natural defence for the city, due to its mostly marshy habitat and subsequently a strategic site of heavy industry, it is mainly known in England for being the home of a small nature reserve: the Lee Valley Regional Park (in the nineteenth century, Ordnance Survey established that either form of spelling could be used to refer to this region.) Here you can go rafting, cycling or horse-riding and admire splendid specimens of Bitterns, Tufted Ducks, Pochards, Goosanders, Great Crested Grebes and Coots, as well as many other kinds of birds and mammals. After that there is nothing, just open countryside, which is mostly deserted and derelict. Soon, however, more visitors than have ever been seen in these parts will begin to flock here, as the Lea Valley has been chosen as the main location for the 2012 Olympic Park. Here, sporting facilities, residential accommodation and an adequate transport infrastructure will be built in an area measuring approximately 2.5 km$^2$. Lara Almarcegui's photographs provide a record of this place before its definitive transformation. She often

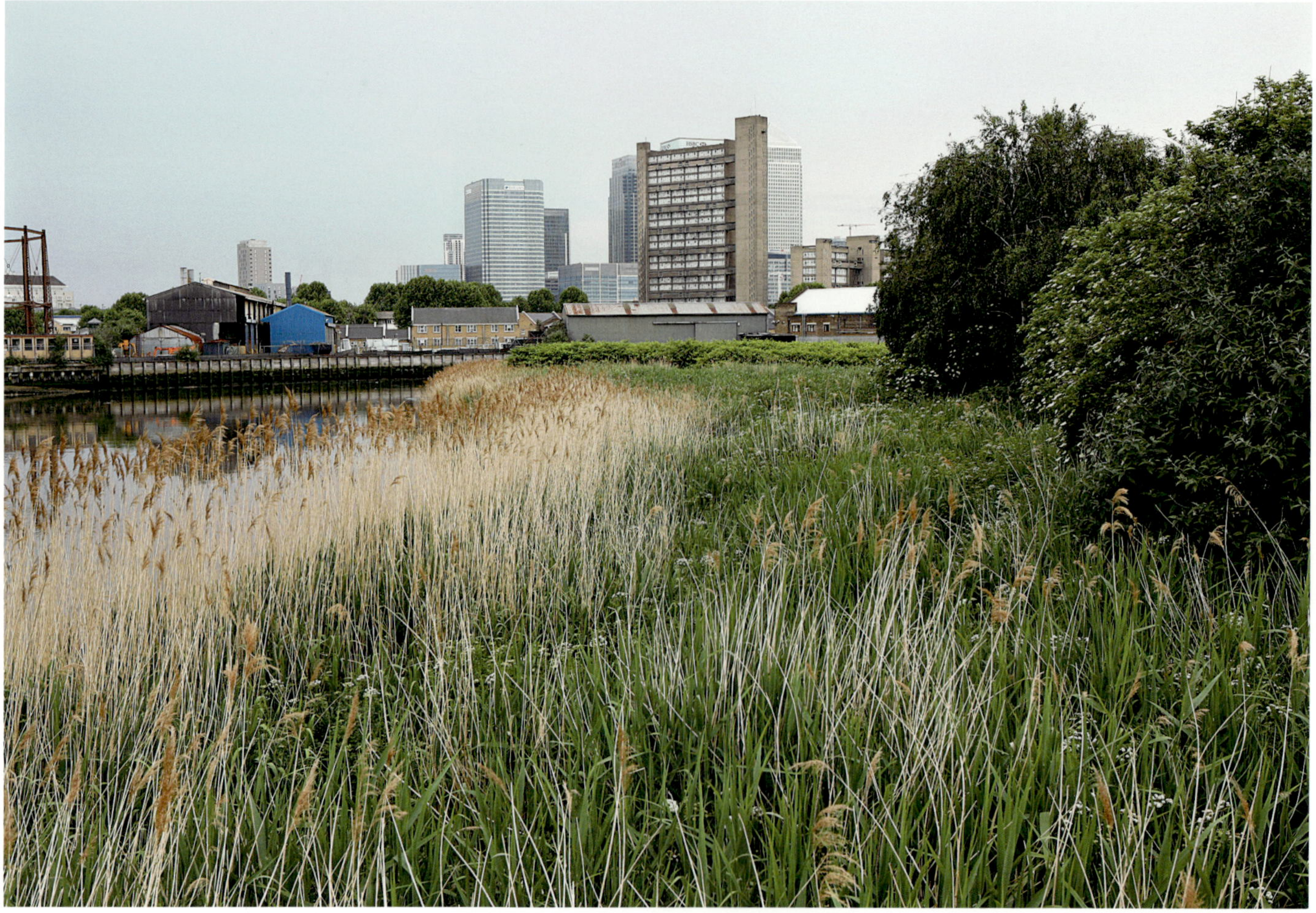

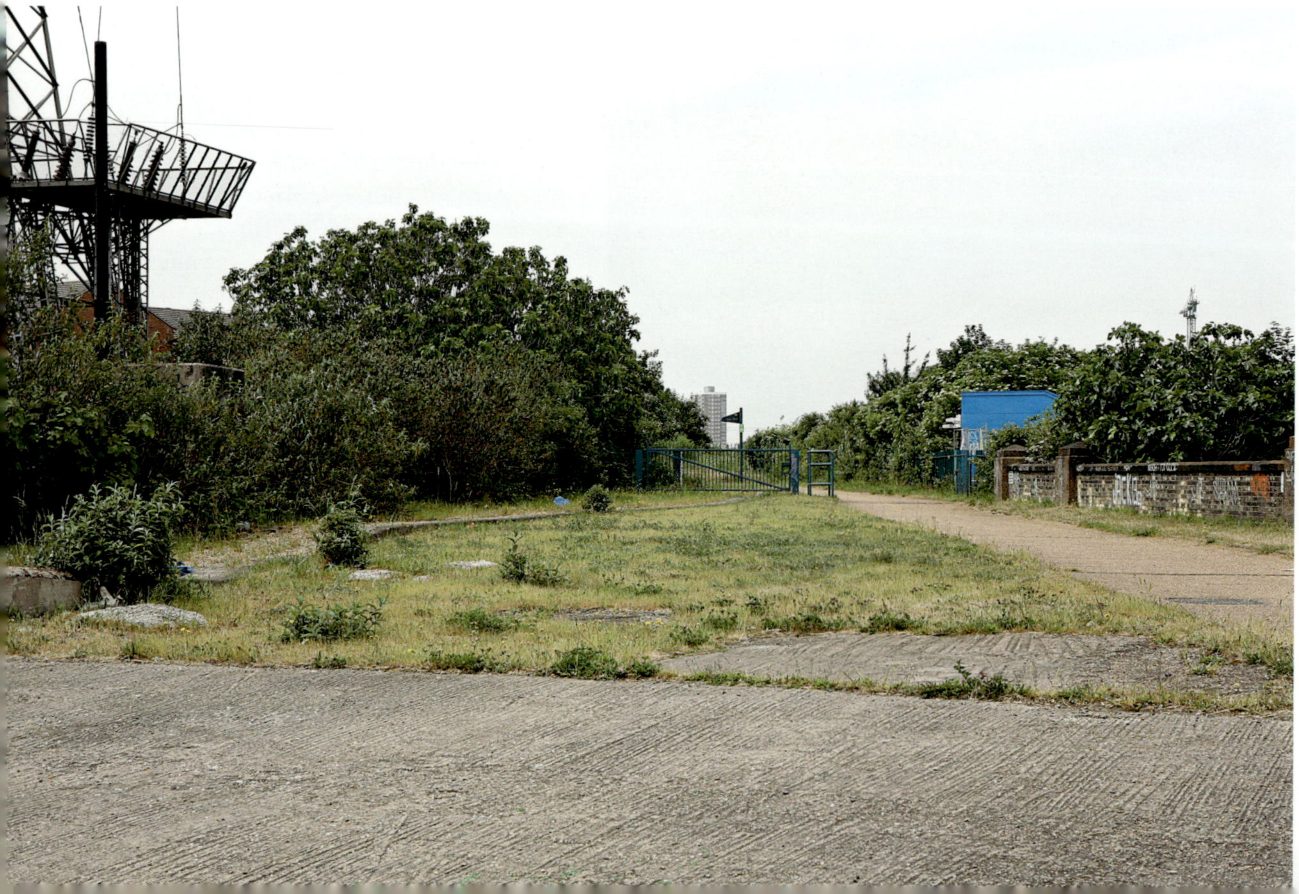

*Above* Guide to the Wastelands of the Lea Valley: 12 Empty Spaces Await the London Olympics: Twelvetrees Crescent, Lea River, Prologis, Newham. *Below* Guide to the Wastelands of the Lea Valley: 12 Empty Spaces Await the London Olympics: The Greenway. Hackney Wick, Stratford, West Ham

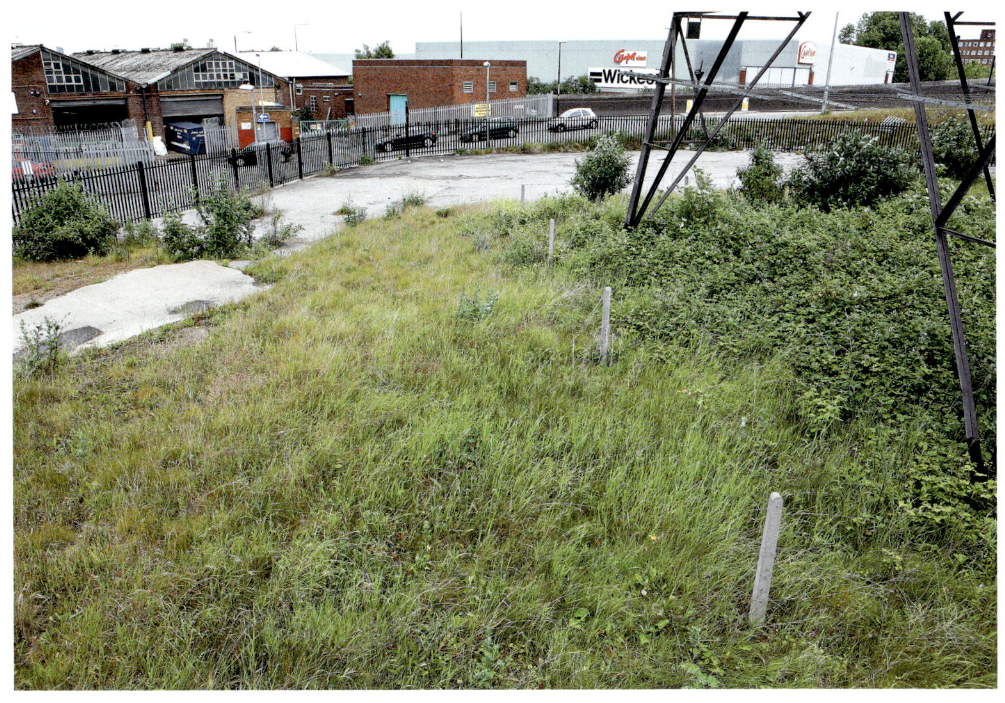

explores neglected sites in her work, indexing each location's tendency towards degradation. In this case the status will change: from an undefined, generic space into the stage of one of the most popular media ceremonies. What Almarcegui describes instead is precisely the intermediate nature of this terrain, its essential lack of precision. Her unique reportage tackles the very idea of suspension and entropy which rules a system lacking in any actual form of control. It is a carefully disciplined study (the laborious researches of the artist which precede her work on the field become the absolute protagonist of a set of images void of any relevant content) on the lack of any discipline.

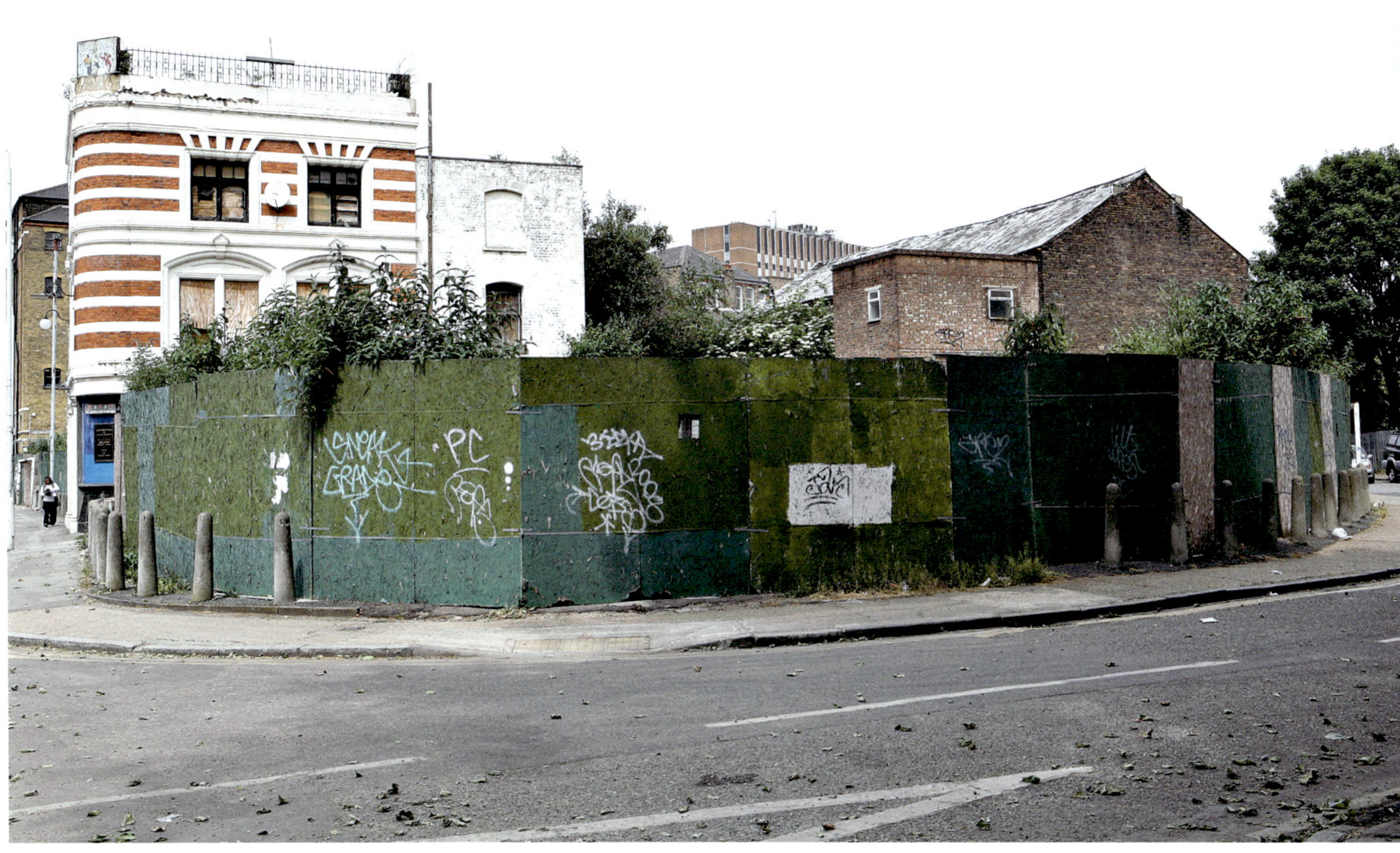

*Top* Guide to the Wastelands of the Lea Valley: 12 Empty Spaces Await the London Olympics: Pylon site, Bidder Street, Wharfside Road, Barking Road, Canning Town. *Bottom* Guide to the Wastelands of the Lea Valley: 12 Empty Spaces Await the London Olympics: New Mount Street, Bridge Road, Bridge Terrace, New Mount Street, Stratford

*Below* Guide to the Wastelands of the Lea Valley: 12 Empty Spaces Await the London Olympics: Orchard Wharf, Orchard Place, Blackwall Pier, Leamouth, Tower Hamlets

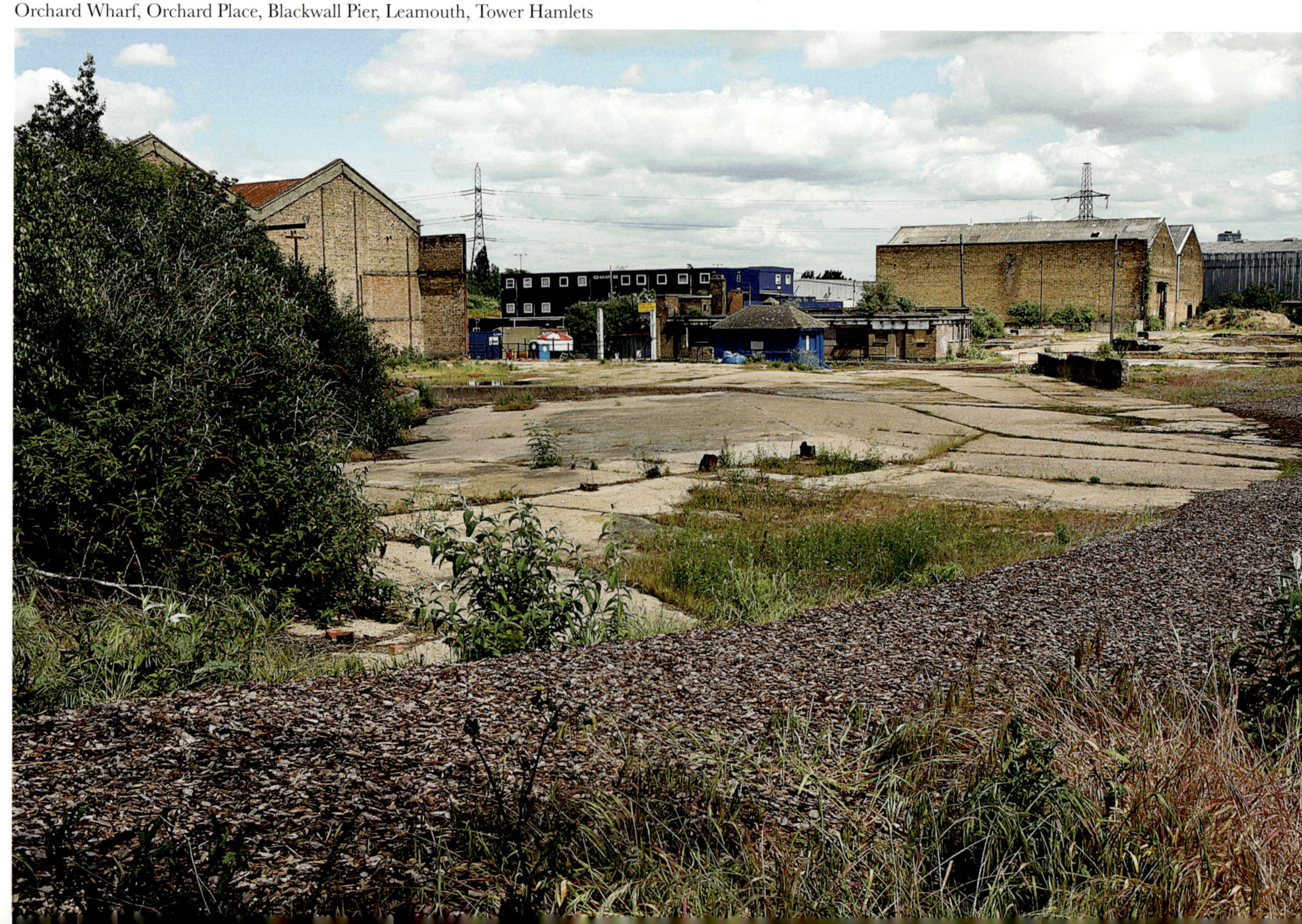

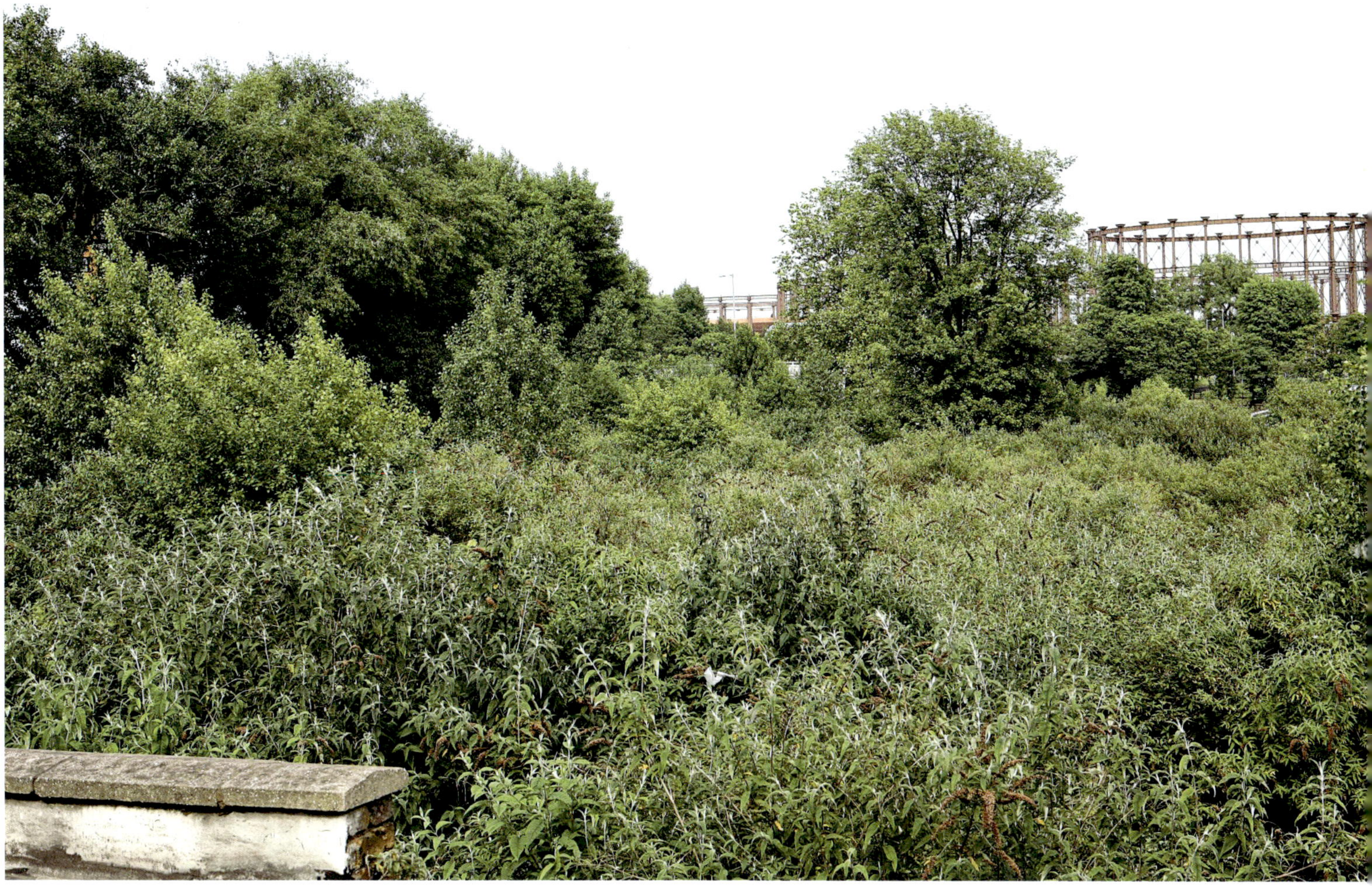

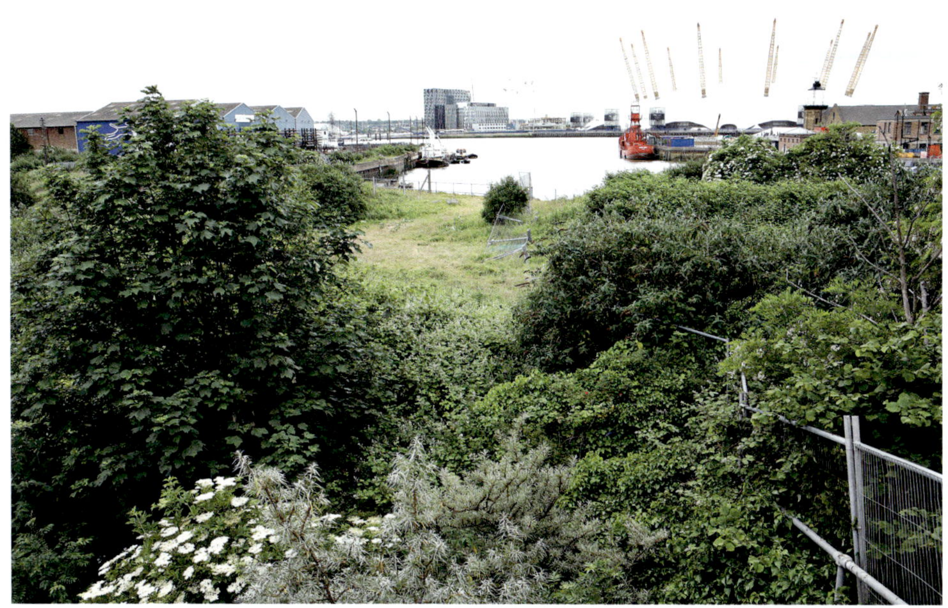

*Top* Guide to the Wastelands of the Lea Valley: 12 Empty Spaces Await the London Olympics: Coventry Cross, Gillender Street, Twelvetrees Crescent, Limehouse Cut, Tower Hamlets. *Bottom* Guide to the Wastelands of the Lea Valley: 12 Empty Spaces Await the London Olympics: Limmo Riverbank, Lower Lea Crossing, Lea River, Canning Town. *All images © the artist, courtesy Ellen de Bruijne Projects, Amsterdam*

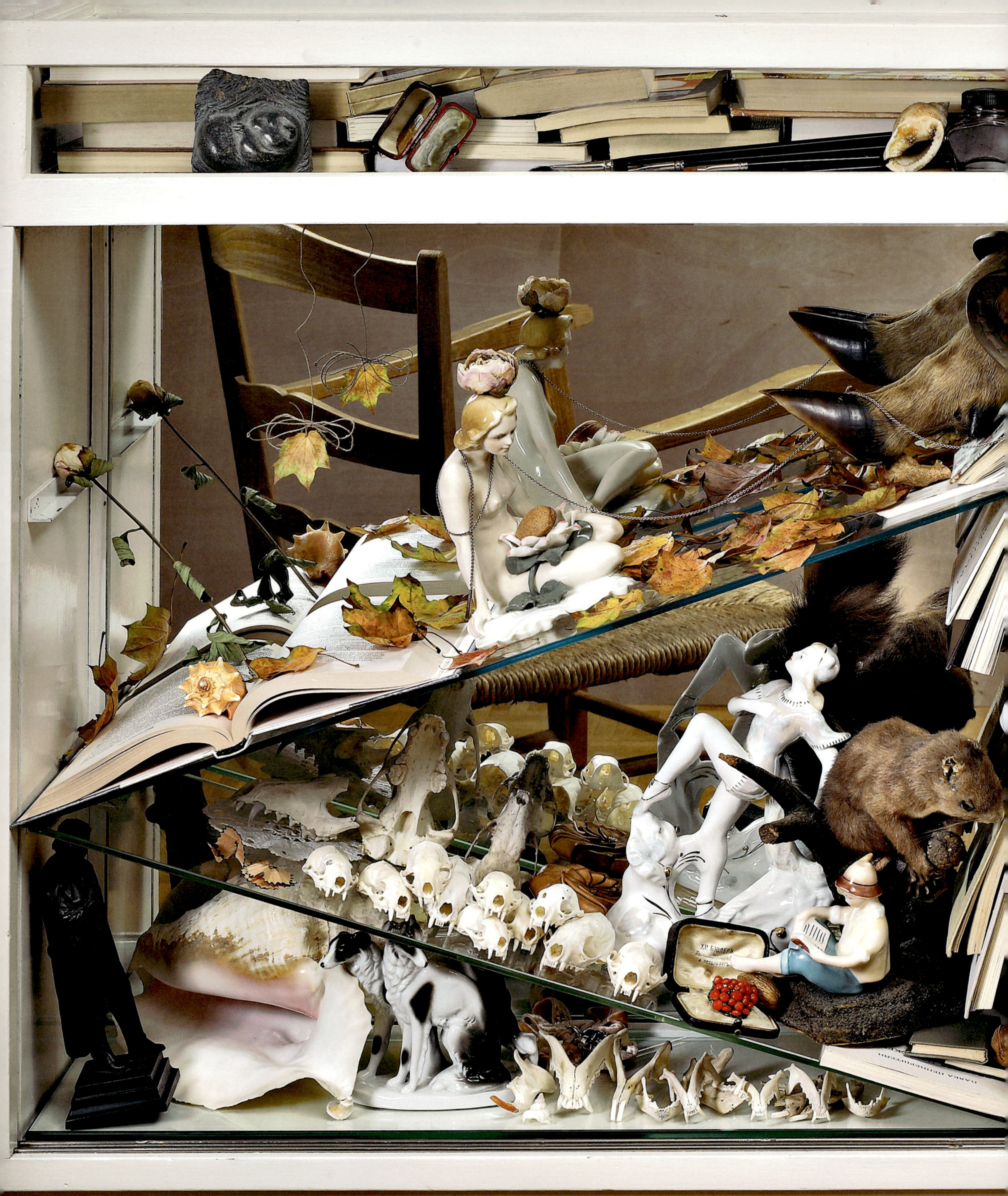

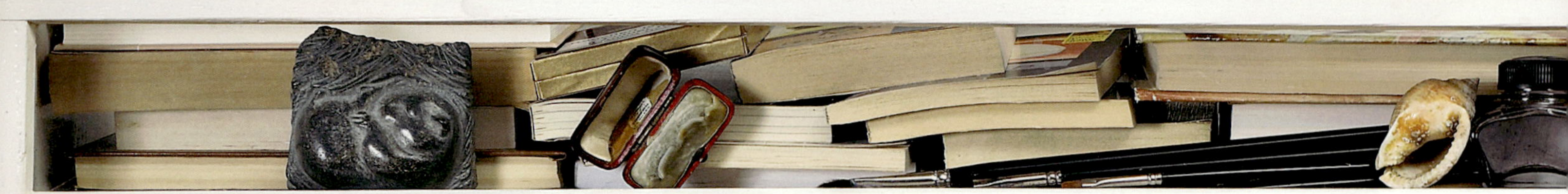

3 Pushkins, 3 Squirrels *from the* Show-Cases *series*, 2009, pigment print, cm 100 x 145. *Image © and courtesy the artist*

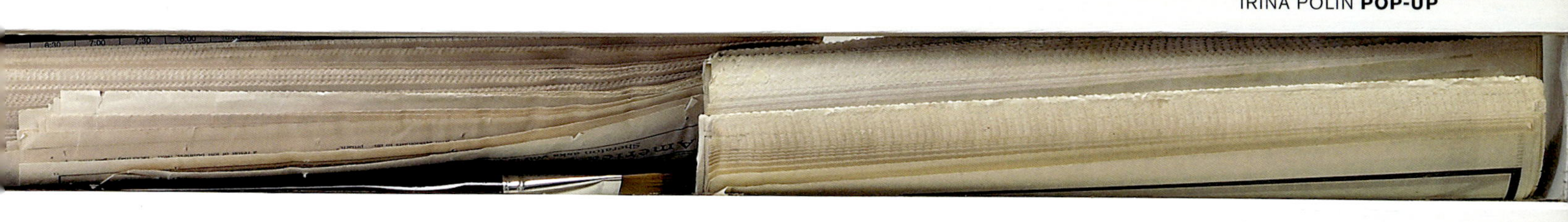

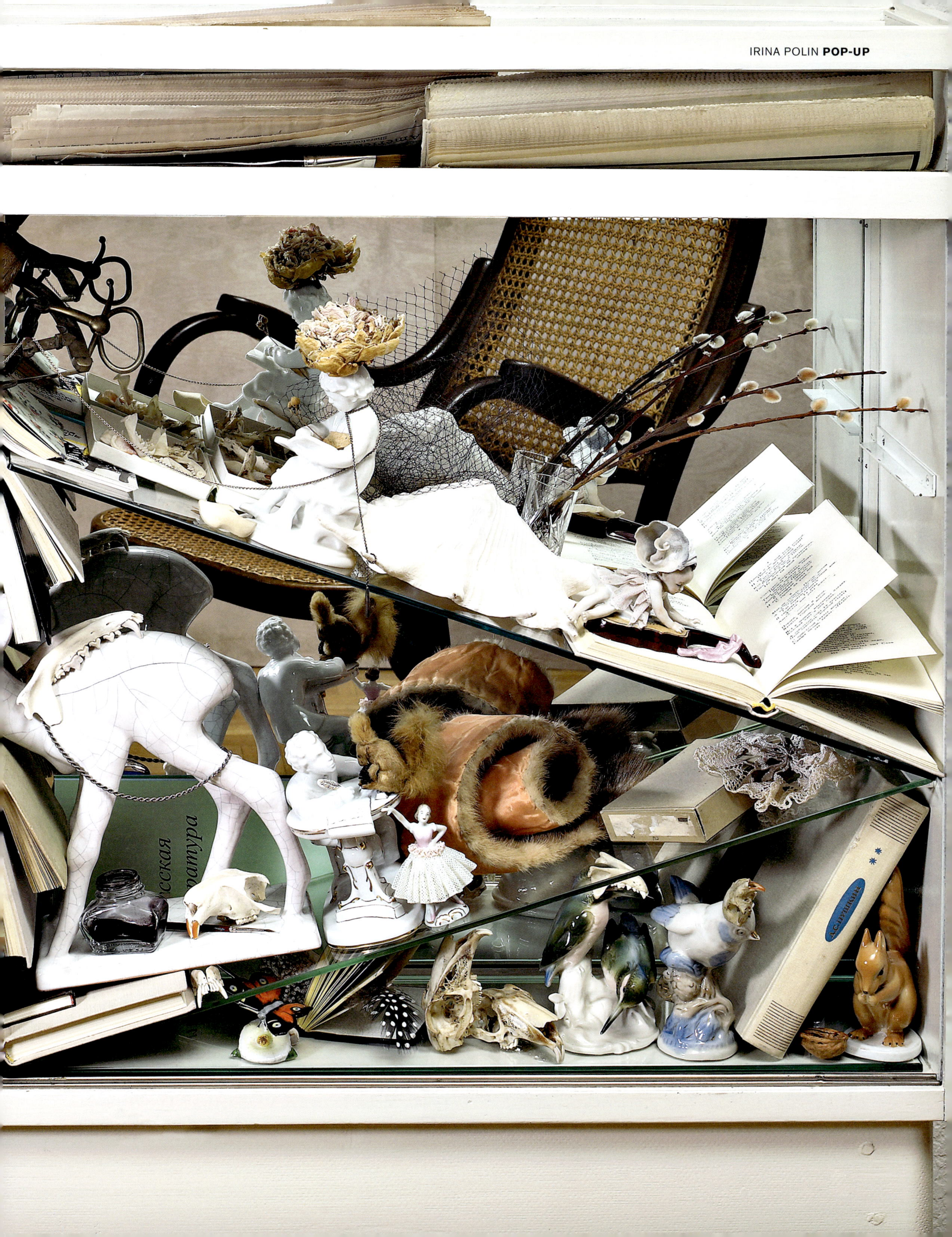

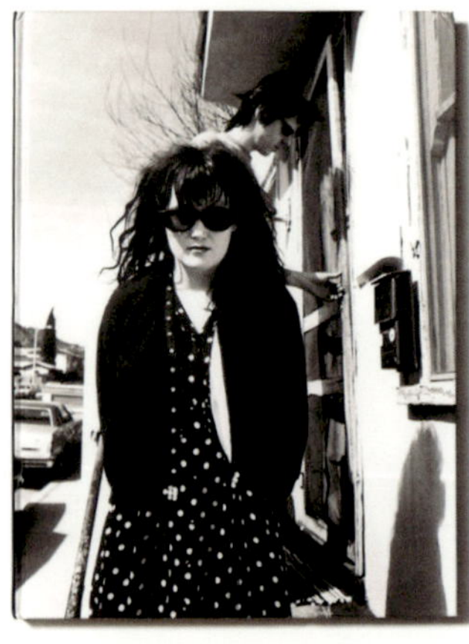
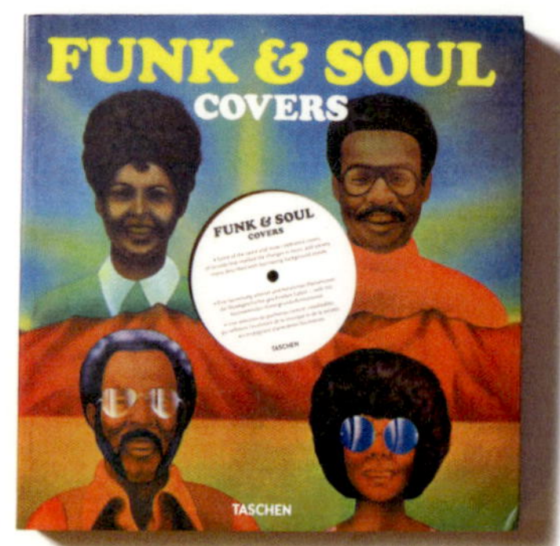

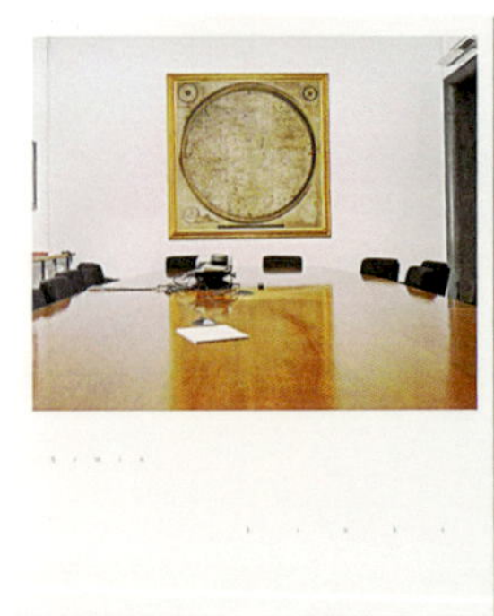
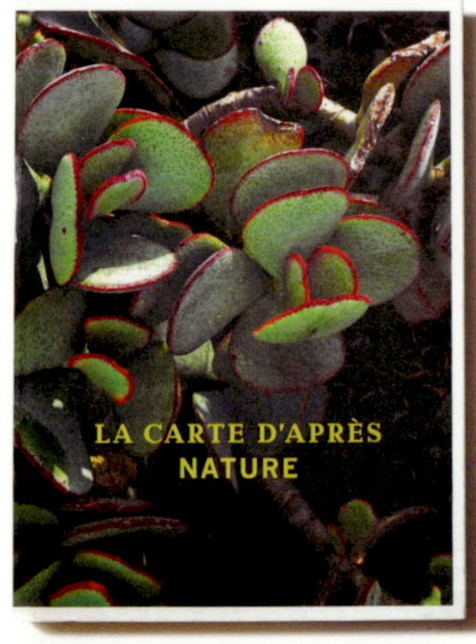


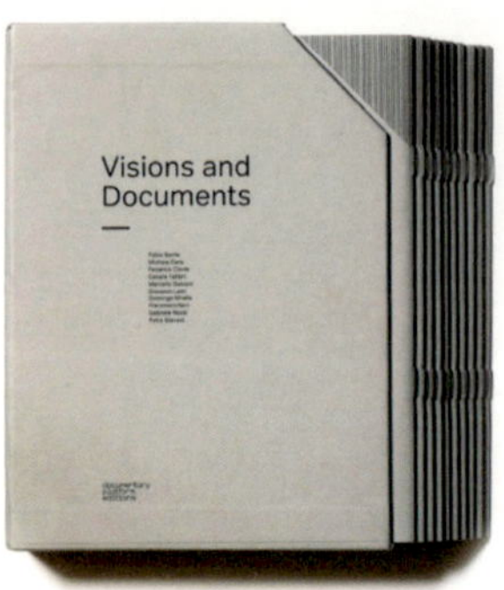

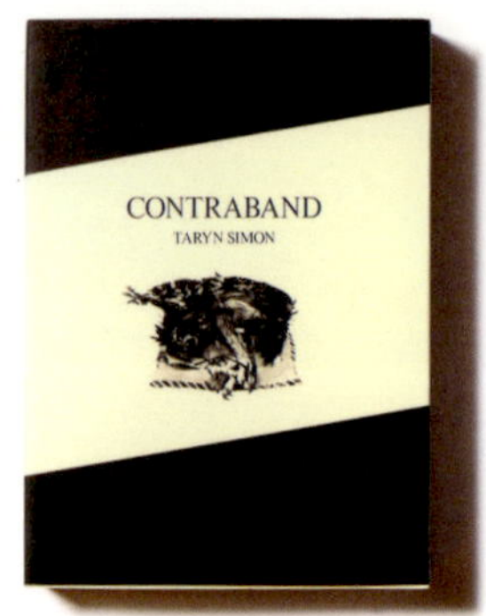

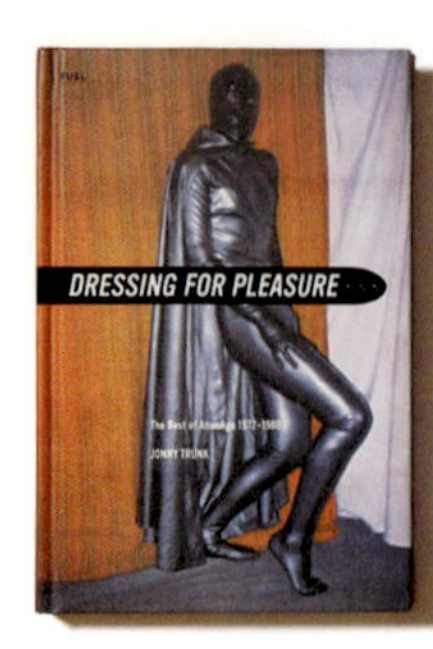

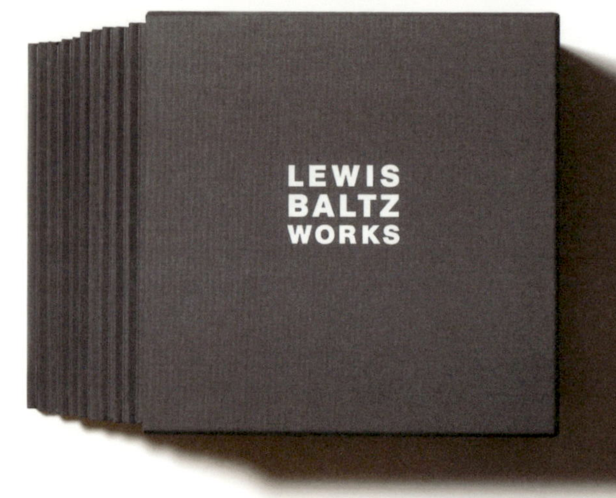


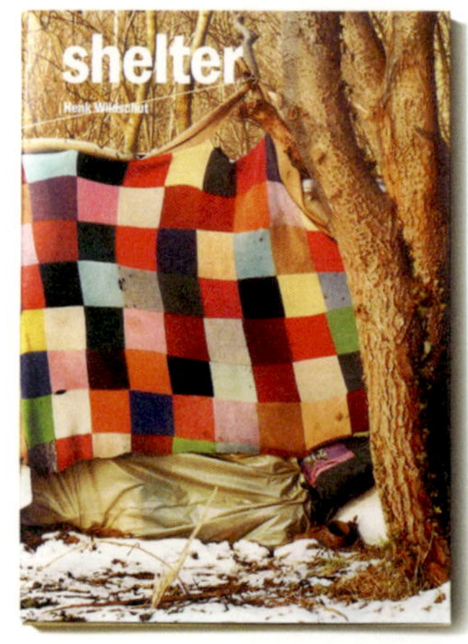

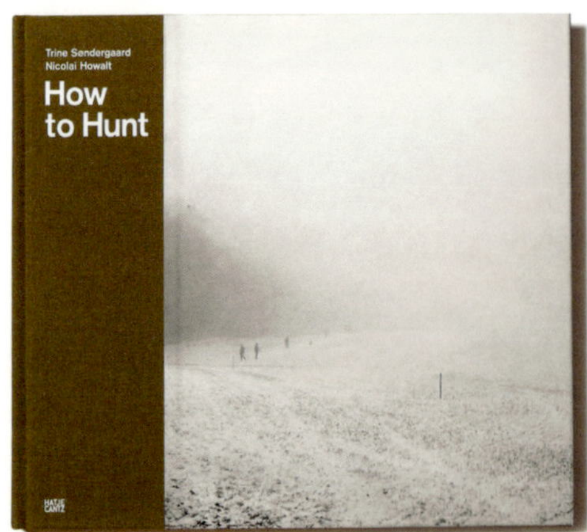

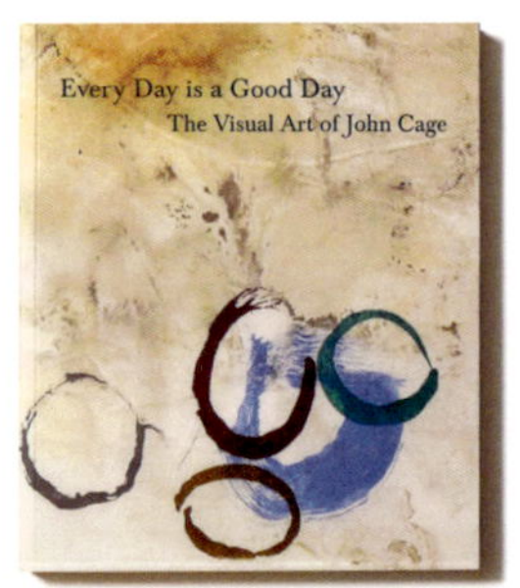

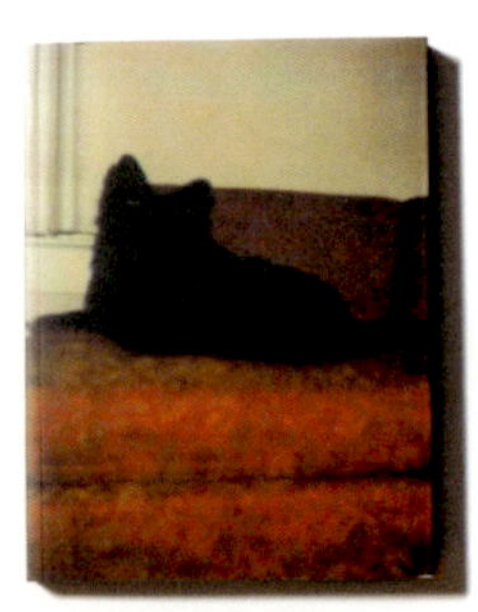

**ON OUR SHELVES** *Top: The Beautiful & The Damned: Punk Photographs by Ann Summa*, edited by Kristine McKenna, foreword by Exene Cervenka, 112 pp., Foggy Notion Books/Smart Art Press *smartartpress.com;* Joaquim Paulo *Funk & Soul Covers*, editor Julius Wiedemann, 432 pp., Taschen *taschen.com;* Armin Linke *Il Corpo dello Stato*, with a text by Giorgio Agamben, 128 pp., JRP|Ringier *jrp-ringier.com; La Carte d'Après Nature*, catalog of an exhibition curated by Thomas Demand, essay by Christy Lange, texts by Thomas Demand, Tacita Dean, Rodney Graham and Luigi Ghirri, 208 pp., Mack *mackbooks.co.uk;* Various Artists *Visions and Documents*, 10 volumes, 200 pp., Documentary Platform Editions *documentaryplatform.com;* Taryn Simon *Contraband*, text by Hans Ulrich Obrist, 480 pp., Steidl/Gagosian Gallery *steidlville.com;* Jonny Trunk *Dressing for Pleasure: The Best of AtomAge*, 208 pp., Fuel *fuel-design.com;* Lewis Baltz *Lewis Baltz Works*, 10 volumes, 964 pp., Steidl *steidlville.com;* Henk Wildschut *Shelter*, 112 pp., Post Editions *post-editions.com;* Trine Søndergaard and Nicolai Howalt *How to Hunt*, texts by Liz Wells, 116 pp., Hatje Cantz *hatjecantz.de; Every Day is a Good Day: The Visual Art of John Cage*, with texts and contributions by Jeremy Millar, Lauren A. Wright, Helen Luckett, Roger Malbert, 160 pp., Hayward Publishing *cornerhouse.org; In Almost Every Picture #9*, collected and edited by Erik Kessels, 122 pp., KesselsKramer Publishing *kesselskramerpublishing.com*

**IRINA POLIN** (1971) is a Russian-born, Switzerland-based artist, and the protagonist of this issue's Pop-Up section. She studied in Moscow at The Arts College Named After the Memory of Year 1905 and the School of Art and Design in Lucerne. She is the recipient of several photography prizes and her work has been widely published and presented in solo and group exhibitions in Europe, Russia and South Africa. *My Collection*, the series presented here, is a semi-autobiographical project inspired by her migration from Russia to Switzerland. The rediscovery of a box filled with Soviet porcelain figurines, glass objects, postcards, books and ephemera - brought from Moscow and with time, forgotten - prompted the artist's present day reconstruction of her history. What she constructs is a world of objects, and in these objects, the eternity attached to them, to their emotional invocations and to their survival. There within lies the human element - for all of these things are not only universally recognizable, but charged with a painstaking restoration.

**LARA ALMARCEGUI** (1972) her work has recently been exhibitited in group shows like *Portscapes*, Museum Boijmans van Beuningen, Rotterdam, *Radical Nature*, Barbican Art Centre London, at the Athens Biennale, Taipei and Gwangju Biennale, Sharjah Biennale, among others. In the past year, she had solo exhibitions at Secession, Vienna and Ludlow 38, New York. *Ruins in the Netherlands* was presented at Gallery Ellen de Bruijne Projects, Amsterdam, in 2008. She currently resides in Rotterdam.

**GIORGIO BARRERA** (1969) graduated in photography from La Fondazione Studio Marangoni, Florence, where he now teaches. After a period of collaboration with Joel Meyerowitz, he became interested in sociology, focusing on the rituals of daily life as well as landscape photography, video and films. His work has been published in a number of books and international magazines and won several prizes. He participated twice at Les Rencontres d'Arles and showed at the Art Institute of Chicago. His recent solo exhibitions were at Jarach Gallery, Venice, Galleria 42, Modena, and Palazzo delle Esposizioni, Rome.

**MARC FEUSTEL** is an independent curator, writer and blogger based in Paris. A specialist in Japanese photography, he is the editor of *Japan: a self-portrait, photographs 1945–1964*. He is a Creative Director at Studio Equis, an organization devoted to broadening access to the visual arts between different cultures, with a focus on the relationship between Japan and the West. His next exhibitions: *Eikoh Hosoe: Theatre of Memory*, will open at the Art Gallery of New South Wales in Sydney in May 2011. He regularly contributes to photography magazines including *FOAM, Images, Réponses Photo* and *VU MAG*, and blogs as well. *eyecurious.com*.

**ALEX GARTENFELD** is an art critic and Online Editor for *Interview Magazine* and *Art in America*. He is the co-founder of an independent space called West Street Gallery in New York. *weststreet.info*

**NATALIE MARIE GEHRELS** was born and raised in Northern California and moved to Europe at the age of eighteen. She is a photographer, art director, and co-founder of the creative studio Ouruse. She lives and works in New York.

**JORDAN HRUSKA** is a Brooklyn-based arts writer, critic and journalist. His writing has appeared in various books and anthologies as well as periodicals such as *The New York Times, Purple, Next American City* and the online editions of *The Economist, Vogue Italia, T Magazine, Art in America* and *Interview*, among others. He is the co-author of a forthcoming book on architect Philip Johnson's Glass House library collection.

**FRANCESCO JODICE** graduated in 1997 with a degree in Architecture. His research investigates the changes in social landscapes comparing similar phenomena in different parts of the world through photography, film, maps and texts. He teaches at the Università di Bolzano and at NABA (Nuova Accademia di Belle Arti), Milan. In 2008, he was commissioned by the UN to create a short film on the occasion of 60th anniversary of the Universal Declaration of Human Rights. He has participated in Documenta, La Biennale di Venezia, Bienal de São Paulo, Liverpool Biennial, ICP Triennial of Photography and Video. He has also exhibited his work at the Tate Modern, Museo Reina Sofia, Castello di Rivoli, Maison Européenne de la Photographie, Bard College and MAMbo. He lives in Milan.

**STEPHANIE SNYDER** is the Anne and John Hauberg Director and Curator of the Douglas F. Cooley Memorial Art Gallery at Reed College in Portland, Oregon. In 1991 she graduated from Reed College, and received her MA from Columbia University and she is currently completing her Ph.D in Art History at the University of the Arts, London. She has curated numerous exhibitions including; *Terry Winters: Linking Graphics, Liza Ryan, Spill, David Reed, Lives of Paintings, Marc Joseph, New and Used*, and *Sutapa Biswas: Birdsong*. In 2007 she was awarded a Curatorial Research Fellowship from the Getty Foundation to support her work on Post-WWII Conceptual Art.

**DAVID TUNG** works as a Director for the Long March Space, in Beijing.

## COLOPHON

**EDITORS**
Cay Sophie Rabinowitz, Selva Barni
editorial@fantomeditions.com

**CONTRIBUTING EDITOR**
Francesco Zanot
francesco@fantomeditions.com

**ART DIRECTOR**
Davies Costacurta
sm-work.com

**VISUAL EDITOR AT LARGE**
Pino Pipoli
pipoli@fantomeditions.com

**EDITORIAL ASSISTANT**
Didier Falzone
didier@fantomeditions.com

**DESIGN ASSISTANT**
Pietro Malacarne

**EDITORIAL INTERNS**
Arianne Di Nardo (Milano)
Erin Tao (New York)

**TRANSLATIONS**
Judith Mundell

**THANKS TO**
Agnese Bossi, Alberto Pellegrinet, Christian Rattemeyer, Ember Rilleau,
Luca Cipelletti, Luca Martinazzoli, Martina Scapinello, Mary Skinner,
Massimo Mezzavilla, Pasquale Marini, Roberto Rossi Gandolfi,
Sean Beolchini, Skype, Sofia Sizzi and Iacopo Falai, Stefano Pitigliani,
Susanna Cucco and Ivanmaria Vele

**FANTOM OFFICE MILANO**
Via Lanzone 22, 20123 Milano, Italy

**FANTOM OFFICE NEW YORK**
137 Grand Street, 10013 New York, NY, USA

**ADVERTISING ENQUIRIES**
info@fantomeditions.com

**WWW.FANTOMEDITIONS.COM**

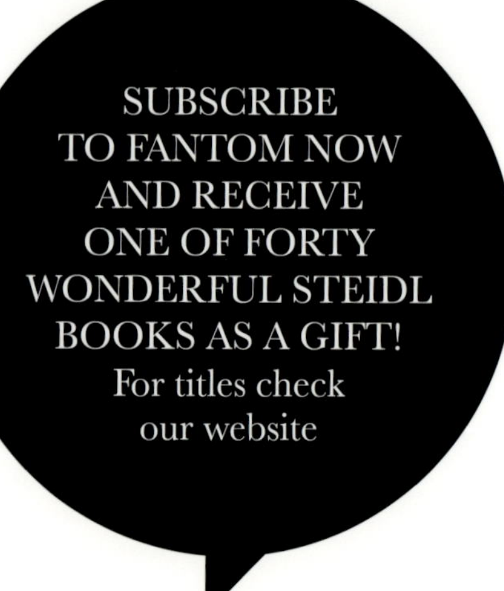


**SUBSCRIPTIONS**
Bruil & van de Staaij
PO Box 75, 7940 AB Meppel, The Netherlands
T +31 522 261303 - F + 31 522 257827
www.bruil.info

**DISTRIBUTION**
Italia and International: S.I.E.S. Srl
Via Bettola 18, 20092 Cinisello Balsamo (MI), Italy
T +39 02 66030400 - F +39 02 66030269
sies@siesnet.it - www.siesnet.it

North America: D.A.P./Distributed Art Publishers
155 Sixth Avenue, 2nd Floor, 10013 New York, NY, USA
T +1 212 627 1999 - F +1 212 627 9484
www.artbook.com

**PUBLISHED BY**
Boiler Corporation Srl
Piazza Castello 19, 20121 Milano, Italy
Numero di Iscrizione al R.O.C. 19.061 del 12/10/2009

**PUBLISHER & EDITOR AT LARGE**
Massimo Torrigiani
m.torrigiani@boilercorporation.com

**ASSISTANT PUBLISHER**
Pier Mario Simula
p.simula@boilercorporation.com

**BOILER INTERN**
Simone Castelli

Printed in Italy by Grafiche Antiga, Via delle Industrie 1
31035 Crocetta del Montello (TV), Italy
www.graficheantiga.it

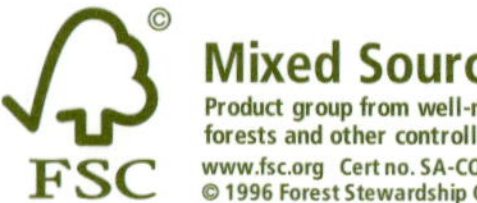


Periodico registrato presso il Tribunale di Milano
N° 436 del 07/10/2009
Direttore Responsabile: Selva Barni

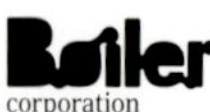


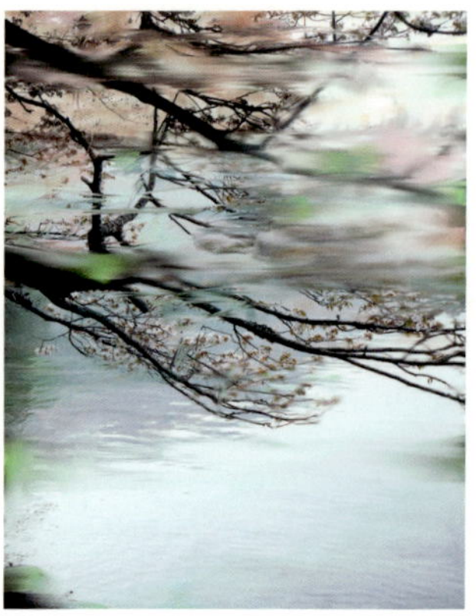

*Fantom* cover author Sandra Kantanen will be feautered in our next issue, out
in Spring 2011. On this cover: Untitled (Sakura 2), pigment print on paper.
Image © the artist, courtesy Gallery Taik, Helsinki

# FANTOM

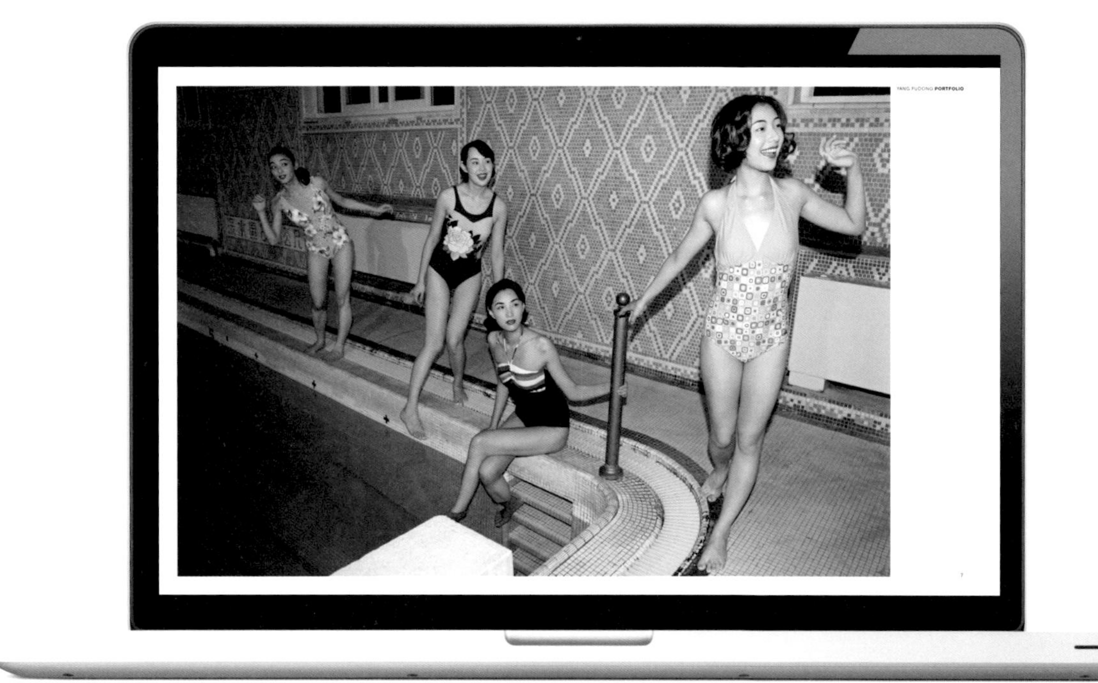


ENJOY ANYTIME, ANYWHERE
DOWNLOAD NOW AT
OTHEREDITION.COM

Other Edition.com

FUSING ORIGINAL CONTENT & MOBILE

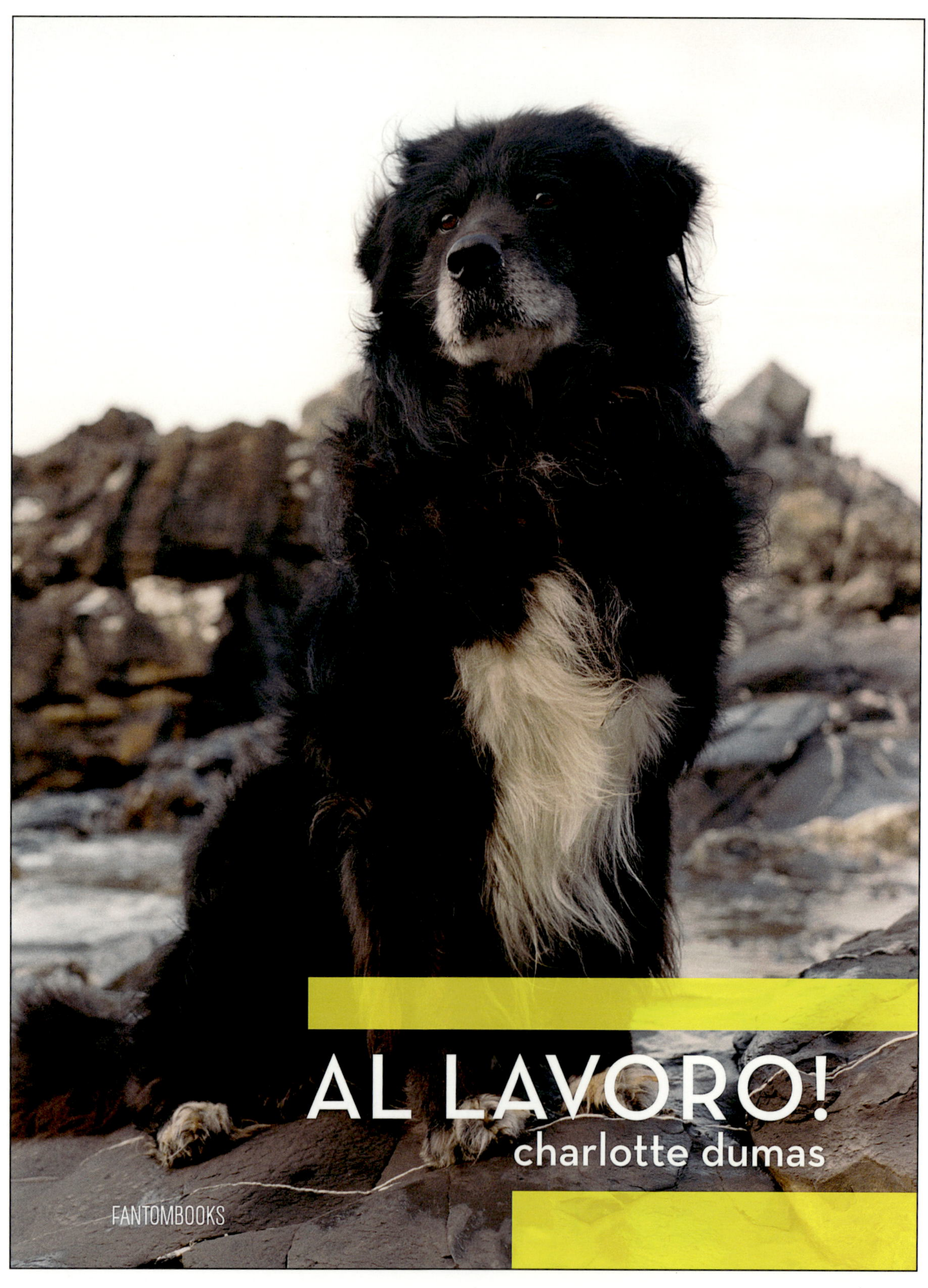

AL LAVORO!
charlotte dumas
FANTOMBOOKS

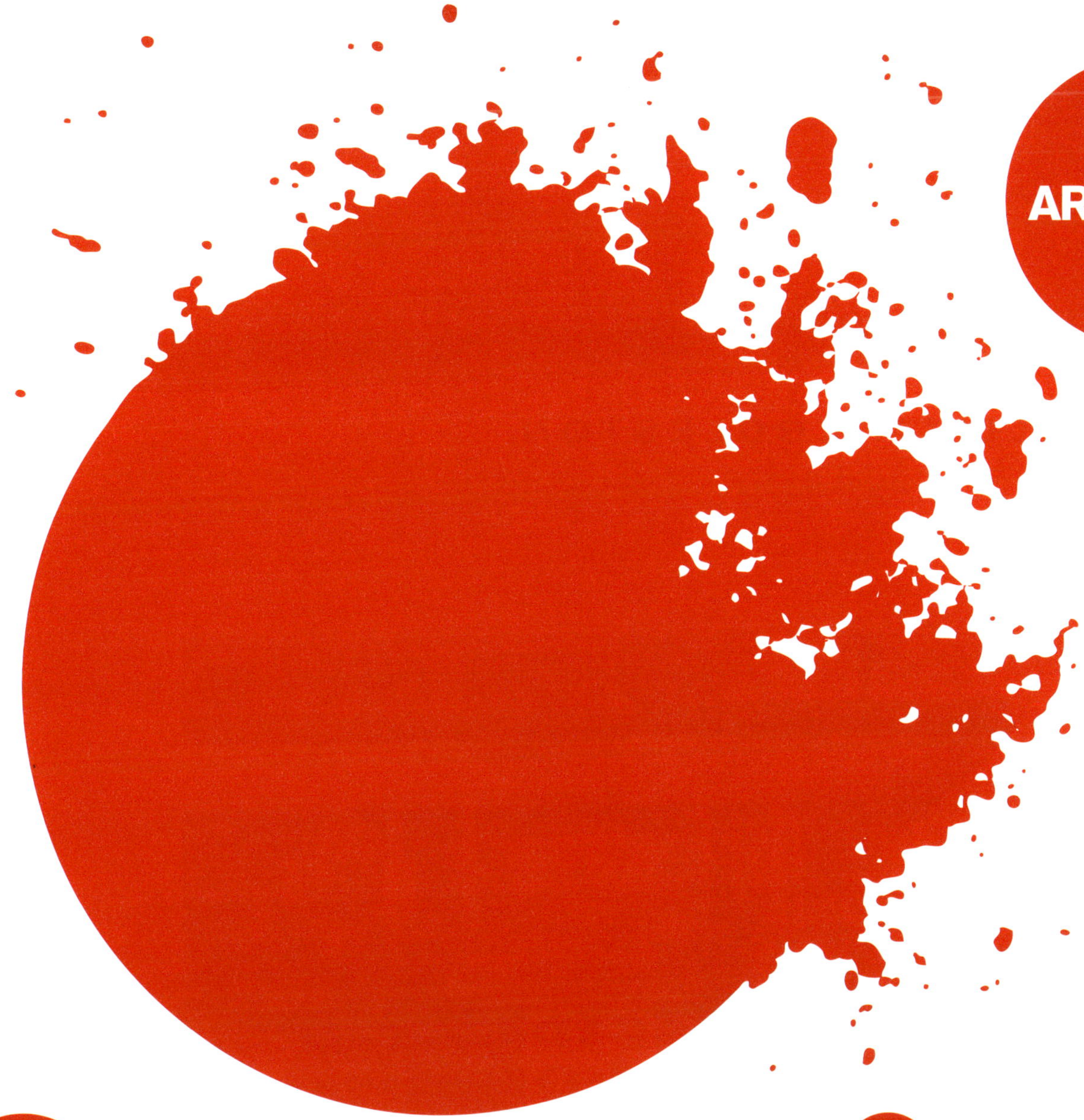

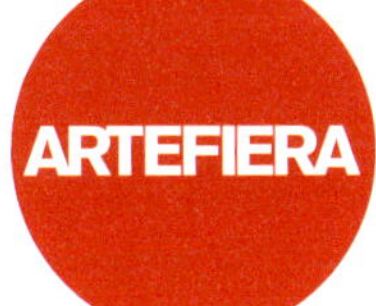




**ARTEFIERA** ART FIRST

Fiera internazionale d'arte contemporanea
International exhibition of contemporary art

# 28/31
# GEN
# JAN
# 2011
**BOLOGNA ITALY**

Main Sponsor

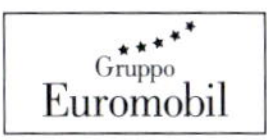
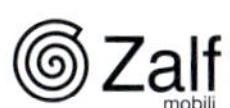
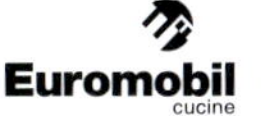
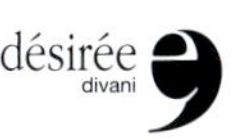



**Dal 28 Gennaio al 27 Febbraio 2011** torna in città la 6° edizione di Bologna Art First. **Se un giorno d'inverno un viaggiatore**, a cura di Julia Draganovic, è un percorso per immagini tra arte e storia attraverso installazioni site specific. Un'unica grande mostra collettiva per creare un dialogo tra arte contemporanea e location inusuali del centro storico della città e dei suoi dintorni.



**Sabato 29 gennaio**, dalle 20 alle 24, la notte cambia colore. Bologna si illumina e l'arte contemporanea invade il suo centro storico per la **notte bianca di Arte Fiera**. Apertura straordinaria delle installazioni di Bologna Art First, di musei, palazzi storici, gallerie d'arte e negozi, mostre, iniziative ed eventi.

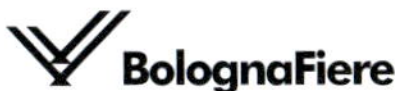


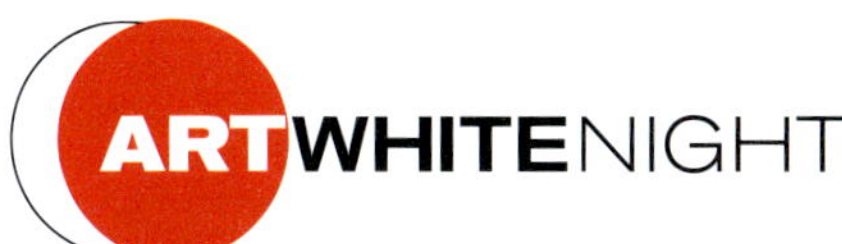

WILLIAM EGGLESTON

BEFORE COLOR


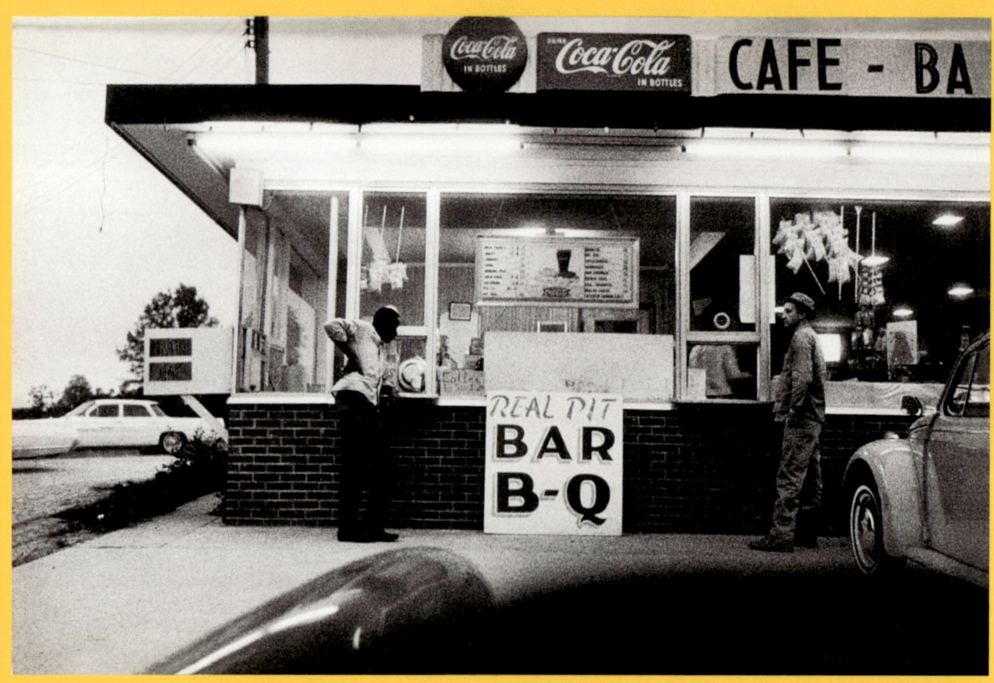


STEIDL BOOKS
www.steidlville.com

# Art | 42 | Basel | 15–19 | 6 | 11

**Vernissage** | **giugno 14, 2011** | **unicamente su invito**
**Art Basel Conversations** | **giugno 15 a 19, 2011** | dalle ore 10 alle 11
**Ordinazione del catalogo** | Tel. +49 711 4405204, Fax +49 711 4405220, www.hatjecantz.de

**Follow us on Facebook and Twitter** | www.facebook.com/artbasel | www.twitter.com/artbasel

The International Art Show – La Mostra Internazionale d'Arte
Art 42 Basel, MCH Fiera Svizzera (Basilea) SA, CH-4005 Basel
Fax +41 58 2062686, info@artbasel.com, www.artbasel.com

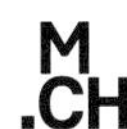

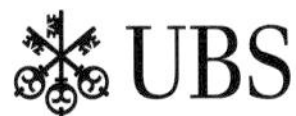

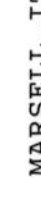

marsèll 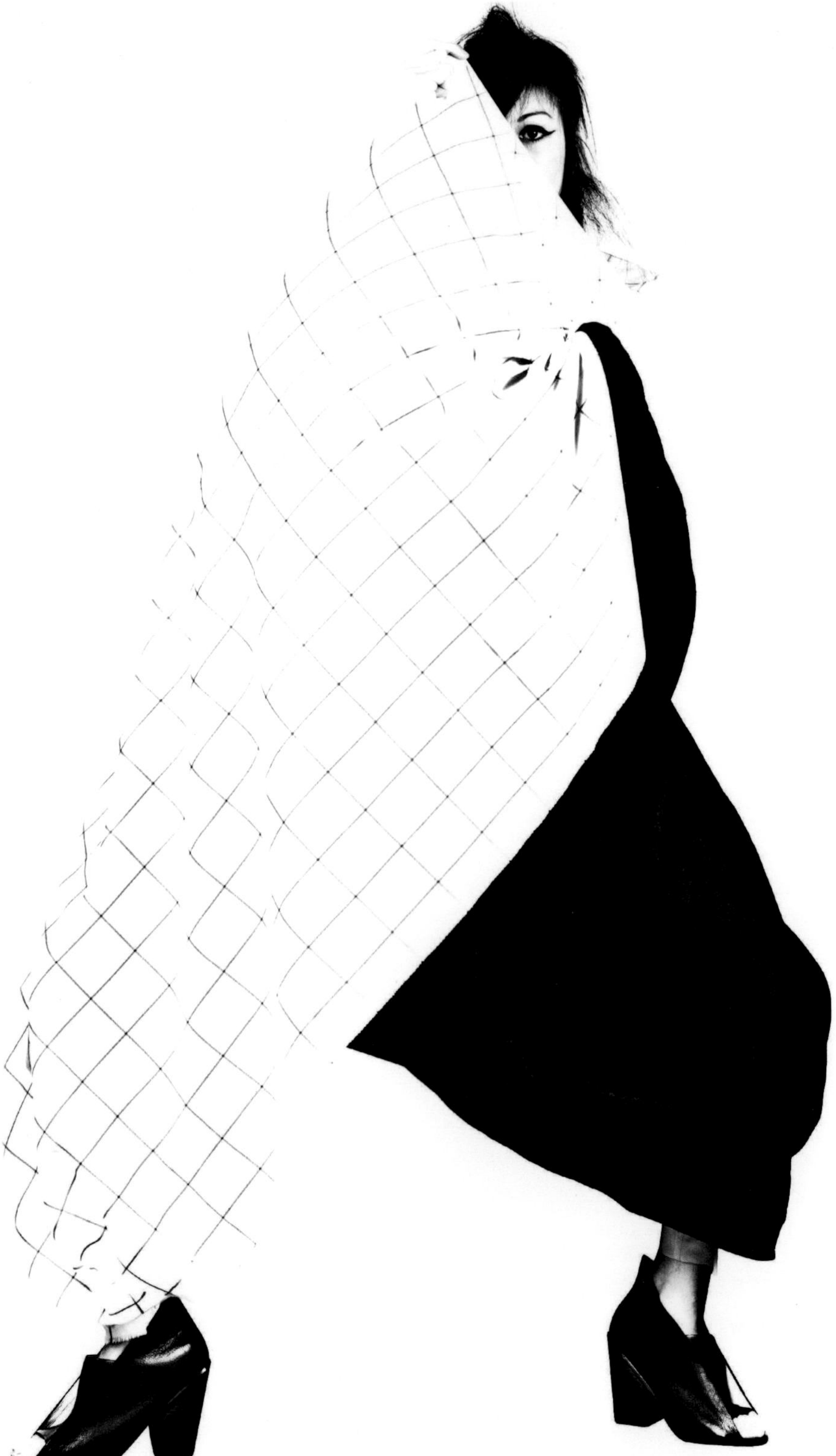
MARSELL.IT
VALENTINA SUMA, LUCA LEGNANI